A First Course in Programming
with Pascal

A First Course in Programming with Pascal

Bert Mendelson   *Smith College*

ALLYN AND BACON, INC.   Boston   London   Sydney   Toronto

Production Editor: Lorraine Perrotta
Preparation Buyer: Linda Cox

Library of Congress Cataloging in Publication Data

Mendelson, Bert, 1926–
    A first course in programming with Pascal.

    Bibliography: p.
    Includes index.
    1. PASCAL (Computer program language)   I. Title.
QA76.73.P2M46   001.64′24   82-3880
ISBN 0-205-07823-0 (pbk.)   AACR2

Printed in the United States of America.
10 9 8 7 6 5 4 3 2 1 87 86 85 84 83 82

Contents

Contents

Contents

Preface

This text is intended for the beginning student. It began as a set of notes prepared for a one-semester introductory course at Smith College. There are no prerequisites for the course, and the material is designed for the general liberal arts student as well as the prospective computer science major.

The first week of the thirteen-week semester is spent familiarizing students with some of the fundamental commands of the operating system level and a text editor. Thereafter, the material is covered roughly at the rate of two chapters a week, omitting the chapter on pointers and material such as variant records. Previously, parameters were introduced with procedures. There are good reasons for exposing students to parameter passing mechanisms at the time that procedures are first introduced, but many students have had considerable difficulty with this topic. There seems to be less confusion if the topic of parameters is postponed to a later chapter.

A useful assignment for the first week of the course is the production of a bibliography for some other course. Thereafter students are given weekly programming assignments. A number of these assignments requires the completion of a program of reasonable length (100-200 lines). This has the advantage of giving the student examples of program fragments that must be read carefully. I have also found that it is useful to give quizzes and a final examination.

Many students at Smith College contributed to this text. My daughter, Irene, assisted greatly both by criticism of the manuscript and by pedagogical discussion. My wife, Marion, aided in many ways. Elizabeth Boogusch was a tireless assistant. My colleague, Phyllis Cassidy, was a constant source of encouragement and last-minute aid. Another colleague, Patricia Skarda, got the project started. The staff at Allyn and Bacon, especially Mike Meehan, Nancy Murphy, Deborah Schneck, and Darlene Bordwell, have contributed their skills.

In this era of the computer, not only can we perform fantastic amounts of processing, but we can also make and multiply errors faster than ever before. The errors in this text are my responsibility.

CHAPTER 1

General Introduction

Sections

1.1   General Remarks

An introductory course in the design of computer programs is normally intended for individuals with little or no previous experience programming a computer. Such a course is almost always tied to a particular programming language such as BASIC, FORTRAN, COBOL, PL/I, etc. This course is tied to the language Pascal.

One goal is to develop an appreciation of the programming language as a tool to facilitate the implementation of well-designed programs. While the mastery of certain grammatical or technical details are necessary, the language should become an aid to description of the instructions and a means of reducing and hiding complexity. The use of a specific language to program a computer is part of a larger general concern, that of problem solving. Automating the solution of a problem forces precision at each stage of the problem solving process.

Readers of this book will have a variety of other goals. Some may be interested in creating and writing useful programs or modifying existing programs. They will want to become aware of many

of the schema for accomplishing certain manipulations, structuring
data, organizing complex procedures into subprograms, and so on.
Some may be interested in gaining insight into the general problems
faced by the computer programmer, so that they may more easily
communicate with the professional programmer when purchasing a
program or specifying the design of a program. Some may be
consumers of program packages such as word processing applications,
statistical packages, or ledger and inventory accounting packages,
and wish to learn more about how these applications are created.
Some may wish to obtain some general knowledge about computers.
Some may find that building useful, well-conceived, complex programs
is exciting and challenging.

    Regardless of the category or categories in which you place
yourself, you will find that learning to write computer programs can
be a worthwhile exercise in the art of developing precision of
thought. The language used presents you with a machine which
performs certain instructions. The exact form in which these
instructions are presented to the machine is the grammar or syntax
of the language. The effect that these instructions have is the
meaning or semantics of the language. Both the syntax and the
semantics will bear some resemblance to ordinary English and
Mathematics, and will also have certain annoying dissimilarities.

    At the time this book is being written, the "Pascal User Manual
and Report" is a de facto standard for the Pascal language. One
purpose of a standard is to ensure that a program may be written
without regard to the machine on which it is to be performed. The
standard language can be thought of as a means of instructing a
hypothetical or virtual machine implemented on many different
physical machines. Having a standard language permits text to be
written without concern for the idiosyncrasies of specific
implementations. In the case of Pascal, and one of its parent
languages ALGOL, it has furnished a frequently used language for
describing algorithms. The International Standards Organization is
close to agreement on a formal standard which should be essentially
the same as the Report.

1.2 Programs

    The instructions to the Pascal machine in the Pascal language
constitute a program. A Pascal program has two major divisions or
parts, a declaratory part and an executable part. The declaratory

part describes data objects available for use in the program. The executable part describes the actions that are to be taken and the effect they have on the data.

The actions may deal with communication with the world external to the program, that is, input and output; with manipulation of values of the data objects; or with modification of the order in which other instructions are performed.

As an example of a small complete Pascal program, here is a program which allows the user to enter a sequence of numbers, to to terminate entry, and prints the total, the average, and a count of the number of entries.

```pascal
PROGRAM SmallSample (Input, Output);

{ See text for description of program }

VAR
    Entry, Total, Average : Real;
    Count : Integer;
    Response : Char;

BEGIN
Count := 0;
Total := 0.0;
Writeln ('Enter a number');
REPEAT
    Count := Count + 1;
    Readln (Entry);
    Total := Total + Entry;
    Writeln ('Do you wish to enter another number?');
    Writeln ('Enter Y for yes, N for No');
    Readln (Response);
    IF (Response = 'Y') OR (Response = 'y')
        THEN
            Writeln ('Enter another number')
    UNTIL Response = 'N';
Writeln ('Total is ', Total : 10 : 2);
Average := Total / Count;
Writeln ('Average is ', Average : 10 : 3);
Writeln ('Number of entries is ', Count : 5)
END.
```

Listing 1.1

The program begins with a heading and a comment enclosed in braces. The declaratory part describes five variables, three of which are declared to be real numbers, one to be an integer, and one to be a character. The executable part contains instructions which either manipulate these variables or determine the instructions to be performed.

The input statements use a standard procedure, Readln, to obtain values for either the variable Entry or the variable Response. There are output statements which use the standard procedure Writeln to write a line of output. There are expressions such as "Count + 1" and "Total / Count" which are evaluated using the current values of the variables involved. Assignment of a new value to a variable may be accomplished not only by obtaining a new value as input using Readln, but also by an assignment statement. For example,

        Average := Total / Count

assigns the value of the expression to the right of the operator ":=" to the variable appearing to the left of ":=". Combinations of words such as "REPEAT..UNTIL" and "IF..THEN..ELSE" control the execution of other instructions.

The program contains a variety of grammatical marks, such as colons, semicolons, parentheses, commas, periods, and single apostrophes. It also contains the pair of words "BEGIN..END" used to group together several instructions.

The executable part of this program has a general form consisting of three parts. The first part performs some necessary preliminary actions, such as setting appropriate values of Total and Count and signaling the user to commence input. The second part interacts with the user as long as there is further input. Finally, a third part displays the results.

Groups of actions may be incorporated into units called procedures. These procedures may be supplied as part of the language, such as Writeln and Readln, or they may be defined within the text of a program. The parameters in a procedure may be thought of as placeholders which will be replaced by variables or values of variables, permitting the procedure to be activated several times, each time with different data. These procedures may then be initiated by using the name of the procedure and, when required, a list of parameters enclosed by parentheses.

Procedures may activate other procedures. In fact, Pascal permits a very powerful form of procedure call, one in which a procedure contains within its executable part a call to itself. Such a procedure is said to be a "recursive" procedure.

There is a comparable pyramiding in the declaration of data objects. At the most primitive level, Pascal supplies the user with five data types: Real; Integer; Char (for character); Boolean (with two constant values, True and False); and a type called Pointer. The user may define new data types by enumerating or listing all of the possible values. The user may also combine previously defined data types into indexed sequences, called arrays, create a sequential structure called a file, group various component types into records, and create subsets of many data types.

1.3   Environment

The Pascal program that a student writes becomes the input to a program called the Pascal compiler. The job of the compiler is to produce from the program, written in Pascal and called the source program, another program consisting of instructions in the instruction set of the host computer. This latter program must be equivalent in meaning to the source program. The source program must be presented to the compiler in machine readable form. A common method of doing this is to use another program called a text editor to create a file that contains a stream of characters, formatted into lines. Typical text editor functions are insertion, deletion, replacement, etc. This file becomes the source file and is the input to the compiler. (In card oriented systems, the source file may be on punched cards.)

The user may be required to interact with the operating system by issuing several commands before a run of a program is actually obtained. It may be necessary to initiate a step called linking which takes the machine instructions and incorporates many necessary system procedures, such as those connected with input and output. Many of these system procedures will guard the integrity of the operating system by aborting a running program which, perhaps because of improper input or impossible demands on system services, cannot continue to execute normally.

A distinction is frequently made between a syntax error in the source program, which prevents successful compilation of the program, and run-time error, which occurs during the execution of a successfully compiled program when the program cannot continue normal execution.

Pascal makes extensive use of two predefined files called Input and Output. In an interactive, time-shared environment, these files will be connected to a terminal. Pascal views these files as streams of characters, including both those that are printable and those that are capable of controlling formatting (such as the signal generated when the return key is depressed at the terminal).

Finding syntax errors in a program can be facilitated by obtaining a listing of a file, called a list file, generated by the compiler as it performs the translation of the source file. Sometimes the creation of the list file is a default setting of the compiler, that is, the list file is automatically created without a specific request. Otherwise, the system command to compile the source file must be qualified to indicate that a list file is desired.

A syntax error at one point in a program will frequently trigger a cascade of subsequent error messages. The compiler attempts to make some sort of "graceful" error recovery so that the remaining portion of the program may be examined, but this may be done by skipping a segment whose absence destroys the validity of later portions. It may be advisable to repair several errors and recompile a program. Some of the later error messages may then disappear.

Finding bugs in a program, that is, repairing a program which runs but does not perform as one had hoped, is a more difficult task. A number of computer systems now include Debuggers, or programs which monitor the execution of a program while allowing the user to halt execution and examine current values of variables. These can be extremely useful if one has developed a well-designed strategy to isolate the sources of the difficulties. Two other debugging techniques are usually easier to apply to the types of programs that are written in a first course. One is to hand simulate or trace an execution of all or a portion of a program. We have included material on tracing. The other is to include as additional output the current values of significant variables. Sometimes this must be done carefully so that the programmer is not overwhelmed by a flood of unnecessary output.

1.4 Conventions and Notation

Pascal is a language. The language instructs a machine to organize data into certain structures and to perform certain operations on this data. The language contains words and grammatical symbols. There are 35 words, called reserved words, which have a fixed and unalterable meaning. These words will be printed in uppercase, alphabetic characters.

A Pascal program is a specific set of instructions in the Pascal language. Portions of programs will be set off from the running text and, with the exception of reserved words, printed in italics. They will be numbered in the form C.N, where C is the number of the chapter and N is a positive integer indicating the position in the listings for that chapter. The same numbering scheme will be used for figures.

Frequently, a distinction must be made between the object being named and the name itself. For example, Chicago is a large city which has several million inhabitants, whereas 'Chicago' has seven letters, two of which are 'C'. As the example indicates, the name is denoted by enclosing the characters within a pair of apostrophes.

Special symbols may be employed to distinguish references to parts of a language from words and phrases in the language. As an example, the sentence

She declined the verb.

can be described as being of the form subject, verb, object. To distinguish this latter use of "verb" from the former use in the sentence, we frequently enclose the linguistic term in angle brackets. The above sentence would be an instance of:

< subject > < verb > < object > .

1.5 Why Pascal?

The programming language Pascal was developed by the Swiss computer scientist Niklaus Wirth. His preliminary draft appeared in 1968. The first compiler for the language appeared in 1970. In

1974 Wirth and his colleague, Kathleen Jensen, published "Pascal
User Manual and Report". The manual is a terse, complete, and
readable tutorial to the language.

The success of the language is evidenced by its availability on
a very large number of different types of computing machines, from
large mainframes to micro-computers. In addition, Pascal has become
the language of choice for an increasing number of college level
introductory and advanced computer science courses. The new
Department of Defense supported language ADA is based on Pascal;
and, of course, it has given birth to a devoted Pascal users' group,
(PUG).

The first two paragraphs of the introduction to the report are
worth quoting:

"The development of the language Pascal is based on two
principal aims. The first is to make available a language
suitable to teach programming as a systematic discipline
based on certain fundamental concepts clearly and
naturally reflected by the language. The second is to
develop implementations of this language which are both
reliable and efficient on presently available computers.

The desire for a new language for the purpose of
teaching programming is due to my dissatisfaction with the
presently used major languages whose features and
constructs too often cannot be explained logically and
convincingly and which too often defy systematic
reasoning. Along with this dissatisfaction goes my
conviction that the language in which a student is taught
to express his ideas profoundly influences his habits of
thought and invention, and that the disorder governing
these languages directly imposed itself onto the
programming style of the students."

Pascal achieves these, and other, objectives in a number of
ways. It forces the programmer to distinguish between the data that
the program is acting upon and the algorithm by which the program
acts upon the data. For example, all variables must be declared,
and the data type (such as integer, real, character, etc.)
explicitly given. This may seem like an onerous task to someone
accustomed to programming in a language such as FORTRAN or BASIC,
but it is a beneficial constraint. According to Anthony Hoare's
recent Turing lecture, a program error traceable to an undeclared
variable in a FORTRAN program resulted in the loss of a Mariner
spacecraft.

Pascal is a compact language, yet it permits the user to build complex data structures by enumerating new data types and by defining new data types from previously defined data types. The structuring may be accomplished by means of the array, the sequential file, the set construct, and the record. The record allows for the grouping together of data items of differing data type.

To implement systematic discipline, Pascal emphasizes what has become known as structured control. Use of the "GoTo" statement, to transfer control from one portion of a program to another portion, makes programs difficult to understand and introduces a frequent source of error in the control or logic of a program. Although the GoTo statement is included in Pascal, it is almost never used. Instead, so-called structured control statements are used to govern choice (IF..THEN, IF..THEN..ELSE, and CASE..OF) and iteration (WHILE..DO, REPEAT..UNTIL, and FOR..DO). One of the characteristics of structured statements is that the execution of each such statement starts at a single point in the text of a program and also terminates at a single point.

In Pascal, procedures, sometimes called subroutines, are a part of the entire program. A procedure is defined, normally prior to its use, and is invoked by including its name, as well as parameters if called for, in the text of a program. Pascal includes recursion, so that procedures may invoke themselves. Along with free format and the facility to chose meaningful names for variables, programs can be written which are readable and often self-documenting.

Many are convinced that programs written in Pascal are easy to modify and maintain, and are more likely to be correct. There is a growing body of literature in which various Pascal programs are proved to be correct, much as one proves a mathematical theorem. Many excellent examples are given in the text, "The Design of Well-Structured and Correct Programs", by Suad Alagic and Michael Arbib.

For students who wish to consult other texts, the "User Manual and Report" is a concise and complete presentation. Another compact text is "A Practical Introduction to Pascal" by A. M. Addyman and I. R. Wilson. Three texts, two by Wirth and one by Edsger Dijkstra, present many carefully constructed examples. The book by Dijkstra is "A Discipline of Programming". The books by Wirth are "Systematic Programming" (1973) and "Algorithms + Data Structures = Programs" (1976). The last of these is essentially a text in what has come to be known as Data Structures, a course which frequently follows an introductory course. A recent text in Data Structures, specifically oriented towards the use of Pascal, is "Data Structures Using Pascal" by M. J. Augenstein and A. M. Tenenbaum.

CHAPTER 2

Initial Programs, Messages

2.0   Introduction

A computer program is a set of instructions which can be executed by a computer. In this chapter, we shall give some examples of a very simple set of programs, those which instruct the computer to output one or more messages.

2.1 The First Program

Compiling a Program

A compiler is a translation program which attempts to translate a program written in a programming language such as Pascal, called the source program, into the instruction code of the particular computing machine that is being used. Successful compilation of a Pascal program indicates that there are no grammatical errors.

After grammatical errors have been removed, the translated program of actual machine instructions can be executed. If all goes well, the program performs as desired. Things rarely go well. As the problems that are to be solved by a computer program become more complicated, and as more complex computer language features are used to solve these problems, running a program frequently reveals that the program does not solve the given problem. Sometimes it may be that the program gives erroneous results. In this event, the results may give some clue as to what part of the program is in error. Other times the program unwittingly attempts to perform some illegal operation (division by zero is an example). In this case, the computer's operating system may abort the running of the program and give a run-time error message.

Initially, many of the programs in the early chapters will not solve very interesting or important problems. They may be thought of as exercises, similar to beginning musical exercises. Some exercises, however, illustrate techniques that have many and varied applications.

Input, Output File

The purpose of a computer program is to solve a given problem or set of problems and to communicate the solution so that the solution is readable by human beings. To communicate with its external world, such as printers, card readers, terminals, and eventually humans, Pascal a program assumes the existence of two files called Input and Output. Input and Output are sequential streams of printable characters and certain control characters, similar to a carriage return on a typewriter. The characters may be encoded on punched cards, but more frequently they are entered into the input stream from a typewriter-like keyboard at a computer terminal and appear as output on the display at a terminal.

Program Hello

    The initial sample program will communicate with the user by
simply producing a short message, that is, a stream of characters
sent to the output file. Listing 2.1 contains the source program:

        PROGRAM Hello (Output);
        BEGIN
        Write ('Testing: 1, 2, 3, 4.')
        END.

                    Listing 2.1

    We have written this program on four separate lines. Pascal
programs are written in free format. The appearance of the program,
i.e., the number of lines, the indentation, and the portions of the
program that occur in various columns, are immaterial. Listing 2.2
produces exactly the same output as listing 2.1:

        PROGRAM Hello (Output); BEGIN Write
                ('Testing: 1, 2, 3, 4.') END.

                    Listing 2.2

    In the future, we will frequently include in our listings line
numbers. The line numbers are not part of the actual source
program, but allow us to refer to a particular line in the listing.
We shall also include, when appropriate, the output produced by the
program. Using these conventions, we obtain listing 2.3:

    1   PROGRAM Hello (Output);
    2   BEGIN
    3   Write ('Testing: 1, 2, 3, 4.')
    4   END.

Output:
        Testing: 1, 2, 3, 4.

                    Listing 2.3

Program Structure

    Line 1, in listing 2.3, is a segment of the program, called the
program heading. The remainder of listing 2.3, that is, lines 2, 3,
and 4, is called a block. In this instance, the block consists of
the delimiters BEGIN and END surrounding the command to send the
string of twenty characters, 'Testing: 1, 2, 3, 4.', to the Output

file.   (In this previous sentence, to emphasize that we are
referring to the string of characters, we have used the convention
of enclosing the string within apostrophes).   The source program is
terminated by a period.

     Line 3 is an example of a statement, where statement is a
precisely defined term in the grammar or syntax of Pascal.   To
denote grammatical entities such as program heading or statement, we
shall surround the name of the entity with angle brackets.   Using
this notation, we can describe the program of listing 2.3 by the
form:

     < Program heading >   BEGIN   < statement >   END .

where line 1 can be substituted for < Program heading > and line 3
for < statement >.   In turn, the form BEGIN < statement > END is an
example of a < block >.   In the body of the text, we shall usually
omit the angle brackets in referring to these generic objects.

Literal Strings

     The string of twenty characters delimited by apostrophes in
'Testing: 1, 2, 3, 4.' is called a literal string or string
constant.   Note that the blanks or spaces have been counted as
characters.   The exact character set that comprises the characters
available for output by inclusion in a literal string depends on the
particular computer system.   It must include the twenty-six
uppercase alphabetic characters, the ten digits, and a number of
special characters which include the blank, period, semicolon,
colon, open and closed parentheses, and other symbols such as the
symbols for arithmetic operations.

     Using other literal strings, we can create a large number of
programs which print one-line messages.   Substituting, for line 3:

          Write ('Can you read me?')

will result in printing the sixteen characters contained in the new
literal string.

     By using the apostrophe as a delimiter for literal strings, the
apostrophe is no longer available as a printable character inside a
literal string.   For example, the phrase

     Write ('Don't use one apostrophe within a literal string')

would be flagged by the compiler as an error. To place an
apostrophe as a printable character within a literal string, use two
consecutive apostrophes. Thus,

    Write ('Don''t use one apostrophe within a literal string')

produces the output:

    Don't use one apostrophe within a literal string

    The failure to terminate a literal string properly can result
in some bizarre compiler error messages. Given an error message
that cannot be explained in an obvious fashion, check that literal
strings are properly terminated, i.e., that apostrophes occur in
matched pairs.

Program Heading

    The program heading starts with the word PROGRAM. This is
followed by the program name (in this case Hello). The program name
is followed by a list of the files used (in this case Output)
enclosed in parentheses. The form in which we have used program
heading is:

    PROGRAM < Program name > (Output) ;

The program name is an example of a more general entity called an
identifier.

Identifiers

    An identifier is defined as an alphabetic character followed by
one or more alphabetic characters or digits. Each of the following
is an example of an identifier:

    Hello   OneLiner   Try25   SortaList
    Message   X2Y55   ClassList   MusicalChairs

whereas each of the following is not a legal identifier and is,
therefore, not to be used as an instance of Program name:

    2YX55   One Liner   Try2.5   Class List
    Why?   M+T   2*Again   Never-Never

The first and seventh example above begin with a digit, the
second and fourth contain embedded blanks, and the third and the
fifth through the eighth contain special characters. Identifiers
may not contain special characters or blanks. Some extensions of
Pascal will allow the underline, _, or the dollar sign, $, as
embedded characters within an identifier.

An uppercase alphabetic character and the corresponding
lowercase alphabetic character are considered identical in the text
of a Pascal program, apart from characters in literal strings.
Thus, Hello and HELLo represent the same identifier.

Certain identifiers, such as Output, are predeclared. 'Output'
is the name of a standard file to which the procedures Write and
Writeln send output. Programs may communicate with other files, in
which case other identifiers for these files will be included. In
particular, we shall often use another predeclared file, Input,
which, as one might expect, is a file containing input to a program
from an input device.

2.2 Compound Statements

As a second sample program, consider the source program in
listing 2.4:

```
1    PROGRAM TwoLines (Output);
2
3    { Program produces two lines of output, illustrates the
4        compound statement and the use of the procedure
5        Writeln to output a NewLine signal.  Also includes
6        initial example of a comment
7
8     Date : June 4, 1981
9     Programmer : CS 115 }
10
11   BEGIN
12   Write ('Testing: 1, 2, 3, 4.');
13   Writeln;                              { end current line }
14   Write ('Can you read me?');
15   END.
```

Output:
        Testing: 1, 2, 3, 4.
        Can you read me?

                        Listing 2.4

Comments

    This program includes, on lines 3 through 9 an example of a
comment. A comment is a segment of a program opened by the
character { and closed by the character }. On systems in which the
open and closed braces are not available, the character pairs (* and
*) are used to delimit a comment. Since the compiler ignores
comments in translating the source program, comments have no effect
on the actual program that is produced. Comments are placed in
programs for the convenience and edification of the reader of the
source program. Surprisingly, this is often the person who wrote
the program. In a Pascal program, comments may be inserted anywhere
in a program (except in the middle of an identifier).

    In describing the grammatical form of programs, we shall ignore
comments. The above program is of the form:

    < Program heading >   < block > .

But the block is of the form:

    BEGIN < statement >   ;   < statement >   ;   < statement >   END

    The delimiters BEGIN and END now surround a sequence of
statements separated from each other by semicolons. The semicolon
is used as a separator in many parts of a program. Already we have
seen it used to separate statements from one another and to separate
the program heading from the rest of the program.

Syntax and Semantics

    Generally, the discussion of new language features can be
divided into two parts, the grammar or syntax, and the semantics or
meaning. The previous discussion giving the form that the source
program takes describes the syntax. The semantics of a program
fragment is a description of its effect or action.

    We have mentioned that Pascal programs send their output to the
file Output. This is usually a terminal. Writeln has the effect of
starting a new line at the terminal. The procedure that is being

employed when we use Writeln sends an appropriate signal to the
output device. We say that it has inserted a NewLine character in
the Output file. In the absence of the Writeln on line 13 of
listing 2.4, the output produced would be

     Testing: 1, 2, 3, 4.Can you read me?

The Write and Writeln Statements

    The effect of Write and Writeln can be combined. Lines 12 and
13 can be replaced by the single line

    Writeln ('Testing: 1, 2, 3, 4.');

The effect of this single statement is also to place the literal
string 'Testing: 1, 2, 3, 4.' in the output file followed by the
NewLine character. Writeln by itself may be used to print a blank
line, that is, to skip a line. This is illustrated by the example
Proverb in listing 2.5:

```
1     PROGRAM Proverb (Output);
2
3     { Illustrate write and writeln
4
5       Date : June 5, 1981
6       Programmer : Eryn Perry }
7
8     BEGIN
9     Writeln;                                { skip one line }
10    Write ('To Err ');
11    Writeln ('Is Human');             { complete current line }
12    Writeln;                                { skip one line }
13    Writeln ('To really screw up takes a computer')
14    END.
```

Output:

    To Err Is Human

    To really screw up takes a computer

            Listing 2.5

    Here, the output produced consists of four lines, the second
and fourth containing printable characters. The effect of lines 10
and 11 in the program Proverb could be achieved by the single
statement

                        Writeln ('To Err Is Human')

We have used the two statements together, to emphasize the fact that
the output line is not completed until a Writeln has been processed,
and also to illustrate a technique for writing portions of a line of
output using several write statements followed by a writeln
statement.

     Listings 2.4 and 2.5 have included in the initial comments a
short description of the purpose of the program as well as its date
of creation and the name of the programmer. The specific purpose of
some of the statements has also been explained by comments in the
source file.

     Programs should always be documented. Since many of the
programs in this text are accompanied by textual commentary, in this
area we will not practice what we preach.

Common Errors

     Failure to properly terminate a comment can be a troublesome
source of error. The appearance of the character { or the character
pair (* is a signal to the compiler to ignore all characters until
after the appearance of a matching } or *). If a comment is not
closed properly, the compiler may skip a portion of the program
before encountering the end of another comment, or the compiler may
skip the rest of the program. In the the first case, the resulting
error message is unpredictable. In the second case, some indication
that the end of file was encountered prematurely should be given.

2.3 Reserved Words

     An identifier is an alphabetic character followed by alphabetic
or numeric characters. Identifiers are used throughout the programs
to name the program, to name variables, to name types of data, and
so on. Certain identifiers are reserved for special uses.

     There is no limit to the number of characters in a legal
identifier. In practice, many compilers only distinguish the first
N characters, the value of N being specific to the implementation.
Therefore avoid pairs of identifiers which have long identical
initial segments. For example, TotalNumberofHits and

TotalNumberofMisses should not be used in the same program. Some
compilers will issue warning messages if identifiers have been
truncated.

There are 35 reserved words in standard Pascal. These words
have a fixed meaning and are not available as identifiers. The list
of the 35 reserved words is:

AND	ARRAY	BEGIN	CASE	CONST	DIV
DO	DOWNTO	ELSE	END	FILE	FOR
FUNCTION	GOTO	IF	IN	LABEL	MOD
NIL	NOT	OF	OR	PACKED	PROCEDURE
PROGRAM	RECORD	REPEAT	SET	THEN	TO
TYPE	UNTIL	VAR	WHILE	WITH	

Do not use any of these words in your programs other than in
the prescribed manner.

Extensions of the language, incorporating nonstandard features,
may introduce additional reserved words. For example, some
implementations allow the user to assign initial values to variables
in a separate section of the declaration part. A reserved word such
as DATA or VALUE may then be added to the language.

You may, if you wish, use as identifiers words such as:

Read	Readln	Write	Writeln	Maxint	True
False	Input	Output			

and so on, which are the names of standard procedures, or
predeclared constants or files. If you do use these identifiers as
constants, variables, or procedure names, you will then be unable to
use the standard procedure with the same name. It is best to avoid
using these names as identifiers.

2.4 Summary

A Pascal program consists of a heading, a block, and a period.
The heading consists of the word PROGRAM, an identifier (the program
name), and a list of files used by the program. The list of files
should always include the predeclared file Output, and the list must
always be enclosed by parentheses.

An identifier is a string of characters; the first one must be
alphabetic, and thereafter they must be alphabetic or numeric (with
no intervening blanks). When used in an identifier (or in the text
of the program), there is no distinction between an uppercase letter
and its corresponding lowercase letter.

The block of a program contains the pair of words BEGIN and
END. Between this pair are one or more statements separated by
semicolons. A statement which produces output is:

Write (< literal string >)

where literal string stands for any instance of a string of
printable characters (including blanks) enclosed by a pair of
apostrophes. An example is Write ('Testing 1, 2, 3, 4'). The
output line is displayed by executing the Writeln statement.
Writeln places a control signal or character which we have called
NewLine in the output file following the string of characters sent
to this file. The output file is normally the terminal.

Comments may be placed between words and grammatical marks in a
program by enclosing the commentary with braces. Comments do not
affect the resulting program. They should be used to describe the
program.

Three very common errors are a missing apostrophe for a literal
string, a missing brace for a comment, and a missing semicolon to
separate statements.

An identifier is an alphabetic character followed by alphabetic
or numeric characters. Certain words or identifiers are reserved
words. They can be used only with fixed meanings. Examples of
reserved words are BEGIN, END, and PROGRAM.

Exercises for Chapter 2

1. Many printers print characters in their character set by
printing a matrix or rectangle containing dots. For some printers,
each character fits into the space spanned by a five-column by
seven-row set of dots. The character T would be printed by printing
all five dots in the first row and the middle dot in rows 2 to 7.
The same technique can be used to write large-sized characters using
asterisks. The seven statements:

```
        Writeln ('*****');
        Writeln ('  *  ');
        Writeln ('  *  ');
        Writeln ('  *  ');
        Writeln ('  *  ');
        Writeln ('  *  ');
        Writeln ('  *  ')
```

would produce a large T. Create a program which prints your name in
large characters.

2. Create a program which prints several salutations for a number
of holidays. For example, "Have a fruitful Arbor Day". Include
Washington's birthday.

3. Write a program which prints your name in the center line of a
rectangular box outlined by asterisks.

4. Write a program which prints a smiling face using several lines
and under it the message 'Have a good day!'.

5. What will be the exact output produced by the following program?

```
        PROGRAM Message (Output);
        BEGIN
        Write ('Tic-');
        Write ('Tac-');
        Writeln ('Toe');
        Writeln; Write ('February 30, 2001');
        Writeln ('is a holiday')
        END.
```


6. What will be the exact output produced by the following program?

```
        PROGRAM AllAboutApostrophe (Output);
        BEGIN
        Writeln ('An apostrophe is ''.');
        Writeln;
        Writeln ('To give a variable Ch of type character');
        Writeln ('  the value of an apostrophe use:');
        Writeln;
        Writeln ('Ch := '''''''';')
        END.
```

7. For each character string listed below, decide whether or not it
is a legal identifier.

        GoodyTwoShoes   Demi-God   R2D3
        Junk Mail   Ampy&Sand   Blank
        Program   Ending2   One;Two

8. Give the program headings and blocks for the programs listed in
exercises 5 and 6. How many statements do each of these programs
contain?

CHAPTER 3

Simple Data Types

Sections

3.0   Introduction

Almost all computer programs do more than display messages.
They include instructions which act upon data. Each program or
algorithm has two essential parts: the active part consisting of a
set of instructions; and a passive part consisting of the
collection of data objects.

In this chapter, we shall introduce three simple or scalar data
types: integer, character, and real. The actions that can be
performed on variables of these types are the assignment of an
appropriate value or the retrieval of the current value.
Expressions may be created containing the numeric data types,
integer and real, as operands combined by means of arithmetic
operations.

An explanation of why integers and reals are separate data
types may be appropriate since it may seem unusual to have two
numeric data types. The integers are a subset of the whole numbers
(or counting numbers), their negatives, and zero. The integers are
stored exactly. There is a largest integer, and, as long as we
remain within this maximum limit, an integer N and an integer N + 1
will always be distinct. The reals (as a computer data type) are a
subset of the rational numbers or fractions. They are stored
approximately by storing two parts: the first several significant
digits and the magnitude of the number or the position of the
decimal point. The largest available real number is many times
larger than the largest integer, but is not stored as accurately.
If X is a very large real number, then X and X + 1.0 may be stored
so that they are indistinguishable. Since the range of real numbers
is larger than the range of integers, every integer can be made to
correspond to a real number; there is no reciprocal correspondence
from the real numbers to the integers.

3.1   Variables and Variable Identifiers

The utility of computers lies in their ability to manipulate
data. One purpose of a programming language is to present the user
with certain types of data and with the capability to perform
certain operations on that data. To refer to an instance of some
piece of data, we usually refer to it by a name. Numerical

quantities are referred to by names such as 'cost', 'current temperature', 'grade point average', 'X', and so on. Specific values may be represented by these names, and expressions used to denote operations on these values. The statement "profit is price less cost" could be translated into this equation:

$$Profit = Price - Cost$$

When the value may change during the course of a computation, we think of the value as referring to an object called a variable. If a human being is performing a lengthy or complex computation, the values of the variables are most probably written on paper, so that a suitable location for the current value of each variable has been created. A computer program keeps track of the current values of the variables in its data space in a similar manner.

Storing Values

Each variable will have a name or identifier so that the current value of the variable can be referred to and used in the program. The computer will also assign an appropriate memory location in which to keep the current value of each variable. In describing this situation, we shall sometimes write the name of the variable next to a box which contains the current value. We shall shortly see how to create variables and modify their values. If we create variables named Price, Cost, and Profit in a program, then we can describe this by the picture:

```
         ----------            ----------               ----------
Cost    |          |   Price  |          |   Profit    |        / |
         ----------            ----------               ----------
```

If Cost has been assigned the numerical value 17 and Price the value 20, then our picture becomes:

```
         ----------            ----------               ----------
Cost    |    17    |   Price  |    20    |   Profit    |          |
         ----------            ----------               ----------
```

If later Profit is calculated by assigning it the value of Price less Cost, then our picture becomes:

```
         ----------            ----------               ----------
Cost    |    17    |   Price  |    20    |   Profit    |    3     |
         ----------            ----------               ----------
```

The program may repeat the sequence of assignment and calculation. A "snapshot" of the data space might then appear as:

```
     ----------           ----------              ----------
Cost |   24   |   Price |   22   |   Profit |   -2   |
     ----------           ----------              ----------
```

3.2 Integer Data Type

Listing 3.1 contains a program which uses three integer variables. Two of them are assigned values of constants. The value of the third is computed using an expression involving the first two. The values of all three, along with descriptive material, is sent to the output file.

```
1     PROGRAM Intl (Output);
2
3     { Initial program with integer variables }
4
5     { All variables must be declared }
6
7     VAR Cost, Price, Profit : Integer;
8
9     BEGIN
10    { Assign values to Cost and Price }
11    Cost := 17;
12    Price := 20;
13    { Calculate Profit }
14    Profit := Price - Cost;
15    { Output }
16    Writeln ('Cost is ', Cost);
17    Writeln ('Price is ', Price);
18    Writeln ('Profit is ', Profit )
19    END.
```

```
Output:
      Cost is         17
      Price is        20
      Profit is        3
```

Listing 3.1

Lines 10 through 18 consist of three comments and six statements. Each of these statements is an instruction to the computer to perform an action. Consequently, this portion of the program is often referred to as the executable part.

Assignment Statement

The first three statements are called assignment statements, i.e., instructions to assign the value of the expression on the right of the assignment operator, :=, to the variable named on the left. The expressions used in lines 11 and 12 consist of one or more digits representing the value of an integer. These constants are sometimes called literal constants.

Read the composite symbol := as "gets" or "is assigned the value of". Using the picture of a named box for a variable, the following depicts the situation with respect to the variable Cost, before and after line 11 is executed:

```
         Before              Instruction              After

            -------                                     -------
  Cost  |  ?  |            Cost := 17          Cost  |  17  |
            -------                                     -------
```

We have placed a question mark in the box before the assignment is made to emphasize that there is no way to know what value Cost has before the program gives Cost an initial value.

Field Width

The three Writeln statements on lines 16 through 18 include within the parentheses not only a literal string but also the name of a variable, with a comma separating the two. The instruction outputs the appropriate characters specified by the literal string and then the value of the integer variable or expression, using a number of print positions determined by the particular implementation of the language. The system used in writing this book, the VAX Pascal compiler, provides a width of ten positions for an integer.

Numbers are written with leading zeros suppressed. Integers are right-justified within the field of print positions. Thus, with a ten-column field, the units digit is printed in the tenth column.

The number of columns set aside for the printing of a data item is called the field width. To control the width of this field, one can follow the identifier or expression by a colon and the field width desired. Lines 16 through 18 could be modified to print each of the three integers in a three-column field. The three lines would then be:

```
Writeln ('Cost is ', Cost : 3);
Writeln ('Price is ', Price : 3);
Writeln ('Profit is ', Profit : 3)
```

This would produce the output:

```
Cost is  17
Price is  20
Profit is    3
```

The output could be placed on a single line by replacing lines 16 through 18 with the following:

```
Write ('Cost is ', Cost : 3);
Write ('        Price is ', Price : 3);
Writeln ('        Profit is ', Profit : 3)
```

This would produce the output:

```
Cost is  20        Price is  17        Profit is    3
```

One could produce exactly the same output with the single statement:

```
Writeln ('Cost is ', Cost : 3, '        Price is ',
         Price : 3, '        Profit is ', Profit : 3);
```

Note that each literal string is contained within a single line, although the statement itself occupies two lines.

The field width may be an expression. If we have declared an integer variable N, then we may write Cost in a seven-column field using:

```
N := 3;
Writeln ('Cost is ', Cost : 2 * N + 1)
```

Output List

The general form of the Write and Writeln statements is
described by:

Write (< output list >)

The output list is a list of one or more expressions separated by
commas. Additional spaces may be included between the expressions
to make the source program easier to read. These spaces have no
effect on the output produced. Only spaces included in literal
strings and the field width specifications affect the output.

So far, the instances of expressions that we have used are
literal strings and variables. Expressions also include well-formed
combinations of numerical constants, variables, and operators.
Expressions appearing in an output list may be qualified by a field
width specification. Thus, the following Write statement is
acceptable:

Write ('Total Profit is ', Quantity * Profit : 8);

The expression Quantity * Profit has as its value the product
of the current values of the variables Quantity and Profit. The
asterisk is the symbol for the multiplication operator. The
multiplication operator must be explicit rather than be implied by
juxtaposition of variables, as in a mathematical expressions such as
(A + B)C. A complete enumeration of the arithmetic operators for
integers will be given after the discussion of listing 3.1.

Variable Declaration Part

Every variable occurring in a program must be declared in the
variable declaration part. In listing 3.1, this is line 7:

VAR Cost, Price, Profit : Integer;

The variable declaration begins with VAR and ends with a semicolon.
Between VAR and the concluding semicolon is a list of identifiers or
names of variables and their data type. The requirement that every
variable used in a program be declared forces the programmer to
consciously decide what is the data that the program will use and
act upon. In effect, the programmer must construct the collection
of names and corresponding boxes in which the current values are to
be stored. The programmer does not need to know what size box an
integer requires nor how it is stored in the box, but the programmer

must specify the name and type of each variable.

Many popular programming languages, such as BASIC and FORTRAN, do not impose this requirement on the programmer. In these languages, variables may be used in executable program statements without having been previously declared. One of the dangers of this approach is that a misspelled variable name will not be flagged as an error. The results of such a program are unpredictable and unreliable. This can easily happen in large programs. FORTRAN allows the programmer the option of declaring variables, and many programmers place this restriction upon themselves even if the language does not require that all variables be explicitly declared.

User-Defined Identifiers

The name of a variable (as well as the name of a program) is an example of an identifier. Recall that identifiers consist of an alphabetic character followed by zero or more alphabetic or numeric characters. A numeric character is also called a digit, and a character which is either alphabetic or numeric is called alphanumeric.

The literal constants such as 17 and 20 which we have used as expressions for integer constants are examples of unsigned integers. The formal description of an unsigned integer is:

< digit > < zero or more digits >

An integer constant may be prefixed with a plus or minus sign. Thus, appropriate assignments are:

        Positive := +101;
        Negative := -101

Remember that, for characters used in the source program, except for those contained in literal strings, an uppercase alphabetic character and its corresponding lowercase alphabetic character are considered to represent the same character. Profit, PROFIT, proFIT, and profit, all are names of the same variable.

Arithmetic Operations

There are five integer arithmetic operators in Pascal.
Addition and subtraction use the traditional symbols + and -. As
mentioned earlier, the asterisk, *, denotes multiplication. The
division of one integer by another yields an integer result. The
division operator is denoted by DIV. With positive integers, such
as 7 DIV 2, integer division yields the quotient, in this case 3.
If an exact result is desired, the division operator for real
numbers, to be introduced shortly, is used. The two integers, the
dividend and the divisor, are called operands.

If either or both of the operands are negative, such as in -7
DIV 2, the corresponding positive integers are used to calculate the
positive quotient and the result is negated if exactly one operand
is negative. For example, -7 DIV 2 = -3.

Many compilers can not "understand" 7 DIV -2 since they attempt
to interpret - as the subtraction operator. To do this, a variable
may be assigned the value -2 and then used as the divisor. With the
assignment MinusThree := -3, the following is true:

```
 2 =   7 DIV 3
-2 =  -7 DIV 3
-2 =   7 DIV MinusThree
 2 =  -7 DIV MinusThree
```

The fifth integer arithmetic operator is MOD. With positive
operands MOD yields the remainder. For example:

7 MOD 3 = 1   8 MOD 3 = 2   9 MOD 3 = 0

If both operands are not positive, the rule is the same as with DIV.
Calculate the result using the corresponding positive integers, that
is, the absolute values, and then prefix the result with a minus
sign if exactly one operand is negative. Note that DIV and MOD are
reserved words.

Operator Precedence

There are rules of precedence determining the order in which
portions of expressions are evaluated. Multiplication takes
precedence over addition. 2 + 5 * 3 is evaluated as if it were
parenthesized 2 + (5 * 3) and has the value 17. DIV and MOD have
the same precedence as *. Operators of equal precedence are
evaluated left to right. A DIV B * C is evaluated as if it were

written (A DIV B) * C. Subtraction, which is denoted by the symbol
-, has the same precedence as addition. The left to right rule
requires that 7 - 3 + 2 is evaluated as (7 - 3) + 2, yielding the
value 6.

     The symbol - may also be used as a minus sign. As a minus
sign, it has precedence higher than the multiplier-like operations
*, DIV, and MOD. Let Op be one of the previous operators taking two
operands. - A Op B is evaluated as (- A) Op B. If - is to be used
as a minus sign in the interior of an expression, it must be
parenthesized, as in 7 DIV (- 2); otherwise, it is interpreted as a
binary operator.

Maximum Integer, Maxint

     Since the amount of storage in any computer is finite, there is
a limit to the magnitude of the integers that can be stored and
manipulated. Usually this will be one less than a large power of 2.
The power depends on the design of the computer. Because one is
dealing with a finite set of integers, the usual rules of arithmetic
hold only if the results remain within certain limits. Operations
which yield results exceeding these limits are said to cause
overflow.

     An integer Maxint is predeclared and gives the positive value
beyond which there is an overflow condition. The system on which
this book is being written has a value of 2,147,483,647 for Maxint.
This is the thirty-first power of 2 minus 1. If one includes in a
program the statement:

     Writeln('The largest positive integer is ', Maxint)

the output is:

     The largest positive integer is 2147483647

     Notice that no commas are printed to group the digits into
triads. In a program containing the above statement, Maxint is not
declared as an integer. If it were declared, then it would no
longer have its predefined standard meaning and value. Maxint is
not a reserved word, we are free to invent our own uses for this
identifier if we wish to do so.

3.3   Character Data Type

In the early development of high-speed electronic computers--during World War II, and immediately following the war--the major designers and users of computers were concerned with numerical calculations. Governments supported development work on behalf ot the military and on behalf of scientists who, for military and nonmilitary reasons, were performing enormous amounts of calculation. It was not anticipated that the largest use of computers would be of a nonnumeric nature, as is the case today when computers are used to store, retrieve, and manipulate information. Frequently that information is in the form of characters and symbols, rather than numbers.

While the set of characters that can be handled varies from computer system to computer system, for us the set of characters will always include an alphabetically ordered set of capital Latin letters, the numerical ordered set of digits '0' to '9' and the blank character or space. It must also include sufficiently many special characters, such as '*', ';', '+', '=', etc., to allow for the denotation of the various operators in the language.

Declaration ot Character Variables

This section introduces the data type character. Variables of type character can be declared, just as variables of type integer. The name of such a variable is an identifier, and its value is a character in the character set of the implementation. The declaration:

    VAR   Letter : Char

declares that Letter is the name of a variable whose value may be 'A', 'B', ';', '=', etc. The diagram:

```
                    ----------
        Letter  |   'W'   |
                    ----------
```

would be a possible description of this variable at some point during the execution of a program. Listing 3.2 presents a sample program containing both integer and character variables:

```
1    PROGRAM Character (Output);
2
3    { Sample of the use of integer and character variables }
4
5    VAR                          { Note VAR appears only once }
6        Position : Integer;
7        Info : Char;
8
9    BEGIN
10   Position := 1;
11   Info := 'A';
12   Writeln (Info,' occupies position ', Position : 2,');
13   Position := 20;
14   Info := 'T';
15   Writeln (Info,' occupies position ', Position : 2,');
16   Info := '*';
17   Writeln (Info, ' is not an alphabetic character.' )
18   END.
```

Output:
```
    A occupies position  1
    T occupies position 20
    * is not an alphabetic character.
```

Listing 3.2

Data Space

Returning to program Characters, prior to executing the first line, line 10, in the executable part of the program, the data space of the program can be pictured by:

```
          ----------                  -------
Position |    ?    |        Info    |  ?  |
          ----------                  -------
```

After executing lines 10 and 11, the data space is represented by:

```
          ----------                  -------
Position |    1    |        Info    | 'A' |
          ----------                  -------
```

After executing lines 13 and 14, the data space is:

```
           -----------                    --------
Position  |    20    |          Info     |  'T'  |
           -----------                    --------
```

After executing line 16, the data space is:

```
           -----------                    --------
Position  |    1     |          Info     |  '*'  |
           -----------                    --------
```

Characters as Output

     When the character representing the value of a character
variable is placed in the output file, it occupies a field of only
one print position. In order to separate the various values of Info
from the 'o' of 'occupies' in the output of listing 3.2, a space has
been included as the first character of the literal string. Suppose
that three character variables are declared by:

     VAR Start, Third, Fourth : Char;

and assigned values by:

          Start := 'O';
          Third := 'P';
          Fourth := 'S';

The statement

          Writeln (Start, Start, Third, Fourth, '!')

would produce the output

          OOPS!

     Note that the name of the same variable may appear several
times in the output list of a Writeln statement.

3.4   Real Number Data Type

Many programming languages have two numerical data types. We
have already introduced integers. The other type is called real or
floating point decimal. A variable of type real can have values
such as 0.0, 3.1416, -1.010, and so on.

Integers are stored exactly while most real numbers can only be
stored approximately. These two data types must therefore be stored
in a different fashion.

Scientific Notation

The precision and maximum magnitude of the set of real or
decimal values will vary from computer system to computer system.
In many implementations, the precision is about seven significant
digits. 0.3333333 will be about the best approximation of
one-third, 3.141593 the best approximation of "pi", and 2147483000.0
the best approximation of the integer 2147483647 (Maxint on some
machines). Large numbers, such as the last one, can also be written
in a form of scientific notation, in which a decimal number between
1.0 and 10.0 is followed by a power of ten prefixed with an E to
separate the exponent of ten from the decimal part. In this form,
2147480000.0 = 2.14748E9. The exponent may include a sign, which is
necessary for negative exponents. For example, 0.0214748 =
2.14748E-2.

The range of values for real numbers can be quite large. In
some implementations, the smallest positive number may be of the
order of 1.0E-38 and the largest of the order of 1.0E+38. 1.0E+38
is a one followed by 38 zeros, whereas 1.0E-38 is a decimal point,
followed by 37 zeros, and then a one.

Decimal Form

Unless one is dealing with very large or very small numbers, a
beginning student will undoubtedly prefer to use, and therefore to
print, the decimal form. In order to print a real number in decimal
form, a real expression in the output list must be followed by two
quantities. The first is the field width (the same as with
integers, specifying the number of print columns to be used to
display the entire number), and the second is the number of digits

that are to be displayed to the right of the decimal point.

```
X := 2.333;
Writeln ('Value is ', X : 8 : 3 )
```

will produce:

        Value is   2.333

There will be four blank spaces between s and 2, one because of the
final blank in the literal string and three more since the printed
value occupies five print columns in the eight-column field. The
last digit printed is printed in the rightmost print position of the
field requested.

   If a program contains the two statements:

```
X := 2.333;
Writeln ('Value is ', X : 10 : 5)
```

the nonblank characters representing the value will occupy seven
columns (count the decimal point), and the output will be:

        Value is   2.33300

   Here is another variation of these two statements and the
output produced:

```
X := 9.12345;
Writeln ('Value is ', X : 10 : 3)
```

        Output:
           Value is   9.123

The value printed is 9.12345 rounded off to three decimal places.
Since the trailing digits, '45' which are dropped, represent a
number less than 50, the last digit printed, the 3, is left
unchanged. If, instead, X had been assigned the value 9.56789, then
'89' would be dropped but the 7 would be rounded up to an 8 and
9.568 would be printed instead of 9.567.

   Listing 3.3 contains a sample program using reals:

```
 1     PROGRAM Avg (Output);
 2
 3     {  ------------------------------------------
 4        |                                          |
 5        |      Sample program, real data type      |
 6        |                                          |
 7        ------------------------------------------   }
 8
 9     VAR  T1, T2, T3 : Real;
10
11     BEGIN
12     T1 := 2.33333;
13     T2 := 4.33333;
14     T3 := 5.33333;
15     Writeln( 'Data: ', T1:10:3, T2:10:3, T3:10:3);
16     Writeln;
17     Writeln( 'Average: ', (T1 + T2 + T3) / 3.0 : 10 : 3)
18     END.
```

Output:
        Data: 2.333   4.333   5.333

        Average: 4.000

Listing 3.3

We have used some of the characters available to create a box
enclosing the initial comment. Usually, this should also include
the programmer's name, the date the program was created and possibly
modified, and other general information that could be of use.
Although the comments and formatting of the source program have no
effect on the running program, they are extremely useful in
maintaining and understanding program code.

The symbol for the operator of division of real numbers is /.
In line 15, the expression (T1 + T2 + T3) / 3.0 appears in the
output list. The value of this expression is followed by :#10 :#3,
so that it is printed in decimal form, in a ten-column field
with three digits after the decimal place. As with integers, the
number is printed right-justified in the selected print columns and
leading zeros are replaced by blanks.

The numbers we have used actually sum to 11.99999.
11.99999/3.0 is not exactly 4.000, but the output is rounded off so
that 11.99999/3.0, which is 3.99999666..., is written as 4.000 in
10:3 format. If, as here, a real number is output with three digits
after the decimal point and the fourth digit is 5 or more, the third

digit is incremented by 1 with possible carry into higher positions.
In this fashion, 3.999499 would be written as 3.999, whereas
3.999500 would be written as 4.000.

Real numbers in this program can be distinguished from integer
constants by the presence of a decimal point. The syntax of Pascal
requires that at least one digit precede the decimal point. Thus,
.71 is not acceptable while 0.71 is acceptable.

Arithmetic Operations

Arithmetic operations available on reals are addition,
subtraction, multiplication and division, denoted by +, -, *, and /,
respectively. The operators * and / have higher priority or binding
than + and -. The same precedence rules apply to these operators
used for real numbers as apply when they are used with integers.
Thus A + B / C is interpreted as if it were A + (B / C). If one
intends to calculate the value of A plus B and then divide that sum
by C, one must write (A + B) / C. When in doubt as to how an
expression will be interpreted, use parentheses to make the grouping
explicit.

Note that integer division is denoted by DIV and real division
by /. Arithmetic expressions involving both integer and real
variables are allowed. Suppose Portion is an integer variable and
Pie is a real variable, then in the mixed expression:

        Portion + Pie

the value of the variable Portion is coerced into a corresponding
real number (a best approximation) and the addition is performed as
the addition of two real numbers.

3.5 Constants

Listing 3.4, uses both real and integer variables and
introduces constants, in this case a constant of type real:

    1   PROGRAM Constant (Output);
    2
    3   { Constant section of declaration introduced }

```
4
5    CONST Pi = 3.141593;
6
7    VAR
8       Radius, Diameter : Integer;
9       Area, Circumference : Real;
10
11   BEGIN
12   Radius := 7;
13   Diameter := 2 * Radius          { Mixed expression }
14   Circumference := 2 * Pi * Radius;
15   Area := Pi * Radius * Radius;    { Result is a real }
16   Write ('Area of a circle of radius ', Radius : 3);
17   Writeln (' is ', Area : 10:5)
18   END.
```

Output:
        Area of a circle of radius   7 is   153.93645

Listing 3.4

In listing 3.4, line 5,

        CONST Pi = 3.141593;

is the constant definition part of the program declarations. It
introduces the identifier, Pi, as a synonym for the constant
3.141593. Any attempt to assign a new value to the identifier Pi as
if it were a variable would be flagged as an error by the compiler.
The presence of a constant in the data space of a program indicates
that there is a labeled storage cell with the specified value
contained in the cell. But this cell is contained in a portion of
the program's memory that can only be read. It is as if the value
were entered in the cell with indelible ink for the duration of the
program, whereas the contents of the cell in which a variable is
stored can be replaced with a new value. (Memory which always has
the same value is referred to in computerese as Read-Only-Memory or
ROM.)

    The constant declaration part is introduced by the reserved
word CONST and consists of a list of entries of the form:

        < identifier > = < constant > ;

where a constant is either a number, a constant identifier which has
been previously defined, or a (literal) string. A string can be one
or more characters. A possible constant definition part is:

```
CONST
    LowerLimit = -30;
    UpperLimit =  30;
    EndMarker = '*';
    Maximum = 1.0E12;                    { one trillion }
    Name = 'Dudley Doright';
    Year = 1982;
    NewYear = '1983';
    Blank = ' ';
```

The compiler will automatically type each of the new
identifiers with the type of the constant to which it is being
equated. In the above list, LowerLimit, UpperLimit, and Year are
constants of type integer. EndMarker and Blank are of type
character. Maximum is of type real. Name and NewYear are of type
string.

3.6   Summary

Each variable declared in a program has as its name an
identifier, a data type, such as Integer, Real, or Char (for
character), and an appropriate location in the computer's memory
where the current value of the variable is retained. The
declarations are part of the block of the program and precede the
executable part. The section in which variables are declared is
introduced by the reserved word VAR. It contains lists of data
declarations. Each data declaration is a list of identifiers
(separated by commas), a colon, and a data type. Several
declarations for various types may be included by separating them
with semicolons.

An assignment statement of the form:

< identifier > := < expression >

assigns the variable named by the identifier the value of the
expression.

The values of variables and expressions may be written to the
output file by listing them within the parentheses following Write
or Writeln. The various literal strings, variables, and expressions
in these output lists are separated by commas. The list may extend
across line boundaries (but each string must lie within a line).

A character variable is normally written using one column. A
real or integer expression Expr, which includes variables, may be
written in a field of f columns by using Expr : f. A real
expression Expr can be written in a field of f columns with d digits
after the decimal point by writing Expr : f : d. f and d may be
integer constants, variables, or integer expressions.

Only finitely many numeric values are available. A predeclared
integer Maxint is a positive integer such that operations which
would yield values beyond this limit create overflow.

Five arithmetic operations are defined for integers. They are
tabulated below:

Operation	Symbol	Comments
Addition	+	also used for reals
Subtraction	−	also used for reals
Multiplication	*	also used for reals
Division	DIV	yields the quotient, an integer
Remainder	MOD	yields the remainder, an integer

The symbol for real division is /. Since the multiplication and
division operators take precedence over the other operators, A * B +
C is evaluated as (A * B) + C. Real numbers are of limited accuracy
and rounded off values are outputted.

Character variables take as their values printable characters,
including the blank space. To assign a value to a character
variable, the character is enclosed by apostrophes, as in Ch := 'A'.

Variables must be assigned values of the same data type as the
data type of the variable, except that real variables may be
assigned integer values.

Identifiers may be assigned to constant values. This is done
in a section of the declaratory part that precedes the section in
which variables are declared. The constant section is introduced
by CONST. Constants are listed using the form < identifier > =
< constant >. This includes strings, such as Salutation = 'Ciao'.
The value of a constant is fixed for the duration of the program.

Exercises for Chapter 3

1. Write a program which assigns a value to a real number, displays
the number in both decimal and scientific form on one line, the
square of the number again in both forms on a second line, and
finally the fourth power on a third line.

2. What are the values of the following expressions:

    2.1. 3 - 7 + 5
    2.2. 3 + 7 - 5
    2.3. 3 + 7 DIV 2
    2.4. 3 DIV 7 + 2
    2.5. 3 * 7 DIV 2
    2.6. 11 MOD 4
    2.7. 11 DIV 4
    2.8. 4 * (11 DIV 4)
    2.9. 4 * (11 DIV 4) + (11 MOD 4)
    2.A. 80 DIV 5 DIV 4
    2.B. (80 DIV 5) DIV 4
    2.C. 80 DIV (5 DIV 4)
    2.D. 3 * 4 + 5
    2.E. (3 * 4) + 5
    2.F. 3 * (4 + 5)

3. The volume of a sphere is four-thirds times Pi times the radius
cubed. Write a program which calculates and prints the volume of a
sphere.

4. Write a program which

    A. assigns character values to five variables, Ch1, Ch2, Ch3,
    Ch4, Ch5;

    B. prints an English word by executing the statement

            Writeln (Ch1, Ch2, Ch3, Ch4, Ch5);

    C. prints another English word by using another Writeln
    statement with the output list in B rearranged. (For example,
    B could produce LEMON and the statement

            Writeln (Ch3, Ch2, Ch1, Ch4, Ch5)

would produce MELON.

5.   What happens on your system if you attempt to compile and run:

5.1.   a program in which an integer variable Super is declared
and the assignment Super := Maxint + l is made;

5.2.   a program in which a real variable Super is declared and
the assignment Super := Maxint + l is made;

5.3.   a program in which a real variable Super is declared and
the assignment Super := Maxint + 1.0 is made.

6. Make several character assignments in a program and print a
given message by printing the variables that have been assigned
character values.

7. For each of the following constants, specify whether its data
type is character, integer, real, or literal string.

```
CONST
    Day = '9/23/81';
    Temperature = 7.28E1;
    Weather = 'C';
    Age = 10000;
    Frequency = 10000.0;
    X = 'Y';
    Message = 30;
    Notice = '30';
```

8. For each of the following real numbers written in decimal form,
find the corresponding representation using scientific form:

```
3.14156
12345678.9
0.123456789
0.001020304
0.000006789
```

9. For each of the following real numbers written in scientific
form, find the corresponding decimal representation:

```
1.2345E5
9.8765E-1
5.55E0
5.55E1
```

10. To add two real numbers represented in decimal form by hand,
one usually writes the two numbers so that their decimal points are
aligned. Thus, 123.45 and 0.98765 are added by writing:

```
        123.45
          0.98765
        ----------
        124.43765
```

with the addition of digits starting at the right and moving left,
including a carry digit if necessary.

If real numbers are represented in scientific form with 123.45
= 1.2345E2 and 0.98765 = 9.8765E-1, the number with the smaller
exponent can be aligned by temporarily performing compensating
shifting of the significant digits (called the mantissa) to the
right and incrementing the exponent until the smaller exponent has
been raised to the larger one. The equivalent representations of
0.98765 are 9.8765E-1 = 0.98765E0 = 0.098765E1 = 0.0098765E2. The
last representation can be added to 1.2345E2 by adding digits.
Using this method, find the following sums, rounding the mantissa to
six digits:

```
6.666E2 + 3.333E-1
6.789E2 + 3.456E-1
1.0E10 + 9.99999E1
```

11. Supply the missing declarations for the following program:

```
PROGRAM DeclareIt (Output);

BEGIN
Feet := 29;
Yards := Feet DIV 3;
PricePerYard := 5.49;
Cost := PricePerYard * Yards;
Grade := 'B';
Writeln (Grade, '    ', Yards : 8, Cost : 12 : 2)
END.
```

CHAPTER 4

Standard Function, Tracing

Sections

4.0   Introduction

     Pascal includes a number of standard functions. There are
arithmetic functions such as square, square root, and logarithm.
There are functions, called transfer functions, used to transform a
value of one data type to a corresponding value of another data
type. There are two functions which, when applied to ordered data
such as the integers and characters, yield the successor and
predecessor.

Although not part of the language, techniques for catching errors are part of the general problem solving process. Some of the error checking can be done by the compiler. For example, an attempt to add the value of a character variable to an integer variable can be caught by the compiler because the type of every variable is known. Other errors may be in the design or logic of the program. As the instructions and the data become more complex, programs are more likely to contain errors. There are various aids to the corrective or debugging process. One simple technique is simulating an execution of the program by hand. This simulation is called tracing.

At this stage in the learning process, tracing can also be a good check on whether one understands the effect of various instructions.

4.1 Standard Functions

Arithmetic Functions

There are several standard functions which are available in Pascal. In the program in which the area of a circle was computed, we could have used a function to square the radius. This function is identified by Sqr, and, for any number X, Sqr (X) has the value of X squared, that is, Sqr (X) = X * X. X is said to be the argument of Sqr. The assignment of a value to Area could then have been by the statement:

        Area := Pi * Sqr (Radius)

The square function can take either real or integer arguments, and has as its value a number of the same type. Thus Sqr (4) = 16, Sqr (4.0) =16.0, Sqr (0.2) = 0.04, Sqr (-5) = 25.

Another numerical function is the absolute value function. The absolute value of a number X, Abs (X), is defined by Abs (X) = X if X > 0, Abs (X) = 0 if X = 0, and Abs (X) = -X if X < 0. For example, Abs (-5) = 5, Abs (4.0) = 4.0, and Abs (-3.14160) = 3.14160.

There is a square root function, identified by Sqrt. It takes as its argument either a nonnegative integer or a nonnegative real and has as its value a real number. Thus, Sqrt (4) = 2.0, Sqrt (0.04) = 0.2, Sqrt (1.0E-2) = 0.1.

Sqrt is included in a group of arithmetic functions which also take real or integer arguments, but whose value is always real. There are three trigonometric functions--sine, cosine and arctangent--named by Sin, Cos, and ArcTan, respectively. The numerical value of the arguments of Sin and Cos are the radian measure of the angle. Consequently, Sin (3.141593) = 0.0 and Cos (3.141593) = -1.0. Also ArcTan (1.0) = 0.785398. Here 3.141593 is pi, the radian measure of 180 degrees and 0.785398 is pi / 4, the radian measure of 45 degrees.

The three remaining arithmetic functions are the exponential, logarithm, and square root function. These functions are identified by the names Exp, Ln, and Sqrt, respectively. The logarithm is the natural logarithm, that is, to the base e = 2.71828... Exp uses e as the base also.

To raise an arbitrary number a to the power X, one may use the expression Exp (Ln (a) * X). If the exponent X is a positive integer, this form can be replaced by a simpler expression or computation using multiplication.

Transfer Functions

There are four functions called transfer functions. The name indicates that they take an argument of one type and produce a value of a different type. If X is of type real, Trunc (X) is an integer whose value is X truncated, that is, the result is the greatest integer less than or equal to X for X greater than zero, and the least integer greater than or equal to X for negative X. If X is of type real, Round (X) is an integer whose value is X rounded to the nearest integer. Rounding can be expressed in terms of truncation. Round (X) = Trunc (X + 0.5) for X greater than or equal to zero, and Round (X) = Trunc (X - 0.5) for X less than zero.

Ord, Chr

The two other transfer functions Ord and Chr will be especially useful in dealing with characters. The characters are ordered and each one is associated with an integer, called its ordinal number, which indicates the relative position of the character in this ordering.

The particular ordering of the characters in the character set recognizable by a computer system is called the collating sequence of that system. In many installations, the encoding uses the American Standard Code for Information Interchange, referred to by the acronym ASCII. This code is tabulated in Appendix A. If the ASCII code is used to establish the collating sequence, the first printable character is a blank, ' ', and the last printable character is the tilde, '~'.

The ordinal number of a character Ch is given by Ord (Ch). The requirement that the uppercase alphabetic characters occupy their usual position means that:

$$\text{Ord ('A')} < \text{Ord ('B')} < \ldots < \text{Ord ('Z')}$$

Similarly, for the digits:

$$\text{Ord ('0')} < \text{Ord ('1')} < \ldots < \text{Ord ('9')}$$

The particular integers involved in the above relations are implementation dependent. In most cases, whatever the value of Ord ('A'), Ord ('B') will be the next integer, and so on through the alphabet. If X is an integer which is the ordinal number of a character Ch, then the value of Chr (X) is Ch. Thus, regardless of the implementation:

$$\text{Chr (Ord (Ch))} = \text{Ch} \qquad \text{and} \qquad \text{Ord (Chr (X))} = \text{X}$$

Expressions

The argument of a function may be an expression of a type appropriate to that function. Thus, Sqr (3 * 2.71828), Chr (Ord ('A') + 1), are acceptable. In fact, each of these forms consisting of the identifier for a function and an argument enclosed in parentheses is itself an expression, so it may appear in turn as the argument of a function. For example, if X and Y are appropriate variables, the following are all legal expressions:

```
Sqrt (1 / (Sqr (X) + Sqr (Y)))
Chr (Ord (Ch))
Arctan (Sin(X))
Sqr (Sqr (Sqr (X)))
```

Successor, Predecessor

In processing characters, it is convenient to have a function whose value is the next character. This function is called Succ, for successor. Succ may also be applied to integers. For an integer N, Succ (N) yields N + 1. Applying Succ to an argument which has no successor, such as the character with the largest ordinal, is an undefined operation and may result in a run-time error message.

The following should hold:

Succ ('A') = 'B', ..., Succ ('Y') = 'Z'

Succ ('0') = '1', ..., Succ ('8') = '9'

If lowercase characters are in the character set of an implementation, then the following should also hold:

Succ ('a') = 'b', ..., Succ ('y') = 'z'

The character with the largest ordinal value has no successor. In some implementations, this character is the tilde, ~, so an attempt to evaluate Succ ('~') may result in a run-time error message. The values of Succ ('Z'), Succ ('9'), and Succ ('z') may vary from implementation to implementation.

There is a companion function Pred, for predecessor. For an integer N, Pred (N) = N - 1 (unless the value of N is the smallest integer allowed). For a character variable Ch, Pred (Ch) is constrained by the requirements:

Pred ('B') = 'A', ..., Pred ('Z') = 'Y'

Pred ('1') = '0', ..., Pred ('9') = '8'

and, if lowercase characters are allowed:

Pred ('b') = 'a', ..., Pred ('z') = 'y'

If the ordinal of Ch is the smallest ordinal, then Pred (Ch) may create a run-time error message. In some implementations, the blank is the value for which Pred (' ') is undefined.

A complete table of standard functions is included in Appendix B.

4.2 Tracing

Instructions and Data

A computer program is a description in some language of: (1) a set of actions or executable instructions and (2) the data upon which those actions are to be performed. (More complex programs may also include a description of the interaction of the program with other programs and with the operating system.)

The data plays a passive role, and the extent to which the data must be explicitly described varies from language to language. In Pascal, the descriptions of the data must be explicit, and these descriptions are contained in the declaration section. (So far, we have seen two subsections, one for constants and the other for variables.) The description of the data can be thought of as the environment within which the program executes. We have been calling this environment the data space of the program.

The actions or executable instructions manipulate the data, perform communication functions with devices external to the program (such as creating output), and, as we shall see, control the future execution of instructions within the program. These executable instructions can be thought of as a collection of imperative verbs.

All of this--the data space and the actions--are described in the source program. The compilation or translation of this source program results in a collection of equivalent instructions in the language or instruction set of the host computer. (These machine language instructions can be thought of as strings of zeros and ones. Each zero or one is called a bit.) The translation creates both the environment and the imperatives for the running of the program.

Memory

As we have indicated, each data object declared in the program is assigned to an appropriate memory cell. A declaration such as:

    VAR Count : Integer;

can be depicted by:

```
                              ------------
                   Count    |            |
                              ------------
```

Here, instead of the label Count, the machine substitutes a memory
address, and, instead of a rectangle in which we anticipate placing
the value of an integer, the machine substitutes a sufficiently
large memory cell to accommodate a machine encoding of the value of
an integer.

   The total environment or data of the program can be acted upon
by assignments such as Count := 0. The resultant picture is then:

```
                              ------------
                   Count    |     0      |
                              ------------
```

   A declaration section such as:

```
CONST
    Pi = 3.1416;
    Max = 20;
VAR
    Rad, Area : Real;
    Count : Integer;
```

would be pictured by:

```
          ------------                    ------------
Pi      | 3.1416   |         Count     |            |
          ------------                    ------------
          ------------         Max        ------------
Rad     |            |                   |    20      |
          ------------                    ------------
          ------------
Area    |            |
          ------------
```

   Note that the constants will already have values. Variables
will not initially have meaningful values. Only some program action
which establishes an initial value of a variable will supply a
meaningful value.

   If the first two executable statements in a program are:

```
Count := 0;
Rad := 3.5;
```

then, after executing these two statements, a picture or snapshot of
the data space would be:

```
         ----------                    ----------
Pi     | 3.1416 |         Count     |    0   |
         ----------                    ----------
         ----------         Max       ----------
Rad    |   3.5  |                   |   20   |
         ----------                    ----------
         ----------
Area   |        |
         ----------
```

        A useful analogy is that the data space consists of a
blackboard on which, for the duration of the program, the constants
are written indelibly in appropriately labeled regions, while the
variables are the names of regions which are initially blank or
undefined.

Simulating the Computation

        In simulating the action of a computer, we can devise various
ways of recording successive snapshots of the data space. When
performing this tracing using paper and a writing implement, we are
interested in the most recently assigned values of each variable.
One way of recording this information is to keep the values of each
constant or variable in a separate column. Using the previous
example, the table below represents the initial state of the data
space:

Pi	Rad	Area	Count	Max
3.1416				20

        If we wished to record each executable instruction and its
effect on the data space, we may list an instruction on each row and
enter in the appropriate column the result of the execution of that
instruction. If the first four instructions are:

    (1)   Count := 0;
    (2)   Rad := 3.5;
    (3)   Area := Pi * Rad * Rad;
    (4)   Count := Count + 1;

the simulation or trace would appear as the table:

Action   Data Space

	Pi	Rad	Area	Count	Max
constants	3.1416				20
(1) Count := 0				0	
(2) Rad := 3.5		3.5			
(3) Area:=Pi*Rad*Rad			38.4848		
(4) Count:=Count+1				1	

The current value of each data object is the last entry in the
column headed by the object's name. Although Count had been given
the value 0 at one time, it currently has the value 1. If one has a
source program with numbered lines, the line number of an
instruction may be used as an abbreviation of the instruction. If
one is interested in output produced by a program, a column for
output may be included in the trace.

The format presented here is meant to be a suggestion. One
need not use exactly the same format.

Sample Trace

As a model of a trace, consider the program:

```
1      PROGRAM SimpleSum( Output );
2      VAR Addend1, Addend2, Sum : Integer;
3      BEGIN
4      Addend1 := 5;
5      Addend2 := -2;
6      Sum := Addend1 + Addend2;
7      Writeln (Addend1:3, '+', Addend2:3, ' = ', Sum:3)
8      END.
```

Tracing the execution of this program yields:

Action	Data Space			Output
instruction line #	Addend1	Addend2	Sum	
4	5			
5		-2		
6			3	
7				5+ -2 = 3

    In order to find errors or debug more complicated programs by
this technique, we may surmise that the difficulty is confined to a
certain set of instructions and the portion of the data space to
which those instructions refer. In that case, we may confine the
trace to a portion of the instructions and data. We must, however,
know and enter in the trace all relevant previously defined values
as they exist immediately prior to the beginning of the instructions
we intend to trace.

4.3   Summary

    A number of standard functions are part of the language. Some
are arithmetic--for example, Sqr, Sqrt, Cos, Sin, ArcTan, Exp, and
Abs--taking numerical arguments and yielding numeric values..
Others are transfer functions, taking as arguments one data type and
yielding values of another type. Ord, for ordinal, is a transfer
function. It takes a character as an argument and yields an integer
value. Succ and Pred, for successor and predecessor, are functions
defined for both characters and integers, yielding a result of the
same type. See Appendix B for a listing of the standard functions.

    A useful technique for testing and debugging a program is to
trace or simulate manually the execution of a program. This
involves keeping track of the current values of variables as each of
the instructions in the program is executed.

Exercises for Chapter 4

1. What are the values of the following expressions:

    1.1. Succ (Succ (Succ ('E')))
    1.2. Pred (Pred ('7'))
    1.3. Pred (0)
    1.4. Chr (Ord ('X') + 1)
    1.5. Round (3.4999)
    1.6. Round (3.4999) + 0.1
    1.7. Round (3.4999 + 0.1)
    1.8. Trunc (3.4999 + 0.1)
    1.9. Sqr (11)
    1.A. Sqr (11.0)
    1.B. Sqrt (Sqr (3) + Sqr (4))
    1.C. Sqrt (Sqr (3)) + Sqrt (Sqr (4))
    1.D. Arctan (Sin (0.0))
    1.E. Exp (Ln (10.0))
    1.F. Ln (Exp (Cos (0.0)))

2. Trace the execution of the following program:

```
    1     PROGRAM Trace (Output);
    2
    3     VAR P, Q, Temporary : Integer;
    4
    5     BEGIN
    6     P := 7;
    7     Q := 33;
    8     Writeln (P : 5, Q : 5);
    9     Temporary := P;
   10     P := Q;
   11     Q := Temporary;
   12     Writeln (P : 5, Q : 5)
   13     END.
```

3. A program is said to "bomb" when it creates a run time error
message. This is usually because the program attempts to perform
some instruction on inappropriate data. Try running the following
program several times. See if you can discover the character with
the largest ordinal. (It could be the character which makes the
program bomb. Some implementations may be very forgiving and print
only a blank.)

```
 1    PROGRAM Bomb (Input, Output);
 2
 3    VAR Ch : Char;
 4
 5    BEGIN
 6    Writeln ('Enter a character');
 7    Read (Ch);
 8    Writeln ('The ordinal of ', Ch, ' is ', Ord (Ch) : 3);
 9    Writeln ('The successor is ', Succ (Ch))
10    END.
```

We have included a Read statement in this program. It permits the user to enter the character at the terminal, so that the program can be run many times with different input. The read statement is explained in the next chapter.

CHAPTER 5

Input

Sections

5.0   Introduction

     The assignment statement was introduced in Chapter 3 as one
method of assigning a value to a variable. A much more flexible
method is to obtain the value or values from an input device,
usually a computer terminal. Then, each time the program is
executed, it can manipulate the values that have been entered as
part of that run of the program. Input which is obtained from the
user can be likened to a stimulus, which can be varied within limits
imposed by the program. One hopes that the output produced by the
program is the response that the designer had in mind.

Values of variables of the three types, integer, real, and
characters, may be obtained from the input device. Without regard
to the type of the device, the computer system equates the input to
a standard file called Input.

We shall consider numeric input first. This will be followed
by a consideration of how a Pascal program obtains a character, or
several characters, as input.

5.1 Numeric Input

Many languages, including Pascal, provide standard procedures
for obtaining information from an input device during the execution
of a program. Suppose a program is awaiting input as a result of
executing an instruction to read the value of an integer variable.
If the user enters the string inside the apostrophes, ' 70531 ',
terminated by a carriage return or an equivalent end-of-line mark,
the system reads a string of seven characters (counting the leading
and trailing blanks) as well as the line terminator. The five
numeric characters are automatically read, and a conversion routine
is used to create the appropriate numeric value and to store that
value in the storage location set aside for the corresponding
integer variable.

Input Parameter List

In Pascal, the standard input procedure is called Read. The
form used is:

        Read (< input parameter list >)

The input parameter list is one or more identifiers of variables of
the three data types, integer, character, and real, separated by
commas.

For example, we can take the program Constant of listing 3.4,
which calculated the area of a circle, and modify it to allow the
value of the radius to be an input each time the program is run.
The resulting program, AreaofCircle, is given in listing 5.1:

```
1    PROGRAM AreaofCircle (Input, Output);
2
3    { Obtain radius of circle from input file using
4        the Read statement }
5
6    CONST Pi = 3.141593;
7
8    VAR
9        Radius : Integer;
10
11   BEGIN
12   Writeln ('Please enter integer value for radius');
13   Read (Radius);
14   Writeln ('Area of a circle of radius ', Radius : 3,
15            ' is ', Pi * Sqr (Radius ) : 10 : 5)
16   END.
```

Run:
```
     Please enter integer value for radius
6                                                        !Input
     Area of a circle of radius    6 is   113.09735
```

Run:
```
     Please enter integer value for radius
8                                                        !Input
     Area of a circle of radius    8 is   201.06195
```

Listing 5.1

This program not only uses the output file to communicate with the external world but also accepts information via an input file. The list of files in the program heading is expanded to include the input file. Since the execution of the program now includes input, we have used Run: to indicate the command to initiate the execution of the program. The output produced by the computer is indented whereas the user's input has been set flush to the left and, on the far right of the line, contains an emphatic indication that it is input.

Prompting

The read statement on line 13 is preceded by a prompt to the user. After this prompt, the computer waits for the user to enter an integer. Without the prompt, the user may not know that the computer is waiting for input. Eventually, the user may realize this and enter an integer, if the user guesses that is what the computer is waiting for. On the other hand, the user may become bored, and leave. It is better to include too many prompts, as opposed to too few, so that the user is aware of why the program is in a state of suspension.

Effect of the Read Statement

Assuming that the user has entered 6 (as in the first run of this program), the effect of the Read statement is similar to the effect of an assignment statement. The before and after picture of the data space is given by:

```
           Before            Instruction          After

         -----------                           -----------
Pi       | 3.14156 |                      Pi   | 3.14156 |
         -----------       Read (Radius)       -----------
         -----------                           -----------
Radius   |    ?    |                    Radius |    6    |
         -----------                           -----------
```

The reason why we used an integer variable for the radius in the previous version of this program is that we wished to exhibit the use of expressions with both reals and integers. Here, it would be more reasonable to permit the user to enter a real number for the value of the radius. The appropriate modification of the source program would be to change the declaration of Radius to Real (and probably to change the format by which its value is printed in line 14).

The output list for a Write statement may include expressions and literal strings. The program creates appropriate values (and converts them into appropriate character strings) as needed. An input list, on the other hand, may only contain identifiers of variables. This is a reasonable requirement if one realizes that there must be a memory location assigned and available in which to store the value obtained from the input device.

Reading Several Values

The source program included in listing 3.3 found the average of three real numbers whose values were established by means of three assignment statements. Those assignment statements can be replaced

by a Read statement to obtain the three values from the user. Here
is the new program:

```
1    PROGRAM MoreAvg (Input, Output);
2
3    { Compute and print the average of three real numbers
4         obtained from the user }
5
6    VAR  T1, T2, T3 : Real;
7
8    BEGIN
9    Writeln ('Please enter three real numbers');
10   Read (T1, T2, T3);
11   Writeln;
12   Writeln ('Data: ', T1 : 10 : 3, T2 : 10 : 3, T3 : 10 : 3);
13   Writeln;
14   Writeln ('Average: ',  (T1 + T2 + T3) / 3.0 : 10 : 3)
15   END.
```

Run:
      Please enter three real numbers
1.0   2.0   3.0   !Input

      Data: 1.000   2.000   3.000

      Average: 2.000

Run:
      Please enter three real numbers
5.0   0.0   -5.0   !Input

      Data: 5.000   0.000   -5.000

      Average: 0.000

Listing 5.2

     These are not very exciting results, but they are easy to check
by hand. Although most programs should be checked more thoroughly
than by using two sets of sample data, simple data can often be very
useful in spotting program errors. Again note that we have preceded
the Read statement with a prompt.

     The Read statement of line 10 requires that the program obtain
values for each of the three variables listed, before the program
proceeds to the next statement. If more than three numbers were
entered on a line, the first three values would be the ones that
were read. Thus, we could have the following execution of this

program:

   Run:
       Please enter three real numbers
  5.0   0.0   -5.0   100.0   2000.1   !Input

      Data: 5.000   0.000   -5.000

      Average: 0.000

    The three values required need not be entered on a single line since the Read statement will continue to seek the necessary input until it is found. Thus, the execution of the program could appear as:

   Run:
       Please enter three real numbers
   5.0   !Input
   0.0   !Input
   -5.0   !Input

      Data: 5.000   0.000   -5.000

      Average: 0.000

Possible Errors

    If the values are entered on the same line, at least one blank space must separate them (this allows the routine which reads the characters and converts them to their numeric values to discover where one number ends and the next begins). Normally, we tend to use a comma as a separator when listing several numbers, but the presence of a comma in the input will almost always create a run-time error, which causes the operating system to abort the program and to display some "error message". If one looks carefully at most of these error messages, one can sometimes find a few words which are intelligible, although most of the information displayed is of no help at all. Someday, perhaps, one might obtain the following:

   Run:
       Please enter three real numbers
  10.0, 20.0, 30.0   !Input
      ERROR. Comma or commas encountered while attempting to
        read numeric data. Program MoreAvg aborted at line 10

   Input, presented to the program using the instruction to read
real numbers, can also be in the scientific or E format. Here is
the result of a run of the program using input in that form:

   Run:
        Please enter three real numbers
   5.0E6   0.0E6   -5.0E6   !Input

        Data: 5000000.000   0.000-5000000.000

        Average: 0.000

   In this case, some of the numbers are of fairly large
magnitude, and it might be more appropriate to print out the data
and results in the same form as the input. 5.0E6 is a five followed
by six zeros, i.e., five million. To write all of the characters in
the representation of this number, with three digits after the
decimal point, requires eleven characters. A generous operating
system will override the 10 : 3 format specified and use as many
print positions as is necessary to print the required
representation.

5.2   Character Input

   A general purpose computer system will include one or more
input devices. A common device, which provides for both input and
output to a computer, is a terminal. (Terminals are generally
classified as CRT, if the messages appear on a TV-like screen, or as
hardcopy, if the messages are printed in typewriter-like fashion.)
A terminal, and therefore the individual at the terminal,
communicates with the computer by means of messages composed of an
encoding of a string of characters and some control information such
as linefeeds and carriage returns. This encoding is by means of a
series of electrical signals. The message unit, which may contain
zero or several printable characters, is called a line.

   The maximum number of characters per line on a CRT may vary
from terminal to terminal. If one were using punched cards as
input, a line would be equivalent to up to 80 characters and a card
feed. Most CRT terminals display the same number of characters on a
line. Many terminals allow one to send longer lines to the
computer, perhaps lines containing 132 printable characters, which
corresponds to the line width on many printers. The characters

after the eightieth then appear on a continuation line on the screen
of the terminal but appear on the same at the printer.

Buffered Input

We shall assume that the message unit or line to the computer
is not completed and sent until the RETURN (or an equivalent) key is
pressed. (One of the nice features of this technique is that one
may delete and replace characters in the line provided one has not
yet pressed the return key.) The computer stores the characters as
they are received from the terminal in an area of memory which is
usually called a buffer. Buffers are used to store temporarily
information that is being sent from one device to another. They are
frequently emptied, that is, read from, and frequently written to.
(In certain installations, input may not be buffered, and processing
a read statement may not wait for the Return key to be pressed).

While the input stream is viewed by a Pascal program as a
stream of characters, it is usually transmitted by some standard
code as a sequence of bits encoding a character. A bit may be
thought of as a variable with one of two values, usually represented
by 0 or 1. The memory cells of a computer are storage locations
which can retain a certain number of bits. Characters, either
control characters--such as carriage return--or printable
characters--such as integers, reals, and other data types--are all
represented by groups of bits.

Reading Several Characters

Listing 5.3 contains a short Pascal program which writes a
prompt, reads five characters from the terminal, and then prints the
first five characters that have been read.

```
1    PROGRAM Read5Characters (Input, Output);
2
3    { Read 5 characters from terminal or input device
4        Used to show End-of-line or carriage return,
5        when read as a character, is read as a blank }
6
7    VAR
8        C1, C2, C3, C4, C5 : Char;
9
10   BEGIN
11   Writeln ('Please enter at least five characters.');
```

```
12    Writeln ('Count each return as a character.');
13    Read (C1, C2, C3, C4, C5);
14    Writeln ('The characters read were');
15    Writeln ('....1....2....3....4....5');
16    Writeln (C1 : 5, C2 : 5, C3 : 5, C4 : 5, C5 : 5);
17    END.
```

Listing 5.3

     We will illustrate and comment upon several runs of this
program. Line 13 is an instruction to obtain the first five
characters from the input file and assign them to the character
variables C1 through C5, respectively. The input file may include
control characters in addition to printable characters. In most
systems using terminals, when the Return key is pressed on the
keyboard, a control character which we shall call NewLine, and
abbreviate <EOL>, is entered in the input file. To enable programs
to respond to the end of a line, these control characters cannot be
skipped. As we shall see, when the carriage return control
character is encountered, it is read as a blank.

     Here is a run of this program in which exactly five characters
are entered followed by a carriage return:

```
Run:
      Please enter at least five characters.
      Count each return as a character.
ABCDE                                                    !Input
      The characters read were
      ....1....2....3....4....5
          A    B    C    D    E
```

Line 16 requests that each character be printed in a five-column
field in order to separate the output. Each character is printed in
the rightmost position of its field, so that the five characters
appear in columns 5, 10, 15, 20, and 25. If no field width were
specified, each character would be printed in a single column and
the last line would be ABCDE.

     More than five characters may be entered on a line. In the
next run, only the first five characters are read to establish
values of C1 through C5:

Run:
          Please enter at least five characters.
          Count each return as a character.
     ABCDEFG+++123456789*   !Input
          The characters read were
          ....1....2....3....4....5
               A   B   C   D   E

If there were subsequent Read statements in the program, the next
character read would be F. The Input file has a pointer or window
which is situated so that it points to the character about to be
read. We can picture this by placing a pointer under the next
character that will be read, giving the state of the input file as:

     ABCDEFG+++123456789*
            ^

Reading <EOL> (End-of-Line)

     In the next example, we have entered two characters on a line
and then a Return to move to the next line:

     Run:
          Please enter at least five characters.
          Count each return as a character.
     AB   !Input
     CDEFG   !Input
          The characters read were
          ....1....2....3....4....5
               A   B   C   D

Since the first line of input has not satisfied the requirements of
the Read statement, more characters are read from the second line.
To the program, however, the first line contains not only the two
printable characters but also a third character, the NewLine or
<EOL>. Character variables may only be assigned printable
characters as their values. Since C3 is not allowed to store <EOL>,
it is given the value of the blank character.

     The input file, after the Read statement has been executed, is:

     AB<CR>CDEFG<CR>
          ^

Five characters have been read and the next character is E.

5.3   Readln

There is a variant of the Read procedure called Readln. Readln
completes the reading operation by positioning the file pointer or
file window immediately after the next NewLine in the input file.
This permits the subsequent read operation, if there is one, to
start at the beginning of a new line.

For example, suppose in the following program fragment that
Response is a character variable and Copies is an integer variable:

```
Writeln ('Enter Y for Yes, N for No');
Readln (Response);
Writeln ('If response was yes enter number of copies');
Readln (Copies);
```

A run of this portion of the program could be:

```
    Enter Y for Yes, N for No
  Y                                                         !Input
    If the response was yes enter number of copies
    1234                                                    !Input
```

The second input line begins with three blanks. The input file
produced is:

    Y<EOL>   1234<EOL>

The execution of the first Readln statement leaves the file pointer
in this position:

    Y<EOL>   1234<EOL>
          ^

and the execution of the second Readln statement leaves the file
pointer in this position:

    Y<EOL>   1234<EOL>
                     ^

Note that, since the conversion routine ignores leading blanks the
presence of a leading blank in the second line does not change the
resulting value of Copies. But the presence of a blank in front of
a Y or N in the first line will cause the variable Response to get
the value ' ', that is, the blank character.

One might consider separating the action of reading from the Input file and resetting the Input file to the beginning of the next line. Use a Read statement to get the input, and then a Readln statement, without any parameters, to reposition the file pointer. The following code maintains this distinction:

```
Writeln ('Enter Y for Yes, N for No');
Read (Response);
Readln;   { Move input window to beginning of next line }
Writeln ('If response was yes enter number of copies');
Read (Copies);
Readln;
```

5.4   Summary

Values may be assigned to integer, real, and character variables from an input device using the standard procedure Read. The variables whose values are to be read are named in the input parameter list, and the list is enclosed in parentheses.

The input device is treated as an Input file consisting of a stream of characters. The standard file Input must be named in the list of files in the heading. The Input file always has a pointer positioned at the next character to be read. When reading the value of a numeric variable, intervening blanks are skipped and the digits (along with perhaps a decimal point and an E for exponent) are read. When reading a character, the next character in the input file is read without skipping blanks or control characters. If the character is the control character NewLine, it is read as a blank.

The procedure Readln positions the file pointer or window at the beginning of the next line (i.e., immediately after the next NewLine). Readln may be used with an input parameter list, in which case the input file is first read until the values for all variables listed have been obtained (crossing line boundaries if necessary), and then a skip is made to the beginning of the next line.

Exercises for Chapter 5

1. Write a program which requests as input two integers, prints out
the integers just read, does the same for two characters, and then
finally does the same for two reals.

        (The repetition as output of the value of a variable
immediately after it is read is called echoing. In the development
stage of programs, it is always worthwhile to echo input, thus
verifying that it has been entered properly.)

2. Write a program which requests two integers and finds the
remainder when the first is divided by the second. Use the MOD
operator. The MOD operator may not be familiar to you. It can be
quite useful. You may find it worthwhile to run this program
several times with a variety of inputs.

3. Write a program which obtains from the user a character and an
integer. The integer should be of small magnitude, perhaps in the
range 1 to 25. Have the program output the character whose ordinal
is the ordinal of the given character plus the given integer. If,
in the particular arrangement (called the collating sequence) of the
machine you are working on, the alphabetic characters are ordered so
that they have consecutive ordinals, then, given B and 5 as input,
you should get G.

4. A weighted average of a sequence of numbers X1, ..., XN with
weights W1, ..., WN is obtained by multiplying each number by its
corresponding weight, adding these products, and then dividing this
sum by the sum of the weights. Write a program which allows a user
to enter three real numbers and three corresponding integer weights
and computes the weighted average.

5. Write a program which prompts the user for the measurement of an
angle in degrees, prints the measure of the angle in radians and the
sine, cosine, and tangent of the angle. Label the output file so
that it appears in a format such as:

      Angle   Sine   Cosine   Tangent
     0.78539   0.707   0.707   1.000

CHAPTER 6

Conditional Statements

Sections

6.0   Introduction

    In this chapter, we introduce a fourth data type, one in which there are only two values, True and False. Expressions may be formed using these data types and the logical connectives NOT, OR, and AND. Expressions involving relations between integers, between reals, or between characters, also yield one of these two truth values.

A statement which determines the subsequent instructions that are to be executed is called a control statement. The first control statement introduced is the IF-THEN-ELSE statement. On the basis of the truth or falsity of the governing expression, either the THEN clause or the ELSE clause is executed. Many occasions arise in which if something is true we wish the program to perform some action, otherwise we wish to skip that action. The appropriate control statement is the IF-THEN statement, which can be viewed as a special case of the IF-THEN-ELSE with the ELSE clause suppressed.

Both the IF-THEN and IF-THEN-ELSE statements allow selective execution of instructions. Pascal also includes a multiple branch instruction, the CASE statement. We have postponed the discussion of the CASE statement until user-defined types have been introduced.

6.1   Boolean Data Type

A fourth data type predefined as part of the Pascal language is called Boolean, after George Boole (1815 - 1864), a British logician and mathematician. A Boolean variable may have one of two values, True or False. The concept of a variable which may have either of the two constant values, True or False, may seem unusual to the novice programmer, but variables and expressions that have these values have many uses in a computer program.

Variables

A Boolean variable may be assigned a value and stored in the proper storage cell in whatever manner the system encodes the two possible values, True and False. That value can then be decoded and sent to the output file as an appropriate string of characters. This is illustrated by listing 6.1:

```
1    PROGRAM Perhaps (Output);
2
3    { Assignment to and output of Boolean variables }
4
```

```
 5    VAR   Maybe, Sometimes : Boolean;
 6
 7    BEGIN
 8    Writeln ('  Maybe   Sometimes');
 9    Maybe := True;
10    Sometimes := False;
11    Writeln (Maybe, Sometimes);
12    Maybe := False;
13    Sometimes := True;
14    Writeln (Maybe, Sometimes)
15    END.
```

Run:

```
        Maybe   Sometimes
         TRUE    FALSE
        FALSE     TRUE
```

Listing 6.1

The number of print columns used to print the Boolean values depends on the implementation. In this listing, seven columns are used to print either TRUE or FALSE. Unlike Integer, Real, and Character variables, the standard version of Pascal does not allow the value of a Boolean variable to be read from the input file. Nonstandard extensions may permit the character strings TRUE and FALSE to be read as a Boolean value rather than as a character string.

Expressions

An identifier which names a Boolean variable is subject to the same convention as are the names of other variables. It must begin with an alphabetic character and may be followed by any number of alphanumeric characters. Just as arithmetic expressions containing arithmetic constants, variables, and operators are evaluated and yield arithmetic values, Boolean expressions containing Boolean constants, variables, and operators are evaluated and yield Boolean values. Boolean values may also be obtained by evaluating relations.

Simple examples of Boolean expressions are expressions consisting of a single Boolean variable or either of the two constants, True and False.

Operators, Truth Tables

     More complicated Boolean expressions may be generated using the
Boolean operators NOT, OR, and AND. Since there are only two
Boolean constants, True and False, we can show the effect of these
operators by tabulating all the possibilities. The resulting tables
are called truth tables.

     If E is a Boolean expression, then NOT E is also a Boolean
expression, and, depending on the value of E, the value of NOT E is
determined according to the table:

E	NOT E
True	False
False	True

For example, Found := False; Again := NOT Found yields the value
True for Again.

     If P and Q are Boolean expressions, then both P OR Q and P AND
Q are Boolean expressions. The values of these compound expressions
are determined by the following table:

P	Q	P OR Q	P AND Q
True	True	True	True
True	False	True	False
False	True	True	False
False	False	False	False

For example,

```
     Found := True;
     Done := False;
     Again := (NOT Found) OR Done;
     Leftover := Found OR (NOT Done)
```

assigns the value False to Again and the value True to Leftover.

```
    TimeIsRipe := True;
    ThereIsMoney := False;
    DoIt := TimeIsRipe AND ThereIsMoney;
    DreamIt := TimeIsRipe AND (NOT ThereIsMoney)
```

assigns False to DoIt and True to DreamIt.

P AND Q is sometimes called the logical product of P and Q and also the conjunction of P and Q. P OR Q is sometimes called the logical sum of P and Q and also the disjunction of P and Q.

Relations

The previous examples illustrate how Boolean expressions involving Boolean variables and the operators NOT, OR, and AND have Boolean values. Relations between characters, integers, or reals, also give rise to Boolean values. Six relations and their usual meaning available in Pascal are:

Symbol	Meaning
=	Equals
<>	Is Unequal To
<	Precedes or Is Less Than
<=	Precedes or Equals or Is Less Than OR Equal To
>	Follows or Is Greater Than
>=	Follows or Equals or Is Greater Than OR Equal To

Here are some examples:

```
    Maximum := 50;
    Item := 33;
    Valid := (Item <= Maximum)
```

assigns the value True to Valid;

```
    Top := 20.0;
    Bottom := 5.0;
    X := 12.5;
    Inrange := (Bottom <= X) AND (Top >= X)
```

assigns the value True to Inrange;

```
    Early := 'D';
    InOrder := Early < 'Z';
    XXXXX :=  True AND (Early < 'A')
```

assigns the value True to InOrder and False to XXXXX.

Operator Precedence

    In a Boolean expression, AND takes precedence over OR, and NOT
has the highest precedence. The expression:

        NOT A OR B AND C

is evaluated as if it were the parenthesized expression:

        (NOT A) OR (B AND C)

Like arithmetic expressions, Boolean expressions may need to be
parenthesized. In fact, it is always good practice to parenthesize
Boolean expressions, for the Boolean operators bind more closely
than the arithmetic operators. Therefore, in an expression such as:

        Bottom <= X AND Top >= X

the compiler will first attempt to evaluate the expression X AND
Top, which generates an error. The expression must be written as

        (Bottom <= X) AND (Top >= X)

    Since the uppercase, or lowercase alphabetic characters are
ordered by their alphabetic position, the values of the expressions:

        'A' < 'Z'
        'K' < 'L'
        'p' < 'q'

are all True, whereas the expressions:

```
    'Y' < 'X'
    ('A' < 'B') AND ('q' < 'p')
```

are False.

There are three standard Boolean functions. These functions
are also called predicates. One of them, called Odd, takes an
integer as its argument and yields or returns a Boolean value. Odd
(N) is True if the integer N is odd and False if the integer N is
even. For example, Odd (5) is True, Odd (-10) is False, and, if N =
7, Odd (3 * N) is False.

The two other Boolean functions are identified by Eoln and Eof.
The first one tests for NewLine and the other tests for the end of a
file. They will be discussed in a later chapter.

6.2   IF-THEN-ELSE Statement

On the left side of figure 6.1 is a flowchart of the
IF-THEN-ELSE statement, on the right side is the form the statement
takes in a Pascal program. S1 and S2 are themselves statements
which may be simple or compound.

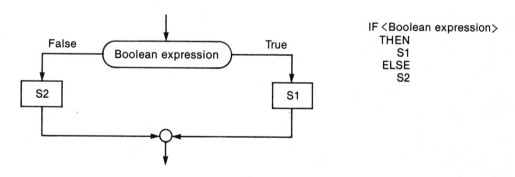

Figure 6.1   Flowchart and Form of the IF-THEN-ELSE Statement

Flowcharts

A flowchart is a collection of nodes and edges. The edges are
directed by arrow heads and usually connect two nodes. A node can
be used to represent a statement or action taken by a program. In
this case, it will have one edge leading toward the node and one
edge leading away from the node. Nodes may also represent decisions
based on testing the value of an expression. This type of node will
have one edge leading towards the node and several edges leading
away from the node, each of the edges labeled with a possible value
of the expression. Edges may be brought together at junctions.

Paths through a flowchart in the direction of the arrows are
intended to represent possible sequences of instructions in a
program. With each new statement, we will include a figure with a
flowchart alongside the syntactic form of the statement.

In each of the programs examined so far, the executable portion
of the program has consisted of a sequence of instructions which are
executed in exactly the same order as the order in which they appear
in the program. The power of the computer lies in the ability of
computer programs to modify the order in which instructions are
executed. Statements which modify the order of execution are called
control statements. There are two major classes of control
statements that we will rely upon to design programs. One class is
the set of statements which provide for making choices--statements
of the form, "If such and such is true then do the following". The
other class, which we shall consider in the next chapter, contains
statements which create repetition.

The IF-THEN-ELSE statement directs the execution of program
statements to take one of two possible courses, depending on the
truth or falsity of a Boolean expression. Because of the two
possible paths that execution may take, the IF-THEN-ELSE is often
characterized as a conditional branch.

Sample Program, TrueOrFalse

Listing 6.2 contains a program which prompts for a response to
a true or false question and then indicates whether a correct answer
has been given:

```
1    PROGRAM TrueOrFalse (Input, Output);
2
3    { Example of an IF-THEN-ELSE statement }
4
```

```
5    VAR
6       Answer : Char;
7
8    BEGIN
9    Writeln ('Washington''s white horse was grey?');
10   Writeln ('Please respond T for true, F for false.');
11   Read (Answer);
12   IF Answer = 'F'
13      THEN
14         Writeln ('Great!, Your answer was correct.')
15      ELSE
16         BEGIN
17         Writeln ('Sorry, your answer is wrong.');
18         Writeln ('Please accept my sympathy.')
19         END
20   END.
```

Run:
    Washington's white horse was grey?
    Please respond T for true, F for false.
F   !Input
    Great!, Your answer was correct.

Listing 6.2

Since we did not want the computer to think we were stupid, we carefully gave the right answer. This meant that, at the time the condition Answer = 'F' was evaluated, the resulting value would have been True. Consequently, the THEN clause was executed. Suppose, for the sake of illustration, that we run the program and supply a T when prompted. The run then appears as:

Run:
    Washington's white horse was grey?
    Please respond T for true, F for false.
T   !Input
    Sorry, your answer is wrong.
    Please accept my sympathy.

This time, Answer = 'F' evaluates to False, and the ELSE clause is executed.

In situations where both uppercase and lowercase alphabetic characters are available, a user might enter the character f rather than F and be surprised when told that the answer was wrong. It would be advisable to replace line 12 by the following:

```
12       IF  (Answer = 'F') OR  (Answer = 'f')
```

With this modification, both a lowercase and uppercase character
would be acceptable. It might be noted that any other character
results in a wrong answer. Thus, correct input preceded by several
blanks will also be treated as though an incorrect answer had been
entered. If one were carefully constructing questions to be
answered interactively, one might consider ignoring initial blanks
here, and also prompting again for an answer if any character other
than F or T is the first nonblank character. To do this, however,
we shall need control statements which provide for repetition.

Form of the IF-THEN-ELSE Statement

     In the program TrueOrFalse, the IF-THEN-ELSE statement occupies
lines 12 through 19. The form is:

     IF < Boolean expression > THEN < statement > ELSE < statement >

The THEN clause is a simple statement on line 14. The ELSE clause
in this program contains two Writeln statements. In order to bind
these two statements together to form a compound statement, they are
preceded by BEGIN and END on lines 16 and 19, respectively. BEGIN
and END may be used in this way very much like parentheses are used
for grouping in arithmetic expressions.

Nested Statements

     Lines 16 through 19 supply an instance of a statement following
ELSE. The entire IF-THEN-ELSE statement encompassing lines 12
through 19 is also an instance of statement. This is an interesting
situation in which certain statements are formed using as
constituent parts other statements. Statements which are embedded
in other statements in this fashion are said to be nested.

     Certain statements are simple, in that they have no statements
within them. In this class are assignment statements and statements
invoking the input/output procedures. Although certain statements,
such as the IF-THEN-ELSE, are defined in terms of other nested
statements, the most deeply nested statements must be simple
statements.

Sample Program, TeeOrEff

We suggested that one should test for the response F and the response T to the question in the program TrueOrFalse. This can be done by nesting an IF-THEN-ELSE statement within another statement. Listing 6.3 is a modified version of TrueOrFalse.

```
 1    PROGRAM TeeOrEff (Input, Output)·
 2
 3    { Example of nested IF-THEN-ELSE statements }
 4
 5    VAR
 6       Answer : Char;
 7
 8    BEGIN
 9    Writeln ('Washington''s white horse was grey?');
10    Writeln ('Please respond T for true, F for false.');
11    Read (Answer);
12    IF (Answer = 'F') OR (Answer = 'f')
13       THEN
14          Writeln ('Great!, Your answer was correct.')
15       ELSE
16          IF (Answer = 'T') OR (Answer = 't')
17             THEN
18                BEGIN
19                Writeln ('Sorry, your answer is wrong.');
20                Writeln ('Please accept my sympathy.')
21                END
22             ELSE
23                Writeln ('ERROR.  Character not T or F.')
24    END.
```

Run:
     Washington's white horse was grey?
     Please respond T for true, F for false.
Yes   !Input
     ERROR. Character not T or F.

Listing 6.3

Although three characters were entered, only the first character was read by the program, and Answer was given the value 'Y'. Therefore, both the expressions

            (Answer = 'F') OR (Answer = 'f')
and
            (Answer = 'T') OR (Answer = 't')

gave the value False. Consequently, the simple statement on line 23 was executed.

The semantics of the IF-THEN-ELSE statement is strongly suggested by the English usage of these words. If the expression is true, then the statement following THEN is executed; otherwise, the statement following ELSE is executed. Thus, the program has a fork with two branches. This situation is diagrammed by the flowchart in figure 6.1.

Pseudo Code

Figure 6.2 is a flowchart of the program TrueOrFalse. The program statements do not appear in the flowchart in complete detail; rather, they are described by English language phrases. Using English language phrases along with the forms of Pascal statements produces a description of a program called pseudo code.

```
Ask question
Get response
IF Answer = 'F'
    THEN
        Express sympathy
    ELSE
        Send congratulations
```

is pseudo code for the program TrueOrFalse. An excellent method for developing programs, especially complex ones, is to write preliminary versions in pseudo code.

Indentation

Without taking explicit note of the technique of indentation, we have been using it in the sample programs. Previously, all programs have been sequential, i.e., the executable part has been of the form BEGIN S1, ..., SN END., where S1, ..., SN were N statements. We have usually been writing each of the statements S1, ..., SN on a separate line. With the introduction of the IF-THEN-ELSE statement, we meet a more complicated statement, one which results in nonsequential execution and which, in turn, may contain or have nested within it other statements. To present visually the structure of this statement, we have indented THEN three spaces with respect to the IF. The statement that constitutes the THEN clause has also been indented three spaces with respect to

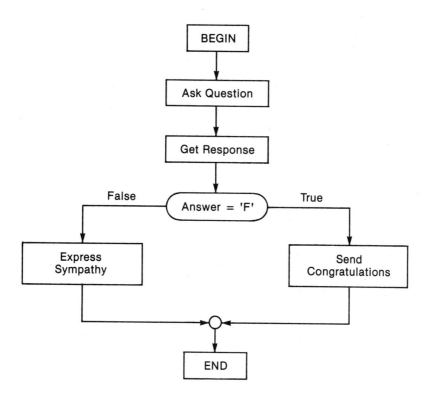

Figure 6.2   Flowchart of Program TrueOrFalse

THEN. In our example, the statement following ELSE is a compound statement of the form BEGIN S1, S2 END. We have chosen to use four lines, indenting each three spaces with respect to the ELSE, to permit a reader of the program to see the structure of the ELSE clause. Indentation should also be used with pseudo code.

Since indentation is not a part of the syntax of a Pascal program, the compiler ignores indentation. It is, nevertheless, an important part of good programming style, making programs more readable and understandable. There is no absolutely correct style and a variety of indentation styles exist. A number of authors will line up the IF and the ELSE of the IF-THEN-ELSE statement. We have chosen a style which emphasizes the IF and indents both the THEN and the ELSE in such a manner that it is easy to distinguish the two clauses.

6.3   IF-THEN Statement

     There are situations in which, if some condition is true, we
wish to take some action, whereas, if the condition is false, we do
not wish to take any action. In this case, the ELSE clause may be
omitted. For example, let N be an integer variable, then

     IF N > 100
        THEN Writeln ('Value too large')

will result in the execution of the statement following THEN being
executed in those instances in which N is greater than 100.   The
syntax of the IF-THEN statement is:

     IF < Boolean expression > THEN < statement >

The flowchart for this statement is given in figure 6.3.

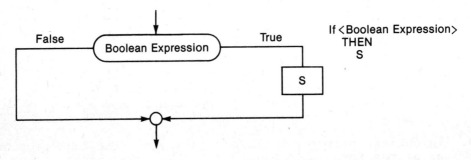

Figure 6.3   Flowchart and Form of the IF-THEN Statement

More on Flowcharts

     A flowchart of the program TeeOrEff (figure 6.4), in which we
have one IF statement nested within another IF statement, shows the
possible branches that execution of the program may take depending
on the input.   There are three possible paths from the initial BEGIN
to the final END.

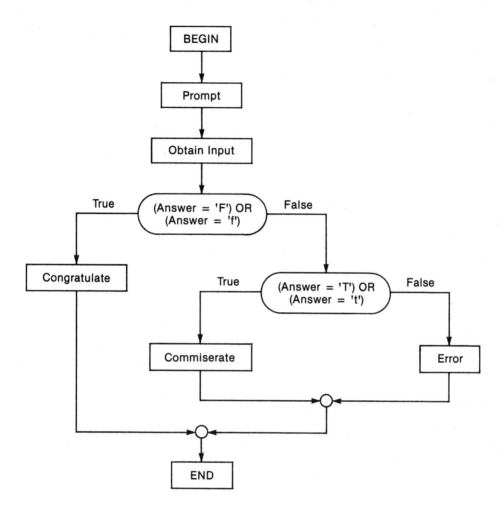

Figure 6.4   Flowchart of Program TeeOrEff

    The first programming language, FORTRAN, was initially
developed at IBM in the period 1954-57. In the next ten years, many
other programming languages were created. As programming languages
proliferated, many computer scientists felt the need for a universal
language. All this time, since flowcharts had been used to diagram
computations, it was natural to think of the possibility of a
universal language based on flowcharts. Programming texts contained

many flowcharts, and many of them adopted conventions which made the
function of a box in a flowchart correspond to its shape. Some
manuals contained flowcharts which spread over many pages and had
special symbols to connect them with other flowcharts. Diagrams of
this complexity are now not thought to aid in the understanding of
the flow of control in the algorithm being described. Today, it is
fair to say that a minimum amount of time is spent on flowcharts in
an introductory computer science course.

A Common Error

     Programmers often create an error condition by placing a
semicolon in front of the ELSE in the IF-THEN-ELSE statement.
(Perhaps this is done because the IF-THEN statement is usually
followed by a semicolon). For example, the semicolon in what
follows is an error:

```
        IF Grade > 'C'
            THEN
                Writeln ('Not too bad');
            ELSE
                Writeln ('Bummer!')
```

The compiler recognizes the first three lines as a complete IF-THEN
statement and attempts to recognize the third and fourth lines as a
statement beginning with ELSE. Since no such statement exists, an
error is created.

The Dangling ELSE

     An expression is ambiguous if it has two possible
interpretations. The potential ambiguity of the arithmetic
expression A+B*C is that it could be interpreted as either (A+B)*C
or A+(B*C). The ambiguity is resolved by deciding that the
multiplication operator * binds more closely than the addition
operator +. Consequently, the product B*C is formed first and this
is then added to A. Similarly, the presence of both the IF-THEN and
the IF-THEN-ELSE statements creates a potentially ambiguous
expression when an IF-THEN and an IF-THEN-ELSE are combined.

     To illustrate this, we will use S1 and S2 for statement and B1
and B2 for Boolean expression. The form:

```
        IF < B1 > THEN IF < B2 > THEN < S1 > ELSE <S2>
```

could be interpreted in two ways. The ambiguity to be resolved is
which of the two possible THEN's should the ELSE be paired with.
Using parentheses only for the sake of illustration here, since the
parentheses in these positions would not be permitted in a Pascal
program, the two interpretations are:

      IF < B1 > THEN (IF < B2 > THEN < S1 >) ELSE < S2 >

      IF < B1 > THEN (IF < B2 > THEN < S1 > ELSE < S2 >)

The convention adopted to avoid the ambiguity is that the ELSE is
paired with the nearest preceding unpaired or free THEN. Thus, the
second interpretation would be selected.

    In our indentation scheme, this interpretation is:

```
IF < B1 >
    THEN
        IF < B2 >
            THEN
                < S1 >
            ELSE
                < S2 >
```

An ELSE in this position is referred to as a "dangling ELSE".

    Here are two ways to arrive at the first interpretation: use
either an empty statement with another ELSE, or the BEGIN-END. The
two appropriate forms are:

```
IF < B1 >                        IF < B1 >
    THEN                             THEN
        IF < B2 >                        BEGIN
            THEN                             IF < B2 >
                < S1 >                                   THEN
            ELSE                                 < S1 >
                { Do nothing }                   END
    ELSE                             ELSE
        < S2 >                               < S2 >
```

The comment { Do nothing } may be omitted.

Tracing IF-THEN-ELSE

    Listing 6.4 is a program which prompts for two integers and always displays them starting with the smaller one. We will use this program to illustrate tracing a program containing an IF-THEN-ELSE statement.

```
1     PROGRAM Smaller (Input, Output);
2
3     VAR Item1, Item2, Small, Large : Integer;
4
5     BEGIN
6     Writeln ('Enter two integers');
7     Read (Item1, Item2);
8     IF Item1 <= Item2
9        THEN
10          BEGIN
11          Small := Item1;
12          Large := Item2
13          END
14       ELSE { Item2 < Item1 }
15          BEGIN
16          Small := Item2;
17          Large := Item1
18          END;
19    Writeln (Small, Large)
20    END.
```

Listing 6.4

    To trace this program, in addition to the data space of the declared variables, we encounter a Boolean expression on line 8 which must be evaluated in order to decide which part of the IF-THEN-ELSE statement is to be executed. Instead of storing the computed value in our head, we shall include a column in the trace in which the value of the expression can be entered. (The computer evaluates the expression and places the result in a working or scratchpad location often called a register.)

    Here is the trace with input 30   20:

Trace of program Smaller

Line	Item1	Item2	Small	Large	Item1 <= Item2	Input	Output
6							Prompt
7	30	20				30 20	
8					False		
16			20				
17				30			
19							20 30

6.4   Summary

The data type Boolean has two values, True and False. Boolean variables and constants are simple Boolean expressions. Boolean expressions may be combined using the logical operators NOT, OR, and AND. Relational operators may be used to compare two expressions, both of the same data type, yielding a Boolean result.

A program may choose which of two statements to execute by testing a Boolean expression. The controlling statement is of the form

```
IF < Boolean expression >
    THEN
        < statement 1 >
    ELSE
        < statement 2 >
```

Indentation is used to highlight the alternatives, i.e., the branches in the possible flow of the program. The effect of this IF-THEN-ELSE statement is to execute statement 1 if the Boolean expression has the value True and to execute statement 2 if the Boolean expression has the value False.

The statements in the THEN or ELSE clauses may in turn contain other IF-THEN-ELSE statements. This nesting of alternatives provides the facility to create many possible execution paths in a program.

The IF-THEN statement provides a method of executing a statement if a Boolean expression is True and skipping the statement if the expression is False. The form of this statement is:

```
IF < Boolean expression >
    THEN
        < statement >
```

Exercises for Chapter 6

1. Create your own program which presents the user with a True-False question, reads the response, and indicates if the user has chosen the correct answer.

2. Information may be coded in various ways. Suppose adult is coded as A, child as C, female as F, and male as M. Write a program which allows the user to enter two characters, the first either A or C and the second either F or M. If the user has entered CF, the program should print:

     The subject is a female child

Appropriate sentences should be printed for three possible choices, CM, AF, and AM.

3. Write a program which allows the user to enter three integers and which indicates correctly in all possible cases if the third integer entered lies strictly between the first two. Test the program with various sets of integers. Draw a flowchart of the program.

4. Write a program which requests one of the four integers 0, 1, 2, 3, and, if the integer supplied is in the requested range, prints one of the directions North, East, South, West according to the correspondence:

     0   North
     1   East
     2   South
     3   West

Have the program print some sort of error message if the integer
supplied is not in the requested range.

5. Using pseudo code, describe what might occur if a credit card
holder attempts to charge a purchase. Include the possibilities
that the card has expired and that the credit limit would be
exceeded.

6. An order for a certain number of units of some particular item
is received. Use pseudo code to describe how this data should be
processed. Include messages such as "all units ordered to be
shipped", "partial shipment, remainder to follow", "no units
available, do you wish to back order?".

7. For each of the four possible messages that might be printed by
the following program fragment, give assignments to Mileage and
Rainy of values which produce that message.

```
        Mileage :=          ;
        Rainy :=         ;
        IF Number < 100
            THEN
                IF Rainy
                    THEN
                        Writeln ('Take the brick road')
                    ELSE
                        Writeln ('Take the yellow road')
            ELSE
                IF NOT Rainy
                    THEN
                        Writeln ('Take the high road')
                    ELSE
                        Writeln ('Take the low road')
```


8. For each of the three possible messages that might be printed by
the following program fragment, give an assignment to Initial of a
value which produces that message. Are there any values for which
no output is produced?

```
        Initial :=        ;
        IF ('A' <= Initial) AND (Initial <= 'Z')
            THEN
                IF (Initial < 'H') OR (Initial > 'W')
                    THEN
```

```
                    Writeln ('Use the first door')
                ELSE
                    BEGIN
                    IF Initial = 'Q'
                        THEN
                            Writeln ('Use the second door')
                    END
            ELSE
                Writeln ('Come back tomorrow')
```

9. Assume the following assignments have been made:

```
        Number := -33;
        Count := 12;
        Letter := 'D';
        Ch := 't';
        Sick := False
```

Find the values of each of the following expressions:

```
        (Number > 0) OR (Count > 0);
        (NOT (Ch < 'z')) AND (Number <= 0);
        NOT (Sick OR ((Ch = 'T') AND (Letter = 'D')));
        (Count <> 0) AND (NOT Sick);
        (Count = 10) OR (Number > 0) OR
                    ((Count > 6) AND (Count < 18));
```

10. Since many real numbers cannot be stored exactly in computer memory, tests involving real numbers should not be based on equality but on some degree of closeness. Write a program which allows the user to enter three real numbers, say a, b, and c--the third one a positive number which describes a possible measure of closeness of the first two numbers. Have the program indicate whether or not the first two numbers are closer together than the measure given by the third. Thus, an input of 2.3, -3.8, and 5.0 should indicate that the degree of closeness is not achieved since $2.3 - (-3.8) = 6.1$, whereas an input of 6.1, 5.9, and 0.3 should indicate that the first two are within 0.3 of each other.

11. Two simultaneous linear equations in two unknowns are equations of the form:

$$a * x + b * y = e$$

$$c * x + d * y = f$$

Multiplying the first equation by d and the second equation by b and
subtracting to eliminate y, one can solve for x and obtain the
formula:

$$x = (e * d - f * b) / (a * d - c * b)$$

provided a*d -c*b <> 0. Similarly, a solution for y can be obtained
in the form:

$$y = (a * f - c * e) / (a * d - c * b)$$

Write a program which (1) requests the values of the six numbers a,
b, c, d, e, f; (2) prints the equation in a reasonable format, such
as:

```
1.5  * x +        -3.5  * y =        4.0
2.0  * x +         1.0  * y =       -2.5
```

(3) calculates the denominator a*d - b*c; and (4) prints the
solutions (if the denominator is different from zero), or else
indicates that there is no unique solution.

12. Write a program which obtains from the user three integers A,
B, and C, and indicates if A = B MOD C.

13. Write a program which obtains from the user a positive integer
intended to represent a potentially large number of minutes and
which then prints the number of hours and minutes this integer
represents. The minutes reported in the output should be an integer
between 0 and 59, inclusive.

CHAPTER 7

Repetition

Sections

7.0 Introduction

To find one item of information in a large store of
information, a computer program may need to perform a comparison
instruction over and over again. All programs which process a
sizeable amount of information must repeat groups of instructions
many times. Today, high-speed computers perform tens of millions of
instructions per second, or in computer jargon, "MIPS". Computer
programs can generate instructions in these quantities by means of
statements which command the repetitive execution of certain
actions.

In Pascal, there are three statement constructs which govern or
control repetitive action: WHILE-DO, REPEAT-UNTIL, and FOR-DO.

7.1 WHILE-DO

The WHILE-DO statement commands the computer to repetitively
execute a statement (possibly a compound statement). The form of
the WHILE-DO statement is:

        WHILE < Boolean expression > DO < statement >

Effect of WHILE-DO

The effect of the WHILE-DO statement is described by the
flowchart in figure 7.1. Let B be the Boolean expression and S the
statement. WHILE B DO S repetitively performs two steps:

    Step 1. Evaluate and test B.
             If B is true, do step 2.
             If B is false, go on to the instruction following
                the complete WHILE-DO statement.

    Step 2. Execute S.
             Return to step 1.

The repetition terminates the first time Step 1 yields the value
False as the value of B. In other words, while B is True, the

statement S following the DO is executed. The two steps correspond
to the two boxes in the flowchart in figure 7.1.

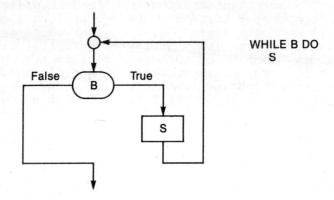

Figure 7.1 Flowchart and Form of the WHILE-DO Statement

     If one is not careful, one can easily write a program which
never terminates. Computers are patient machines, and they never
become bored performing the same operations over and over again.
Therefore, unless Step 2 eventually affects the value of B, the
WHILE-DO statement will never be terminated.

Sample Program, Guess1

     Program Guess1, given in listing 7.1 uses the WHILE-DO
statement:

```
 1     PROGRAM Guess1 (Input, Output);
 2
 3     { User enters a character until it matches
 4         "secret" character.  Illustrates WHILE-DO }
 5
 6     CONST  BigSecret = 'W';
 7
 8     VAR    Guess : Char;
 9
10     BEGIN
11     { Get first guess }
12     Writeln ('Guess my secret character');
```

```
13    Read (Guess);
14    Readln;          { Prepare to read from next line }
15    Writeln ('Your guess is ', Guess);
16    WHILE Guess <> BigSecret DO
17       { Get another guess }
18       BEGIN
19       Writeln ('That was wrong.  Try again.');
20       Read (Guess);
21       Readln;
22       Writeln ('Your new guess is ', Guess)
23       END;
24    Writeln ('You guessed it!')
25    END.
```

Listing 7.1

The WHILE-DO statement occupies lines 16 through 23. The
Boolean expression is Guess <> BigSecret. (Recall that <> stands
for the relation "is not equal to".) The statement following DO is a
compound statement which occupies lines 18 through 23 and consists
of four simple statements delimited by the BEGIN-END pair.

A run of this program could be:

```
Run:
      Guess my secret character
X                                                       !Input
      Your guess is X
      That was wrong.  Try again.
U                                                       !Input
      Your new guess is U
      That was wrong.  Try again.
W                                                       !Input
      Your new guess is W
      You guessed it!
```

Fortunately, we knew the secret character from the beginning.
This is one of those nasty programs which will not let you go on
until you give it what it wants, but, unless you have seen the
source program or have special information, you do not know what is
wanted.

It is not unusual to use the WHILE-DO statement in situations
where the Boolean expression is found to be False the first time it
is tested and, consequently, the statement after DO is not executed
at all. (This is what would happen if we ran Guess1 with initial
input W.)

Flowchart of Guess1

        Pseudo code for the program Guess1 is:

```
        BEGIN
        Prompt for input
        Read Ch
        Echo input
        WHILE Ch <> BigSecret DO
            BEGIN
            Send message
            Read Ch
            END
        Congratulate
        END
```

The corresponding flowchart is given in figure 7.2.

        In these flowcharts, the presence of a loop or cycle indicates
a path that can be repeated many times. As control flows along such
a loop, the statement or statements executed may be either simple or
complex. A WHILE-DO statement can have compound statements,
conditional statements such as the IF-THEN-ELSE statement, and other
WHILE-DO statements nested within it.

WHILE Unacceptable DO

        As an example of this sort of nesting, listing 7.2 contains a
portion of a program which could be used to do the following:

        Prompt the user for some input
        Test the input to determine if it is acceptable
        If it is acceptable proceed with further processing,
            otherwise explain to the user that the input is
            unacceptable (perhaps with a short explanation as to
            why) and then recycle through the input and test
            portions again

Pseudo code for this process is given in listing 7.2:

```
        Unacceptable := True
        Prompt for input
        WHILE Unacceptable DO
            BEGIN
            Obtain input
            Assign Unacceptable a value on the basis
```

```
        of the input just obtained
IF Unacceptable
    THEN
        Send error message
END
```

Listing 7.2

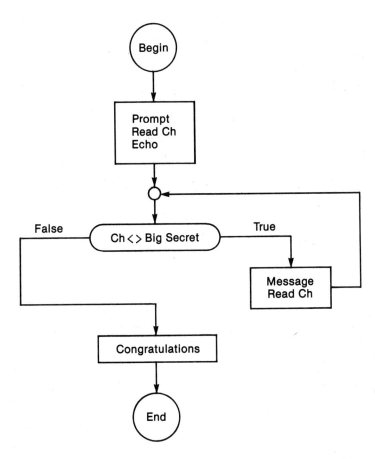

Figure 7.2 Flowchart of Program Guess1

For example, the user may have been prompted to enter an
integer called Choice in the range Low to High. The assignment of a
value to Unacceptable could then be by the statement:

        Unacceptable := (Choice < Low) OR (High < Choice)

An alternate form, which some may find more natural, includes
the determination of acceptable as part of the IF-THEN statement by
expanding it to the following IF-THEN-ELSE statement:

```
        IF (Choice < Low) OR (High < Choice)
            THEN
                Send error message
            ELSE
                Unacceptable := False
```

There is no reason to believe that there is a unique way to
write a program which accomplishes a given task. The previous
statement can also be revised to the equivalent form:

```
        IF (Low <= Choice) AND (Choice <= High)
            THEN
                Unacceptable := False  { Choice is in range }
            ELSE
                Send error message
```

Note that, in all these variations, we have always given
Unacceptable an initial value of True before entering the WHILE-DO
loop. Even though the significant determination of the value of
Unacceptable occurs within the loop, the value of Unacceptable is
used in the first step of the loop. Therefore, it must have a value
assigned to it prior to the entry into the loop.

Do It Again

Both the program Guess1 and this fragment are instances of
programs which do not permit processing to proceed until a certain
condition is satisfied. There are many situations in which we want
the program to give the user the option of requesting another
repetition. The general outline of such a scheme would be a
fragment such as listing 7.3:

```
DoItAgain := True;
WHILE DoItAgain DO
   BEGIN
   { Do Something }
   Writeln ('Do you wish to continue?');
   Writeln ('Respond Y for yes, N for No');
   Read (Response);
   Readln;
   IF (Response = 'N') OR (Response = 'n')
      THEN
           DoItAgain := False
   END
```

                Listing 7.3

Password

     Suppose we do not wish to allow users of a program, other than
those who know the secret character, use of a portion of a program
and the data which that portion of the program may access. In other
words, we wish to protect a portion of a program with a password.
Frequently, if a password is fairly complex, a user is given a few
chances to supply it successfully before an alarm of some sort is
sounded. Listing 7.4 supplies a program which requests a
two-character password, gives the user three tries to supply it, and
sounds an alarm if the user fails the third time.

```
1     PROGRAM Password (Input, Output);
2
3     { Obtain two characters from user, compare them with
4        two predefined characters as a password.  Allow
5        the user at most three tries to match password.
6        Report the result. }
7
8     CONST       First = 'W';       Second = 'I';
9
10    VAR
11       C1, C2 : Char;                    { User's characters }
12       Count : Integer;                  { Number of tries }
13       Locked : Boolean;  { Initially True, set to False if
14                                 password is supplied }
15
16    BEGIN
17    Writeln ('Please enter 2 character password');
18    Locked := True;
```

```
19    Count := 0;
20    WHILE Locked AND (Count < 3) DO
21       BEGIN
22       Count := Count + 1;                    { Increment Count }
23       Read (C1, C2);   Readln;               { Get password? }
24       IF (C1 = First) AND (C2 = Second)
25          THEN
26             Locked := False
27          ELSE
28             Writeln ('Please try again')
29       END;
30    IF Locked
31       THEN
32          Writeln ('Sound the Alarm!')
33       ELSE
34          Writeln ('Pass, you took ', Count:1, ' tries')
35    END.
```

Listing 7.4

This program introduces a technique whereby the program itself
keeps track of the number of times the compound statement extending
from line 21 to line 29 is executed. Before the WHILE-DO loop is
entered, an integer variable Count is initialized to have the value
0. Each time the loop is executed, the assignment statement on line
22 uses the current value of Count to evaluate the expression Count
+ 1. This new value is assigned to Count, thereby increasing its
value by 1.

Two variables, one Count, and the other the Boolean variable
Locked, are assigned values before the WHILE-DO loop is entered.
They both must have appropriate values at the moment that the
Boolean expression

Locked AND (Count < 3)

is first tested. Since Locked will be False and (Count < 3) will be
True, the conjunction of the two will be False. Thus, the compound
statement on lines 21 through 29 will be executed at least once.

Accumulating a Total

The variable Count in this program accumulates a running total
of the number of times the user has attempted to supply the
password. A similar technique can be used to find the sum of a
sequence of numbers. Initially, a variable, such as Total, is set

to zero. The accumulation instruction is performed while there is a
next number to be included. In pseudo code the accumulation
instruction is:

        WHILE There is a next number DO
            Total := Total + NextNumber

Powers of 2

    Another variation would initially set a variable Number to one
and continually double it using the instruction:

        Number := 2 * Number

Listing 7.5 is a program which should print as many powers of 2 as
the particular implementation permits:

```
1    PROGRAM Powersof2 (Input, Output);
2
3    { Print a table of positive powers of 2 determined by
4        the value of Maxint }
5
6    VAR CurrentValue, CurrentPower : Integer;
7
8    BEGIN
9    { Print Heading }
10   Writeln ('      Table of Powers of 2');
11   Writeln ('      Power              Value');
12   Writeln;
13   { Initialize CurrentValue, CurrentPower }
14   CurrentPower := 0;
15   CurrentValue := 1;
16   WHILE CurrentValue < (Maxint DIV 2) DO
17      BEGIN
18      CurrentPower := 1 + CurrentPower;
19      CurrentValue := 2 * CurrentValue;
20      { CurrentValue = 2 ** CurrentPower }
21      Writeln (CurrentPower : 10, CurrentValue : 15)
22      END
23   END.
```

Listing 7.5

    We will not include the output from this program, other than
the last line. When it was run on a 32-bit machine (meaning that 32
bits were used to store an integer), the output was

```
30       1073741824
```

Pascal does not have an exponentiation operator nor a symbol
for exponentiation, therefore, we have borrowed the FORTRAN symbol
** for exponentiation in the comment on line 20. After line 15 has
been executed to give CurrentPower and CurrentValue their initial
values, CurrentValue = 2 ** CurrentPower (since 1 = 2 ** 0). After
the execution of the loop, lines 16 through 22, the relation
CurrentValue = 2 ** CurrentPower is still true. For this reason,
the relation is called a loop invariant. Finding appropriate loop
invariants is an essential part of a more advanced approach to
programming--program verification, or proving the correctness of
programs.

Make sure you understand the effect of the WHILE-DO statement.
A frequent misconception with regard to the WHILE-DO statement is
that somehow the computer continually monitors the controlling
Boolean expression and will terminate the loop immediately after
executing the instruction that makes the expression have the value
False. This is not the case. A WHILE-DO loop is either skipped
completely if the controlling condition is initially False, or
terminated after the entire statement following the DO has been
executed.

7.2   REPEAT-UNTIL

The IF-THEN and WHILE-DO statements together provide the
necessary control statements with which to describe any computation.
It is convenient, nevertheless, to have other control statements.
The typical situation in which the WHILE-DO is natural is WHILE
there is more to do, DO it. The emphasis is on the truth that there
is more to do.

In another typical situation, instructions are to be repeated
until some terminating condition becomes true. The typical form is
REPEAT these instructions UNTIL the task is finished. The emphasis
is now on the truth of the task being finished as the terminating
condition.

Form of REPEAT-UNTIL

Let S1, S2, ..., SN be statements and let B be a Boolean
expression. The syntax of the REPEAT-UNTIL statement is

REPEAT S1 ; S2 ; ... ; SN UNTIL B

The syntax and accompanying flowchart are given in figure 7.3.
Here, the REPEAT-UNTIL loop is the one or more statements between
the REPEAT and the UNTIL. The BEGIN-END construct is not needed
here. As one can see from the flowchart in figure 7.3, the
REPEAT-UNTIL loop is always executed at least once since the test
for termination occurs at the end of the loop.

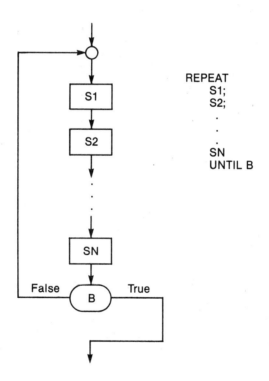

Figure 7.3 Flowchart and Form of the REPEAT-UNTIL Statement

In the form of execution and test for termination, the outline
of the REPEAT-UNTIL loop is:

Step 1 Execute one or more instructions.

Step 2 Test for termination.
            If the terminating condition is true proceed
                to the next instruction.
            If the terminating condition is false return
                to step 1.

Steps 1 and 2 are repeated until step 2 yields true for the
terminating condition.

Sample Program, AskAgain

A useful application of the REPEAT-UNTIL statement occurs in
interactive programs which prompt for data within a certain range or
of a certain type. We mentioned the possibility with respect to the
TrueorFalse program of repetitively prompting for a T or F response.
Listing 7.6 contains a comparable program which prompts for an
integer in a certain range:

```
1    PROGRAM AskAgain (Input, Output);
2
3    { Prompt for an integer in a certain range
4      Continue to request input until the integer is in range
5      Application of REPEAT-UNTIL }
6
7    VAR
8       Number : Integer;
9       Acceptable : Boolean;
10
11   BEGIN
12   Writeln ('Please enter a positive integer less than 100');
13   Readln (Number);
14   REPEAT
15      IF (Number > 0) and (Number < 100)
16         THEN Acceptable := True
17         ELSE
18            BEGIN
19            Acceptable := False;
20            Writeln ('Input out of range.  Please reenter.');
21            Readln( Number )
22            END
23      UNTIL Acceptable;
```

```
24    Writeln ('Thank You')
25    END.
```

Listing 7.6

The REPEAT-UNTIL statement can be simulated by using the
WHILE-DO statement. Let S be a statement and B be a Boolean
expression. REPEAT S UNTIL B is equivalent to the compound
statement BEGIN S; WHILE NOT B DO S END.

7.3   FOR-DO

In both of the previously considered iteration statements, the
precise number of repetitions was not known in advance. Frequently,
the exact number of times that a group of actions is to be performed
is computable in advance. A convenient statement to use in these
cases is the FOR-DO statement. The FOR-DO statement allows one to
use a variable called a control variable and to force it to assume
successive values in a sequence or range of values. The control
variable can be an integer, character, or Boolean variable, as well
as a user-defined scalar (see Chapter 10). Commonly an integer
variable is used as the control variable.

There are two forms of the FOR-DO statement. In one form, the
control variable moves from a smaller initial value up to a larger
final value. In the other form, the control variable moves from a
larger initial value down to a smaller final value.

Figure 7.4 gives the flowchart and the syntax of the "up to"
form of the FOR-DO statement.

Sample Program, BankBook

Listing 7.7 is an example of a program using the FOR-DO
statement:

```
1    PROGRAM BankBook (Output);
2
3    { Produce table of bank book balances }
4
5    CONST  Here = 1984;  Eternity = 2001;
```

```
 6
 7    VAR   Balance, Rate, Interest : Real;
 8          Year : Integer;
 9
10    BEGIN
11    Balance := 100.00;
12    Rate := 0.0625;
13    Writeln ('Table of Bank Book Balances'); Writeln;
14    Writeln ('Initial amount', Balance : 10 : 2);
15    Writeln ('Interest rate', Rate : 10 : 4); Writeln;
16    Writeln ('Year      Balance');
17    FOR Year := Here TO Eternity DO
18        BEGIN
19        Interest := Balance * Rate;
20        Balance := Balance + Interest;
21        Writeln (Year : 4, Balance : 12 : 2)
22        END
23    END.
```

Listing 7.7

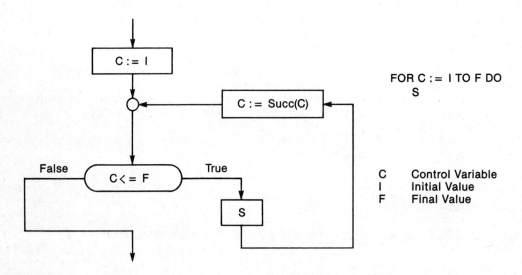

Figure 7.4   Flowchart and Form of FOR-DO Statement,
Increasing Value of Control Variable

Form of FOR-DO

The general form of this version of the FOR-DO statement is:

FOR <identifier> := <expression> TO <expression> DO <statement>

In the sample program, the identifier names an integer variable used
as the control variable, and, therefore, both the expressions must
have integer values. Whenever the FOR-DO statement is used, the
types of the control variable and both of the expressions must
agree.

The actual FOR-DO statement in this sample program occupies
lines 17 through 22. The execution of these lines initially assigns
the value 1984 to Year. Then repetitively, Year is tested to see if
it exceeds Eternity; if not, the compound statement on lines 18
through 22 is executed after which Year is increased by one.

Effect of the FOR-DO Statement

The effect of the FOR-DO statement in which the control
variable is increasing can be outlined as follows:

    Initial action
        Control variable set to the value of first expression

    Repetitive actions
        Step 1   Test if value of control variable exceeds the
                 value of the second expression, and if not
        Step 2   Execute the loop and replace the current value
                 of the control variable by its successor.

This implies that the control variable must be one of the
simple, enumerated types--integer, character, Boolean, or
user-defined scalar.

Note that, the first time Step 1 is executed, if the control
variable exceeds the second expression, the loop is not executed at
all. For example, no output is produced by:

        FOR Index := 10 TO 1 DO
            Writeln ('Golly!')

The above description of the FOR-DO should suggest that the
same effect can be achieved using the WHILE-DO statement. Lines 17
through 22 of the BankBook program:

```
        FOR Year := Here TO Eternity DO
            < statement >
```

are equivalent to:

```
        Year := Here;
        WHILE Year <= Eternity DO
            BEGIN
            <statement>;
            Year := Succ (Year)
            END
```

Remember, however, in the FOR-DO, the control variable is incremented automatically. In the body of a FOR-DO, the appearance of the control variable on the left side of an assignment statement is most likely an error on the programmer's part. This type of irregularity may be officially designated a compilation error in the standard currently under consideration for the Pascal language.

Periodic Output

We have not listed the output of program bankbook. Line 21 is executed eighteen times, producing output starting with the first year's balance, 106.25, and ending with a balance of 297.80 in the year 2001. By 1995, the initial amount has more than doubled, and, in eighteen years, it has almost tripled. Such is the power of compound interest. Since actual bank interest is compounded more frequently than once a year (and may be higher), the growth of a bank balance is faster in reality.

A variation of this program would "run" for fifty years by changing Eternity to 2033. Instead of printing fifty lines of output, we can output the balance every ten years. Line 21 is replaced by the IF-THEN statement:

```
        IF Year MOD 10 = (Here - 1) MOD 10
            THEN
                Writeln (Year : 4, Balance 12 : 2)
```

The resulting output from the modified program is:

Table of Bank Book Balance

Initial amount   100.00
Interest rate   0.0625
Year   Balance
1993   183.35
2003   336.19
2013   616.41
2023   1130.21
2033   2072.27

Finding a Maximum

Another example of repetitive action is finding the maximum value of a sequence of numbers. One technique that may be used is initially to set a tentative maximum to a very small number. Then, in a "king of the hill" fashion, each number is compared to the current maximum. If the new number is larger than the current maximum, it is enthroned as the new maximum.

By prompting the user for a count of the sequence to be examined, we can control the repetition with a FOR-DO statement. The appropriate fragment is:

```
CurrentMaximum := -MaxInt;
Writeln ('Enter number of entries to be processed');
Readln (Count);
Writeln ('Enter ', Count : 3, ' entries');
FOR Place := 1 TO Count DO
    BEGIN
    Read (CurrentNumber);
    IF CurrentNumber > CurrentMaximum
        THEN
            CurrentMaximum := CurrentNumber
    END;
Readln;
Writeln ('The maximum entry was ', CurrentMaximum : 10)
```

Figure 7.5 contains a flowchart for the "down to" version of the FOR-DO statement. The control variable is decremented each time through the loop by replacing it with its predecessor, and termination occurs when the control variable is less than the final value.

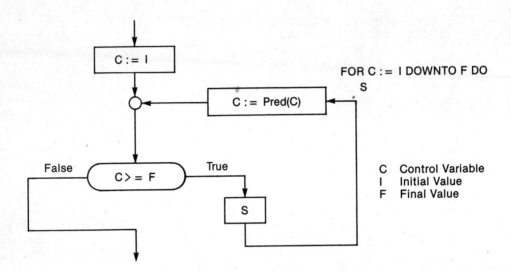

Figure 7.5   Flowchart and Form of the FOR-DO Statement,
Decreasing Value of Control Variable

As an example, the uppercase alphabetic characters could be
printed in reverse order by the code:

```
FOR Ch := 'Z' DOWNTO 'A' DO
   Write (Ch);
Writeln
```

7.4   Reading Input

Pascal includes a function Eoln designed to facilitate reading
a line of characters. As we indicated in Chapter 5, there is a
pointer in the input file which points to the next character that
would be read by the read procedure. If this character is <EOL>
(the control character for end-of-line or NewLine), the function
Eoln has the value True; otherwise Eoln is False.

If Ch is the variable used to hold the value of the last character read, the general form for reading a line is:

```
WHILE NOT Eoln DO
    BEGIN
    Read (Ch);
    Do something with Ch
    END
```

For example, if one wished to determine whether or not a certain character, Special, appeared in a line, the line could be read using:

```
Present := False;
WHILE NOT Eoln DO
    BEGIN
    Read (Ch);
    IF Ch = Special
        THEN
            Present := True
    END
```

In many situations, this scheme is not the most efficient. If this is all that one wants to do, once an occurrence of Special has been found, there is no need to continue reading. A more efficient version is obtained by using:

```
WHILE (NOT Eoln) AND (NOT Present) DO
```

The fragment terminates with Eoln having the value True and the pointer to the next character to be read pointing to <EOL>. If one wishes to read several lines, this pointer must be moved past <EOL> to the beginning of the next line. Readln will accomplish this. For example, to read five lines and determine if the character Special appears in any of the five lines, we would use:

```
Present := False;
FOR LineNumber := 1 TO 5 DO
    BEGIN
    { Read and process a line }
    WHILE NOT Eoln DO
        BEGIN
        Read (Ch);
        IF Ch = Special
            THEN
                Present := True
        END;
    { Move to beginning of next line }
```

```
        Readln
        END
```

Here is another example--one which, in practice, would most likely include additional processing for each line--of a scheme for counting the number of lines up to and including a line ending with an asterisk:

```
        Working := True;
        Count := 0;
        WHILE Working DO
            BEGIN
            Count := Count + 1;
            WHILE NOT Eoln DO
                Read (Ch);
            { Ch is now last character of line }
            IF Ch = '*'
                THEN
                    Working := False;
            Readln
            END
```

The Input file is a special case of a file consisting of printable characters and formatting control characters such as <EOL>. This type of file will be considered in the next chapter, where more examples of reading characters and lines will be given.

7.5   Summary

One characteristic of all of the control statements, except for the GOTO statement (see Chapter 16), is that there is a single entry point and, more importantly, a single exit point. This is one of the properties that makes Pascal a structured language. Programs organized using these control statements are easier to read, easier to write, and easier to prove correct.

Pascal has three control statements which permit the iteration of a statement S. These statements are: the WHILE-DO statement, the REPEAT-UNTIL statement, and the two forms of the FOR-DO statement.

Let B be a Boolean expression and S a statement. The WHILE-DO statement:

    WHILE B DO S

instructs the computer to determine the value of B, and, if B is True, perform S and then determine the value of B again, repeating these two steps as long as B remains True. When B is found to be False, the instruction directly after the WHILE-DO loop is executed. B is tested as long as it continues to be True. If B is True and S never changes B, the WHILE-DO statement will never terminate. If B is false the first time it is tested, S is skipped entirely. The WHILE-DO statement is an appropriate form of iteration for situations in which the number of iterations has not been determined in advance.

The REPEAT-UNTIL Statement:

    REPEAT S1; S2; ... ; SN UNTIL B

executes sequentially the statements S1, S2, ..., SN, then evaluates B. If B is True, execution continues on to the statement following the REPEAT-UNTIL statement, whereas, if B is False, the entire process beginning with the execution of S1 is repeated.

If the number of repetitions has been calculated in advance, a third form of iteration--the FOR-DO statement--is available. Let C (the control variable) be a variable of type Integer, Char, or Boolean, and let I (the initial value) and F (the final value) be expressions of the same type as C. The FOR-DO statements:

    FOR C := I TO F DO S

    FOR C := I DOWNTO F DO S

both repeat the execution of S. In the first form, if I > F, the FOR-DO statement does not execute S at all; if I <= F, S is executed and C, the control variable, successively takes on the values I, Succ (I), ..., F. In the second form, if I < F, the FOR-DO statement does not execute S at all; if I >= F, S is executed and C, the control variable, successively takes on the values I, Pred (I), ..., F.

Processing a line can be done using the function Eoln. If several lines are to be processed, the general scheme is:

```
WHILE Working DO
    BEGIN
    { Read and process a line }
    WHILE NOT Eoln DO
        BEGIN
        Read (Ch);
        Do something with Ch
        END;
    { Move pointer to start of next line }
    Readln
    END
```

Exercises for Chapter 7

1. Write a program which (1) permits the user to enter a character,
(2) permits the user to subsequently enter an entire line of
characters, and (3) prints the number of occurrences of the
specified character in the line.

2. Write a program which permits the user to enter a line of
characters, and, whenever the same character occurs in succession,
prints the character. For example, the line:

        The batter is really too cool

would produce the output: tloo.

3. Write a program which permits the user to enter characters on
one or more lines terminated by a period and which then prints the
number of nonblank characters read up to but not including the
terminating period.

4. Write a program which permits the user to enter a sequence of
positive integers terminated by zero and which then prints the
minimum positive integer that had been entered.

5. Write a program which requests the user to guess a secret
integer between 0 and Maxint. For each guess, have the program
report if the guess is too low or too high until the correct guess

is made.   Can you devise a strategy for minimizing the number of
guesses?

6.   Write a bankbook program which (1) permits the user to enter a
yearly interest rate, an initial principal, a yearly deposit, and a
number of years, and, (2) calculates and prints the current balance
for each year.

7.   Write a loan repayment program which (1) permits the user to
enter the yearly interest rate, the initial amount of the loan, and
the amount of each payment, and (2) for each year prints the current
outstanding loan until the loan is completely repaid.

8.   Print a table of the alphabetic and numeric characters and their
corresponding ordinal numbers.

9.   A certain island is initially populated with 1000 pairs of
rabbits and 100 pairs of foxes. Each year, ten percent of the
rabbits die of natural causes, each pair produces three pairs of
offspring, and each fox kills six rabbits. Each year, twenty
percent of the foxes die of natural causes, and, on the average,
four pairs of foxes will produce one pair of offspring that survive.
Tabulate the population of rabbits and foxes on the island for a
ten-year period.

10.   Trace this program:

```
PROGRAM F (Output);
VAR Sum, Old, VeryOld : Integer;
BEGIN
Old := 1;
VeryOld := 1;
WHILE Old < 50 DO
    BEGIN
    Sum := Old + VeryOld;
    Writeln (Sum);
    VeryOld := Old;
    Old := Sum
    END
END.
END.
```

11. A savings bank is giving out gifts. On a certain day, the
first ten depositors will receive a place setting, the next 100
depositors will receive a Miss Piggy bank, and any depositor who
deposits $500 or more will receive a pocket calculator. Write
pseudo code to describe how this should be done.

CHAPTER 8

Homogeneous Structures, Textfiles and Arrays

8.0   Introduction

Beginning in this chapter, we turn our attention to the structuring of data. We will introduce two data structures. The first is a file, restricted to files of characters (also known as textfiles). The second is the array. The language also includes instructions which act on these structures, assigning values to components and retrieving values from these structures.

Textfiles may be created as empty files, and characters may be appended to the file. Once a file is created, it may be read. Both the writing to and the reading from files are sequential. To change one isolated entry in a file, the entire file must be rewritten. To read one isolated entry in a file, all the preceding entries must be read.

An array is an indexed sequence of data objects of the same type. Isolated data items are easier to access in arrays than in files. An individual array component may be accessed or rewritten directly without moving sequentially through the structure. This ability to directly access each component is sometimes called random access because the average time necessary to access any component is the same irrespective of its position in the array. The space required by an array must be reserved as part of its declaration by prescribing a subrange as the collection of permissible values for the indices.

8.1   Textfiles

Sequential Files

The type of file that Pascal creates is a sequential file or a sequential list of data items. In this chapter, we shall restrict ourselves to files in which the data items are characters. In Chapter 14, we will consider files of arbitrary data types.

In reading or accessing a file, there is a pointer which indicates the position of the next item that will be read. This pointer can be reset to the beginning of the file, and the file can be read character by character to its end. There are also two Boolean functions. One, Eoln (for End-Of-LiNe), permits a program to determine when the next character that would be read is the

NewLine character, <EOL>. The other, Eof (for End-Of-File), permits
a program to determine when there is no next character to read
(because the last character read was the last in the file). We
shall denote this End-Of-File by a special symbol, <EOF>, which is
not to be considered as a character in the file. This special
symbol can be thought of as marking the end of a file.

    To write into a file, the file must initially be created as an
empty file. The file is then written to by appending elements to
the end of the file. This is exactly how we write the standard
Output file, except that we do not create it. If we wish to retain
the information in the file beyond the lifetime of a single
execution of a program, we can read and write to files maintained by
the operating system, called "external" files.

Declaring a File

    Textfiles are declared in the VAR section by either:

        < file identifier > : FILE OF Char

or, since this type of file is so common, the abbreviation:

        < file identifier > : Text

The file identifier, which is constructed according to the rules of
formation of identifiers, may appear in the program heading along
with the standard files Input and Output. If the identifier appears
in the heading, it is the file identifier for an external file. If
the file identifier is not included in the heading, the file is part
of the data space of the program and the lifetime of the file is no
longer than the lifetime of the program.

Writing to a File

    To create a file, a standard procedure, Rewrite, must be used.

        Rewrite (< file identifier >)

opens an empty file. Items may now be appended or written to this
file. An item is appended to the growing file by a statement of the
form:

        Write (< file identifier >, < output list >)

or, if it is desired to place a NewLine mark at the end of the list
of items, this is:

        Writeln (< file identifier >, < output list >)

In the Writeln statement, the output list may be omitted, in which
case only an end-of-line mark is appended to the file.

    For example, assuming appropriate declarations (including the
declaration of DataFile as Text), execution of the following
statements will give DataFile the indicated appearance:

        Number := 12345;
        Rewrite (DataFile);
        Write (DataFile, 'List of Data');
        Writeln (DataFile);
        Writeln (DataFile, 'First', Number : 8)

DataFile will consists of the sequence of 27 characters:

    List of Data<EOL>First   12345<EOL><EOF>
                                          ^

Remember that the end-of-file mark is not an item in the file. We
have appended it at the position in which the next data item, if
there is one, will be placed.

Page Procedure

    Page marks may also be inserted in a textfile by using another
predeclared procedure, Page, in the form:

        Page (< file identifier >)

A page mark is an instruction to a printer to skip to the next page,
or, in the case of a CRT terminal, it is an instruction to erase the
screen and start with a clear screen.

Reading a File

    To read a file, the file pointer must be reset, so that it
points to the first item in the file. With DataFile as above, the
execution of the statement:

        Reset (DataFile)

repositions the file pointer so that we have:

        List of Data<EOL>First   12345<EOL><EOF>
              ^

and the file DataFile is opened for reading. Any attempt now to
append additional information using Write (Datafile, ...) to this
file would be an error. It is also possible to open an empty file
for reading. The situation is then:

        <EOF>
         ^

and, if the name of this file is Somefile, Eof (Somefile) would be
True.

        When using the procedure Read, the file pointer always points
to the next item that would be read, and the truth or falsity of
Eoln (< file identifier >) is determined by whether or not this next
item is <EOL>. In this way, Eoln allows the user to "look ahead"
without actually reading the next character.

        Using DataFile as shown after Reset, we could skip the initial
line of the file by executing:

        Readln (DataFile);

This will move the file pointer just beyond the first <EOL> so that
we have:

        List of Data<EOL>First   12345<EOL><EOF>
                         ^

We would then be ready to read characters in this file, starting at
the beginning of the second line.

Processing a File

        If the characters in a line were to be processed in some way,
this could be done by executing:

```
        WHILE NOT Eoln (DataFile) DO
            BEGIN
            Read (DataFile, NextChar);
            { Do something with NextChar }
            END;
        Readln (DataFile)
```
Without the Readln, the file pointer would be left pointing at <EOL>
and we would have the following situation:

```
        List of Data<EOL>First    12345<EOL><EOF>
                            ^
```

The general scheme for processing an entire file is to
terminate the processing when Eof for that file becomes true. As an
illustration, suppose we wished to count the number of characters in
the file DataFile created above. The following fragment does this.

```
        Reset (DataFile);
        CharCount := 0;
        WHILE NOT Eof (DataFile) DO
            BEGIN
            { Count the characters in a line }
            WHILE NOT Eoln (DataFile) DO
                BEGIN
                Read (DataFile, NextChar);
                CharCount := CharCount + 1
                END;
            { Important!
              Move to beginning of next line }
            Readln (DataFile)
            END
```

Permanent data is placed in files external to, but accessible
by, a program. In this case, the file identifier is included in the
program heading, and the computer operating system must then
establish the connection between the permanent files and the file
identifier as it is used in the program.

Sample Program TextCount

The text of this book is being created in computer files using
a program called a text editor. The files are text and can be
processed by a program as external files. For example, we can
establish the connection between the file identifier Chapter, and

the file which contains Chapter 2 of this text. We can then run the
program given in listing 8.1 below to count the number of printable
characters and the number of lines in this file:

```
 1    PROGRAM TextCount (Input, Output, Chapter);
 2
 3    { Count the number of noncontrol characters
 4        and number of lines in text Chapter }
 5
 6    VAR  Chapter : Text;
 7         CharCount, LineCount : Integer;
 8         Ch : Char;
 9
10    BEGIN
11    Reset (Chapter);
12    CharCount := 0;
13    LineCount := 0;
14    WHILE NOT Eof (Chapter) DO
15       BEGIN
16       { Count a line }
17       WHILE NOT Eoln (Chapter) DO
18          BEGIN
19          Read (Chapter, Ch);
20          CharCount := CharCount + 1
21          END;
22       LineCount := LineCount + 1;
23       Readln (Chapter)
24       END;
25    Writeln ('Lines       ', LineCount : 8);
26    Writeln ('Characters ', CharCount : 8)
27    END.
```

```
Run:
    Lines           623
    Characters    26616
```

Listing 8.1

Default Files, Input and Output

    When Read and Readln are used without a file identifier as the
first entry or parameter, they refer to the input file. One can
refer to them explicitly by using:

    Read (Input, NextNumber)

Similarly, Write and Writeln, when used without a file identifier as
the initial parameter, refer to the Output file. Parameters which
are supplied in the absence of a specific indication are called
default parameters. Input is the default for Read and Readln and
Output is the default for Write and Writeln. Eoln uses Input as a
default file, therefore Eoln and Eoln (Input) can be used
interchangeably. The same is true for Eof, with the understanding
that the computer system provides the user with some means of
setting end of file for the input device.

It is an error to attempt to Reset the Input file and an error
to attempt to Rewrite the Output file. Consequently, there are no
default files for these procedures.

Information about declaring and communicating with textfiles is
collected in figure 8.1.

8.2   Subrange

Before introducing the next structured form of data, the array,
it is necessary to describe subranges of certain simple data types.
Three scalar or simple types--integer, Boolean, and character--can
be enumerated in the sense that, except for the last element of each
type, the successor of each value is well defined. For each of
these three enumerated data types, it is possible to specify a
subrange. (It is not possible to specify a subrange for reals.) The
form of the specification is:

        < initial value > .. < final value >

Both the initial value and final value must be constants of the same
enumerated data type, and the final value must not precede the
initial value.

Here are some examples of variables declared by using
subranges:

```
VAR
    Power : 0..31;
    Year : 1983..2001;
    UpperAlpha : 'A'..'Z';
    Position : -10..10;
```

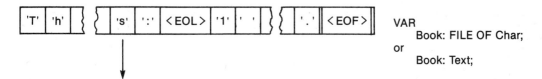

VAR
    Book: FILE OF Char;
or
    Book: Text;

(a) Reading from a file
    Read (Book, Ch)   assigns Ch the value under the
                       pointer and moves the pointer one
                       position to the left

    Readln (Book)   moves the pointer to the position
                       immediately after the next <EOL>

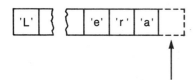

(b) Writing to a file
    Write (Book, Ch)   appends the value of Ch to the end
                       of the file and prepares pointer for next
                       insertion

    Writeln (Book)   appends <EOL> to the end of the file
                       and prepares pointer for next insertion

Figure 8.1   Declaring and Communicating with Textfiles

Range Checking

Declaring a variable by specifying a subrange implies an
intention not to assign a variable a value outside the subrange. A
standard implementation of Pascal would include range checking, by
terminating a program at the instruction which attempted to make an
assignment out of range. Consequently, with the above declarations,
either of the following two assignments would generate a run-time
error message:

        Year := 1982;
        UpperAlpha := 'a';

A value may also be assigned to a variable by a Read statement.
If a user entered 20 in response to the instruction Read (Position),
a run-time error message that the value is out of range would be
generated. A more graceful method would have entailed reading the
input using a variable declared as an integer and having the program
check that the entered value was in the appropriate range. If it
was not in the appropriate range, the program would then give the
user an opportunity to recover and supply a value in the required
range.

A program like this provides a useful fragment for inclusion in
an interactive program. We will want to include such fragments when
we discuss segments of programs called procedures. The scheme for
the entire program is given in Listing 8.2.

```
1     PROGRAM CheckInRange (Input, Output);
2
3     { Obtain input in a specified subrange }
4
5     CONST  Low = 1;  High = 100;
6
7     VAR
8         Number : Integer;
9         Choice : Low..High;
10        Acceptable : Boolean;
11
12    BEGIN
13    Writeln ('Please enter value in range ', Low :3,
14            ' to ', High : 3);
15    REPEAT
16       Readln (Number);
17       If (Low <= Number) AND (Number <= High)
18          THEN
19             Acceptable := True
20          ELSE
21             BEGIN
22             Acceptable := False;
23             Writeln ('Please reenter value between ',
24                     Low : 3, ' and ', High : 3)
25             END
26       UNTIL Acceptable;
27    Choice := Number;
28    Writeln ('Value entered is ', Choice : 3)
29    END.
```

Listing 8.2

Associated Scalar Type

As one can see from this listing, appropriate constants may be used as the initial and final values for subranges. Thus, borrowing from the earlier bankbook program, we could make the following declarations:

```
CONST  Here = 1983;  Eternity = 2001;

VAR  Year : Here..Eternity
```

Just as defining a constant implies the data type for that constant, declaring a variable by subrange implies a data type called the associated scalar type. For the above declarations, the associated scalar type for Power, Year, and Position is Integer and for UpperAlpha it is Char.

The program in Listing 8.3 uses declarations by subrange.

```
1     PROGRAM Graffiti (Input, Output);
2
3     { Example of Subrange }
4
5     VAR  Index : 1..10;
6
7     BEGIN
8     FOR Index := 1 TO 10 DO
9         Writeln ('Romans Go Home!')
10    END.
```

Listing 8.3

This program will produce ten identical lines of output.

The order of characters in a given implementation is called the collating sequence for that implementation. If characters are stored using the ASCII code, (see Appendix A), uppercase characters are consecutive in the code and in the same order as in the alphabet. The same is true for lowercase characters. The subrange 'A'..'J' consists of ten characters. If lines 5 and 8 above are replaced by:

```
5    VAR  Index : 'A'..'J';

8    FOR Index := 'A' TO 'J' DO
```

the output from the program would still be ten lines each containing Romans Go Home!.

For a Boolean variable, the declarations:

Acceptable : Boolean

Acceptable : False..True

are equivalent, though there is little reason to use the subrange
for a Boolean.

8.3   Arrays

Most programming languages have features which allow us to
store a sequence of homogeneous data items. To store this
information, memory locations must be assigned. Most languages
require that the amount of storage that will be needed during the
execution of a program be fixed at the time the program is compiled.
This is called static storage or memory allocation.

The form of the array declaration and the resulting memory
allocation are shown in figure 8.2:

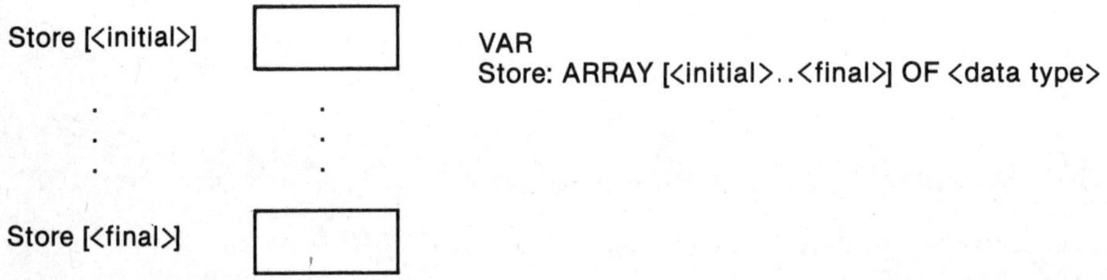

Store [<initial>]   ┌──────────┐   VAR
                         │   │   Store: ARRAY [<initial>..<final>] OF <data type>
                         └──────────┘

       .   .
       .   .
       .   .

Store [<final>]   ┌──────────┐
                         │   │
                         └──────────┘

Figure 8.2   Diagram and Declaration of ARRAY OF < data type >

A declaration such as:

VAR Word : ARRAY [1..6] OF Char

reserves six memory cells, Word [1] through Word [6], each of which
may store a character. Initially, as in the case of a scalar, the
content of each cell is undefined, meaning that the cell contains

whatever the computer may have stored in that location previous to
the execution of the program. The set of assignments:

```
        Word [1]  :=  'O';
        Word [2]  :=  'u';
        Word [3]  :=  'c';
        Word [4]  :=  'h';
```

results in these six cells appearing as:

```
    Word [1]   Word [2]   Word [3]   Word [4]   Word [5]   Word [6]
    --------   --------   --------   --------   --------   --------
    | 'O' |    | 'u' |    | 'c' |    | 'h' |    |  ?  |    |  ?  |
    --------   --------   --------   --------   --------   --------
```

The question marks in the last two boxes indicate that we do not
know what they contain. If we intend to fill the last two elements
of the array with blanks, then the assignments:

```
        Word [5]  :=  ' ';
        Word [6]  :=  ' ';
```

must be made. Only then can we assert that the contents of the
entire array is given by the storage picture:

```
    Word [1]   Word [2]   Word [3]   Word [4]   Word [5]   Word [6]
    --------   --------   --------   --------   --------   --------
    | 'O' |    | 'u' |    | 'c' |    | 'h' |    | ' ' |    | ' ' |
    --------   --------   --------   --------   --------   --------
```

Form of ARRAY Declaration

The syntactic form of the array declaration is:

   < identifier > : ARRAY [< subrange >] OF < date type >

This creates a structured variable, an array, whose name is the
identifier and whose elements or components are of the specified
data type, called the base type. Each component of the array can be
directly referenced by the name of the array variable followed by
the index of the component enclosed by square brackets. The index
may be either a constant or an expression, provided its value is in
the designated subrange.

Here are some examples of array declarations:

```
List : ARRAY [1..20] OF Integer;
CostofLiving, Rainfall : ARRAY [1910..1981] OF Real
Occupied : ARRAY [-20..20] OF Boolean;
Frequency : ARRAY ['A'..'Z'] OF Integer;
LastName : ARRAY [1..20] OF Char
```

If Frequency is declared as above, the assignment:

```
Frequency ['C'] := 345
```

is appropriate. 'C' is an index of type Char in the subrange
'A'..'Z' and 345 is of type Integer. Similarly, in the array List
the assignments:

```
List [1] := 100;
List [2] := Maxint;
List [3] := -100
```

are all permissible. Each index--in this case 1, 2, and 3--is in
the subrange 1..20, and each of the expressions on the right side of
the assignment operator--in this case 100, Maxint, and -100--is of
type Integer.

Do not confuse the associated data type of the subrange, that
is, the data type of the indices, with the data type or base type of
each array element. They may be the same, as is the case of the
array List, or they may be distinct, as in the case of the other
arrays.

Errors

The following assignments would create run-time error
conditions because the index is out of range:

```
Frequency ['*'] := 5;
LastName [21] := 'm';
List [0] := 10
```

Although it is possible to detect these three particular errors
before the program executes, there are situations in which the value
of the index is not known until the assignment is executed. The
index can be an expression that must be evaluated, such as in List
[10 + Offset] or List [Position], and the value of the expression
may or may not be in range depending on the current values of

variables appearing in the expression. Therefore, the compiler does
not attempt to detect even the obvious out of range errors.

    The following assignments would create compilation errors
because a value incompatible with the base type is assigned to an
array element:

        Frequency ['C'] := '*';
        List [10] := 'X'

The base type of both of these arrays is Integer. The compiler has
sufficient information to check that an attempt would be made to
assign a character value to an array component of base type integer.
Similarly, if Offset were an integer variable, it can be determined
that

        LastName [1] := 666 + Offset

is an assignment of incompatible types, without knowledge of the
value of Offset. These errors, involving inappropriate data types,
are flagged as errors by the compiler.

Copying Arrays

    In the previous array declarations, both CostofLiving and
Rainfall are declared to be ARRAY [1910..1981] OF Real. They are
compatible arrays, since they have the same indices and the same
associated data type. Compatible arrays may appear on both sides of
an assignment statement. The components of the array appearing to
the right of the assignment operator are copied into the
corresponding components of the array appearing on the left of the
assignment operator. As an example, the entire 72-element array
CostOfLiving could be copied into the array Rainfall by the single
assignment:

        Rainfall := CostOfLiving

This single assignment statement has the same effect as:

        FOR Index := 1910 TO 1981 DO
            Rainfall [Index] := CostOfLiving [Index]

Reading and Writing Arrays

Only integers, reals, and characters can be read from the Input file and written to the Output file. The following must then be used in standard implementations to read and write these arrays:

```
FOR Position := 1 TO 20 DO
   Read (LastName [Position])

FOR Year := 1950 TO 1975 DO
   Writeln (Rainfall [Year])
```

If one wanted to create an array such as the 41-element array Occupied, one might permit the user to enter a sequence of T's and F's, with a T indicating that the corresponding position is occupied and an F indicating that the position is unoccupied. An appropriate loop would be:

```
FOR Position := 20 DOWNTO -20 DO
   BEGIN
   Read (Indicator);
   IF NOT ((Indicator = 'T') OR (Indicator = 'F'))
      THEN
         { Output an error message for this position }
      ELSE
         IF Indicator = 'T'
            THEN
               Occupied [Position] := True
            ELSE { Indicator = 'F' }
               Occupied [Position] := False
   END
```

Example, Total

Listing 8.4 contains a complete program using an array. The user enters a sequence of real numbers, ended by an entry of 0.0 to signal the termination of this portion of the program. The sequence is read into the components of an array and the length of the sequence is established. Each value and its corresponding position in the array is printed. The user is then given an opportunity to change any array component, irrespective of its position in the array. Finally, the revised version of the array along with the total of the array components is printed.

```
 1    PROGRAM Total (Input, Output);
 2
 3    { Read a sequence of at most Limit reals from the Input
 4         file, terminating input by entering 0.0.
 5      Sequence is stored in an array.  The array is printed
 6         and user is given an opportunity to change entries.
 7      Final version of the array and the total are printed }
 8
 9    CONST  Limit = 100;
10
11    VAR
12       List : ARRAY [1..Limit] OF Real;
13       NewEntry, Total : Real;
14       Index, Length : 0..Limit;
15       NewIndex : Integer;
16       Response : Char;
17
18    BEGIN
19    { Prompt for input }
20    Writeln ('Enter at most ', Limit : 3, ' real numbers');
21    Writeln ('Terminate input by entering 0.0');
22    { Obtain input }
23    Index := 0;
24    Read (NewEntry);
25    WHILE (NewEntry <> 0.0) AND (Index < Limit) DO
26       BEGIN
27       Index := Index + 1;
28       List [Index] := NewEntry;
29       IF Index < Limit
30          THEN
31             Read (NewEntry)
32          ELSE
33             Writeln (Limit : 3, ' numbers entered')
34       END;
35    { Establish length of array and
36      Reposition pointer to Input file }
37    Length := Index;
38    Readln;
39    { Print current array }
40    FOR Index := 1 TO Length DO
41       Writeln (Index : 3, List [Index] : 10 : 3);
42    IF Length > 0
43       THEN { Let user make changes }
44          BEGIN
45          Writeln ('Do you wish to change any entries?');
46          Writeln ('Y for yes, anything else is no');
47          Readln (Response);
```

```
48              IF (Response = 'Y') OR (Response = 'y')
49                 THEN
50                    REPEAT
51                    Writeln ('Enter position and new entry');
52                    Readln (NewIndex, NewEntry);
53                    IF (1 <= NewIndex) AND (NewIndex <= Length)
54                       THEN
55                          List [NewIndex] := NewEntry
56                       ELSE
57                          Writeln ('Entry ignored,',
58                                ' position out of range');
59                    Writeln ('Are you finished with changes?');
60                    Writeln ('Y for yes, anything else is no');
61                    Readln (Response)
62                    UNTIL (Response = 'Y') OR (Response = 'y')
63              END
64           ELSE
65              Writeln ('No numbers entered');
66        { Print final version of array and Total }
67        Total := 0.0;
68        FOR Index := 1 TO Length DO
69           BEGIN
70           Total := Total + List [Index];
71           Writeln (Index : 3, List [Index] : 10 : 3)
72           END;
73        Writeln ('Total is: ', Total : 10 : 3)
74        END.
```

Listing 8.4

There are several features of this program that should be
noted. The use of an array has forced the designer of the program
to decide in advance on a maximum length of possible input. A user
who is about to exceed that limit is so informed by the ELSE clause
on line 33.

The portion of the program which obtains the input performs two
initial actions: the value of Index is set to zero, and the first
entry is read from the input file. Therefore, both these variables
have meaningful values when the Boolean expression controlling the
WHILE-DO loop is tested.

In the WHILE-DO loop, lines 25 through 34, Index is incremented
before it is used to reference a component of List. After each
execution of the body of this loop, Index has as its value the
position of the last list element stored. As a result, the actual
length of the intended input is the value of Index after the loop
has been completed and the variable Length is given this value on

line 37. If the body of the loop is executed 100 times, so that
Index has the value 100, the user is informed that the limit has
been reached. The next test of the controlling Boolean expression
will yield False because Index < 100 is False.

    Line 38, the Readln statement, is crucial when mixing the
reading of numbers and characters. The previous Read statements
read real numbers and will leave the Input file pointer pointing to
the character after the last digit that has been read. This will
most probably be <EOL> if the user followed the last 0.0 with a
carriage return. In any event, after having read the numbers in the
first segment of the program, we want to reposition this pointer at
the beginning of the next line; otherwise line 47, Readln
(Response), may not obtain the intended character from the Input
file.

    In the unlikely event that the user enters 0.0 immediately, the
WHILE-DO loop will be skipped completely and Length will be given
the value zero, as it should. Testing a program should always
include extreme sets of input. This program can easily be tested to
see if it works properly with what amounts to an empty list, by
entering only 0.0. To test the other extreme, one might consider
patiently entering 100 numbers. This can be tedious. Since a
constant has been used as the value of the upper limit, we can
change the value of this upper limit to a much smaller constant
value, say 5. In this fashion, we obtain an alternate version of
the program which can be quickly tested to see if it properly
handles an attempt to enter more than the limited set of numbers.

    The advantage of using an array is shown in lines 52 and 55,
which are

```
52              Readln (NewIndex, NewEntry);
55                 List [NewIndex] := NewEntry
```

If the value of NewIndex obtained is in the appropriate range, line
55 changes the value of the specified component of the array by
directly accessing that component.

Example, Character and Line Count

    As we remarked earlier, the indices of an array may also be a
subrange of the character set. For example, the indices could be in
the subrange 'A'..'Z'. This would be appropriate if one wished to
count the frequency of occurrence of each of these characters in
some text. As a sample program, the program in listing 8.5 will

count and print the frequency of occurrence of the uppercase
alphabetic characters.

```
1     PROGRAM CharCount (Input, Output);
2
3     { Count the frequency of occurrence of uppercase
4       alphabetic characters in input terminated by a period }
5
6     CONST  Period = '.';
7
8     VAR  NextCharacter, Ch : Char;
9          Frequency : ARRAY ['A'..'Z'] OF Integer;
10
11    BEGIN
12    { Initialize }
13    FOR Ch := 'A' TO 'Z' DO
14       Frequency [Ch] := 0;
15    { Prompt }
16    Write ('Enter a sentence consisting of only upper');
17    Writeln (' alphabetic characters and blanks.');
18    Writeln ('Use a period to terminate the sentence.');
19    { Get and process input }
20    Read (NextCharacter);
21    WHILE NextCharacter <> Period DO
22       BEGIN
23       IF ('A' <= NextCharacter) AND (NextCharacter <= 'Z')
24          THEN
25             Frequency [NextCharacter] :=
26             Frequency [NextCharacter] + 1;
27       Read (NextCharacter)
28       END;
29    { Produce output }
30    Writeln ('Character  Frequency');
31    FOR Ch := 'A' TO 'Z' DO
32       Writeln (Ch : 9, Frequency [Ch] : 11)
33    END..
```

Listing 8.5

   To avoid the problem of recognizing and converting lowercase
characters, we have deliberately restricted the program to counting
uppercase characters. Later we shall develop a function which will
allow us to perform such a conversion.

   Note that, on line 23, each character read is first tested to
see if it is in the range 'A'..'Z' before the appropriate array
element is incremented. This ensures that only characters in this
range will be counted.

   In the output portion, lines 29 through 32, each of the frequencies is printed by using an index which successively takes on the values 'A' to 'Z'. Ch may be used as many times as we wish in the For-Do loop (it is used twice in the Writeln statement on line 32).

Line by Line Processing

   If T is a textfile that is to be processed line by line, the characters in a line can be stored in an array. The term buffer is frequently used for a temporary storage array in which information is being placed. We shall use this name for the array in the next fragment. The schema would be:

```
        Reset (T);
        WHILE NOT Eof (T) DO
            BEGIN
            { Get a line }
            Position := 0;
            WHILE NOT Eoln (T) DO
                BEGIN
                Position := Position + 1;
                Read (T, Buffer [Position])
                END;
            Readln (T);
            BufferLength := Index;
            Make use of the current line in Buffer
            END
```

   "Make use of the current line in Buffer" is pseudo code to be further refined in a manner that depends on the specifics of the program in which the above fragment is embedded.

8.4 Summary

   A file of characters, or a textfile, can be created by first using the Rewrite procedure to create an empty file and then appending characters to the end of the file using the Write procedure. Using T for the textfile and Ch for a character, the general schema is:

```
Rewrite (T);
WHILE There is more to enter DO
    BEGIN
    { Enter a line }
    WHILE Line not finished DO
        BEGIN
        { Get a character }
        Write (T, Ch)
        END;
    Writeln (T)
    END
```

A textfile is read by first placing a file pointer at the first
file component using the Reset procedure and reading sequentially.
The general schema is:

```
Reset (T);
WHILE NOT Eof (T) DO
    BEGIN
    { Get a line }
    WHILE NOT Eoln (T) DO
        BEGIN
        Read (T, Ch);
        Use the character Ch
        END;
    Readln (T)
    END
```

Files may be stored permanently. Such files are called
external and the file identifier must be listed in the program
heading.

A subrange is a consecutive sequence of values of one of the
enumerated data types--integer, character, or Boolean. If a
variable is declared using a subrange, assignments will be checked
to insure that values are in the specified subrange.

The indices of an indexed sequence of similar data objects can
be specified by a subrange and an identifier for the aggregate or
array of objects. The name of the array followed by an expression
enclosed in brackets selects a particular array element. In this
fashion, components can be referenced individually, as in Max :=
List [7], or within repetitive statements, as in:

```
FOR Index := 1 TO 100 DO
    List [Index] := 0
```

Arrays are advantageous for storing homogeneous data when individual components are to be directly referenced in a nonsequential order. Arrays have the disadvantage that the size must be declared in the source program. This requirement entails guarding against reference to an out of range index and reserving large amounts of memory space.

Exercises for Chapter 8

1. Let X and Y be external textfiles. Write a program which produces an external file Z whose initial segment is identical to X and which is completed by a second, final segment identical to Y. (The file Z will be X with Y appended.)

2. Write a program which counts the number of lines and computes the average number of characters per line in a textfile. Have the program ignore blank lines.

3. Let X be an external textfile. Write a program which produces another external textfile by prefixing each line of X with five blanks. Produce a version which only prefixes nonblank lines.

4. A certain text editing program requires the user to embed commands to the text editor in the file being edited by starting a line with a period. Write a program which will purge a file of all these command lines. That is, if X is a textfile, the lines of X that start with a period are discarded and the result is written to some textfile Y.

5. Write a program which obtains a sequence of integers from the user, stores them in an array, finds a maximum, and prints the maximum and its position in the array. Decide what you would want the computer to do if two or more entries are equal to the maximum.

6. Write a portion of a program which uses an integer N and an array, List [1..100] of Integer, and determines whether or not there is some Index such that List [Index] = N. Embed this portion in a program for testing.

7. Write a program which rearranges the components of an integer array so that the smallest value is stored as the last array component.

8. Write a program which reads two lines of input, and outputs on one line the characters of the second input line followed by the characters of the first input line.

9. If Ch is a character variable whose value is in the range 'A'..'Z', then the expression

        Ord (Ch) - Ord ('A')

will be an integer in the range 0 to 25. Write a program that obtains a line of uppercase alphabetic characters from the user, stores them in an array of characters, then uses this array to produce a corresponding array of integers in the range 0 to 25. Print out the array to test the program. Now extend the program by adding some constant to each integer array component and taking the remainder MOD 26. Convert each of these integers N back to a character by taking

        Chr (Ord ('A') + N)

You will have produced an encoding known as a linear substitution or Caesar code.

10. Write a program which determines whether or not there are two components of an array that have the same value.

11. Write a program which accepts a specific character and a line of text from the user, prints the line of text, and, on a second line below the first, prints asterisks directly underneath each appearance of the specific character.

CHAPTER 9

Strings and Multidimensional Arrays

Sections

9.0   Introduction

A character string is a sequence of characters. Words,
phrases, and lines are all examples of strings. Individual
characters can be stored in arrays of characters and treated as
strings. This type of storage can be inefficient. A directive
PACKED may be used as an adjective in the declaration to inform the
compiler that information should be compressed. Literal strings are
stored as these packed arrays of characters. Individual characters
may be read and then packed into a string variable. An advantage of
using string variables is that they may be compared in dictionary
order.

Arrays may be created with two or more indices. In the case of two-dimensional arrays, the two indices are commonly called rows and columns, respectively.

9.1   String Constants and String Variables

The atomic or smallest unit of information stored by a computer is called a bit. A bit has one of two values and can be represented in a number of ways, such as ON/OFF, YES/NO, TRUE/FALSE, 0/1, etc. (We have included a section in Appendix C on this topic.)

The Directive PACKED

To store a character in memory, only a byte or eight bits are needed. Since the normal unit of memory is several times larger than this for most medium and large sized computers, it is inefficient to store a single character in such a large space. For example, if this space contains 32 bits for a given computer, then four characters could be stored in this space. To permit implementation dependent efficient storage, Pascal includes a compiler directive PACKED which may qualify the declarations of variables.

If one wished to store a name consisting of at most 20 characters (possibly padded with blanks if the name were shorter than this maximum length), the name could be stored as a PACKED ARRAY [1..20] OF Char. In a 32-bit computer, only five 32-bit storage units would be needed to store a name of this length.

String Variables

We have used literal strings, that is, strings of characters delimited by apostrophes, to include literal output in Write and Writeln statements. A literal string of a given length is a data type, which we can refer to as a string constant whose length is the number of characters in the literal string. The range of lengths is restricted to the maximum number of characters in a line. A string constant of length one is a character constant.

Pascal permits the declaration of string variables, that is, identifiers which may be assigned a value consisting of a string constant of the appropriate length. These string variables must be declared as PACKED ARRAY [< subrange >] OF Char. The subrange must start with the integer 1. A string variable is used in the program in listing 9.1:

```
1     PROGRAM Message (Input, Output);
2
3     { Printing messages using string variables, that is,
4         PACKED ARRAY OF Char }
5
6     CONST  Message1 = 'ROMANS GO HOME';
7            Message2 = 'LONG LIVE ROME';
8
9     VAR
10       Message : PACKED ARRAY [1..14] OF Char;
11
12    BEGIN
13    Message := Message2;
14    Writeln (Message);
15    Message := '*-----*------*';
16    Writeln (Message);
17    Message := Message1;
18    Writeln (Message)
19    END.
```

Run:
```
      LONG LIVE ROME
      *-----*------*
      ROMANS GO HOME
```

Listing 9.1

Two 14-character string constants are declared in the constant section. Both strings, including embedded blanks, are the same length. If this were not the case, and we wished to be able to assign to a variable either of these two phrases, we would pad the shorter one with blanks. On line 10, a string variable called Message has been declared. It can have as its value either Message1 or Message2, as in the assignments made on lines 13 and 17, respectively: or it can have as its value any other of the rather large number of different string constants of length 14. As indicated on line 15, the right hand side of an assignment statement can contain a literal string 14 characters long and that string can be assigned as the value of Message.

Individual characters in a packed array of characters may be accessed in the same way as in unpacked arrays. For example, if we had included:

    Message := 'ABCDEFGHIJKLMN';
    Writeln ('The last character is ', Message [14]);

the output would be:

        The last character is N

An individual component of a packed array may be assigned a new value. If, after the above assignment to Message, we had included:

    Message [10] := 'Z'

Message would then have the value 'ABCDEFGHIZKLMN'.

Information in arrays of the same basic type may be moved from unpacked to packed structures and conversely. Suppose again that Message is a packed array of 14 characters whose current value is 'ABCDEFGHIJKLMN', and that Buffer is an 80-element array of characters consisting entirely of blanks, then the following assignments are permissible:

    Message [10] := Buffer [80];
    Buffer [65] := Message [12];

The effect of these assignments would be to replace the J in Message by a blank and the sixty-fifth element of Buffer would be L.

The Pack and Unpack Procedures

To access or store individual characters in a packed array, the computer must build instructions to address a portion of a memory cell. This can be an inefficient process. To move 14 consecutive characters from an array such as Buffer to a packed array Message, the loop:

    FOR Position := 1 TO 14 DO
        Message [Position] := Buffer [Position + 30]

would involve 14 "packing" operations. There is a standard procedure Pack that is more efficient. The above could be done by using the procedure in the form:

        Pack (Buffer, 31, Message)

This single statement also moves the 14 characters starting at index
31 in Buffer to the packed array Message of 14 characters.

        In general, Pack requires three items, called parameters: the
first is the unpacked source array; the second is the position in
the source at which the first item of information is to be obtained;
and the third parameter is the packed array into which the
information is to be copied. The base type of the source and target
arrays must be the same. The upper limit of the source array must
be such that the position parameter plus one less than the length of
the packed array is no greater than the upper limit of the source
array. This restriction prevents any attempt to access an element
out of range. The size of the packed array determines how many
pieces of information are copied, since Pack will fill up the packed
array. Using the form:

        Pack (< unpacked source array >,
               < position of first item to be moved >,
               < target packed array >)

fills the target array completely.

        There is a corresponding Unpack procedure which will copy
information from a packed array to an unpacked array. The position
that must be specified is the position in the unpacked array where
the first item is deposited, and the three parameters appear in this
order:

        Unpack (< packed source array >, < target unpacked
                 array >, < position where first item to
                 be moved is deposited >)

Again, the unpacked array must be sufficiently large to hold as many
items as are necessary to exhaust completely the packed array.

Reading into Strings

        Packed arrays, including strings, may not be read directly from
the input file (unless the implementation includes a nonstandard
feature to permit this). To read a string from the Input file using
only standard features, individual characters must be read into an
unpacked array and then packed. If LastName is a packed array of 20
characters, in order to read a value for LastName, we can set up an
array Buffer of 20 characters, read the characters into Buffer, and

then pack the array Buffer into LastName. Here are the details:

```
FOR Position := 1 TO 20 DO
    Read (Buffer [Position]);
Pack (Buffer, 1, LastName)
```

This fragment unfortunately demands that the user enter 20
characters, presumably padding the input with sufficiently many
blanks in the case that the last name is less than 20 characters. A
user who is not aware of this requirement may not know how to
continue execution of the program. A preferable scheme is to have
the program do the padding. This is done in listing 9.2:

```
{ Obtain LastName, padding with blanks if necessary }
Position := 0;
WHILE NOT Eoln DO
    BEGIN
    Position := Position + 1;
    Read (Buffer [Position])
    END;
Readln;
FOR Padding := Position + 1 TO 20 DO
    Buffer [Padding] := ' ';
Pack (Buffer, 1, LastName)
```

Listing 9.2

Ordering Strings

A useful feature of string variables and string constants is
that they can be compared with respect to the ordering established
by the collating sequence. Suppose that LastName and SearchName are
both PACKED ARRAY [1..20] OF Char. Then, one can make a comparison
to test if LastName precedes, is equal to, or follows SearchName, by
using the relational operators <, =, and >, respectively. The
characters must all be of the same case. Usually the uppercase
alphabetic characters precede lowercase alphabetic characters, e.g.,
'z' < 'a'. In particular, it would follow that if the following
assignments are made:

```
LastName   := 'superman II          ';
SearchName := 'Zod                  '
```

the comparison, LastName < SearchName, would yield the result False
because 'Z' < 's'. The comparison is made lexicographically; that
is, the leftmost characters are compared, and if these characters

are equal, the next characters (to the right) are compared. The comparisons are continued until two unequal characters are encountered or until all corresponding characters have been found to be equal. Given the assignments:

```
        LastName   := 'Superman II          ';
        SearchName := 'Superman III          '
```

if LastName is compared with SearchName, the relational order will be based on the comparison of ' ' with 'I' in the eleventh positions. If, as is customary, the blank precedes any letter, Superman II will precede Superman III. Similarly, the string 'AB ' would precede the string 'ABA'.

Efficient Storage

     PACKED is a directive to the compiler to optimize storage. The directive may be applied to most structured data objects.

     Storing arrays of Booleans is a case in which packing most likely leads to efficient storage. When packed, a Boolean occupies a single bit. On a 32-bit computer, an ARRAY [1..100] OF Boolean will occupy 100 storage units, whereas a PACKED ARRAY [1..100] OF Boolean will occupy only four storage units.

     Only three bits must be used to represent one of the eight possible values in the range 0..7. Again, if storage is crucial, then it would be advisable to use PACKED ARRAY [1..50000] OF 0..7 rather than an unpacked array.

Converting Lowercase to Uppercase

     It may be convenient to convert each lowercase alphabetic character in a string to the corresponding uppercase character. This would permit a dictionary comparison to be made of any two strings of the same length. The transformation that must be made is:

```
        'a'   ----->   'A'
        'b'   ----->   'B'
                ...
        'z'   ----->   'Z'
```

The difference between the Ord values of the lowercase character and

its corresponding uppercase character is the same in all 26 cases.
In particular, the shift in position is equal to:

         Ord ('A') - Ord ('a')

Consequently, if Ch is in the range 'a'..'z',

         Ord (Ch) + Ord ('A') - Ord ('a')

is the position of its uppercase counterpart. The final conversion
uses the transfer function Chr to supply this uppercase character.

     If S is an array of characters of length L, this replacement
can be accomplished by the code contained in listing 9.3:

```
Shift := Ord ('A') - Ord ('a');
FOR Index := 1 TO L DO
   IF ('a' <= S [Index]) AND (S [Index] <= 'z')
      THEN { S [Index] in 'a'..'z' }
         S [Index] := Chr (Ord (S [Index]) + Shift)
```

                    Listing 9.3

9.2 Multidimensional Arrays

     The ARRAY, along with SET, FILE, and RECORD, constitute the
data structuring facilities available in Pascal. The base type of a
structured type may be a structured type. (FILE OF FILE will
usually not be allowed). Confining ourselves to ARRAY for the
present, this means that we may construct arrays of arrays.

     For example, a name could be an array of 20 characters and a
roster of names could be an array of names, that is, an array of
arrays of 20 characters. The appropriate variable declarations
would be:

```
Name : ARRAY [1..20] OF Char;
Roster : ARRAY [1..100] OF ARRAY [1..20] OF Char
```

A specific character in a specific name would now be indexed by two
integers: the first in the range 1..100 indicating the position in
the roster; and the second in the range 1..20 indicating the
position in the name. Since an array of arrays occurs so

frequently, there is a provision for shortening definitions of
variables such as Roster to:

        Roster : ARRAY [1..100, 1..20] OF Char

    The first character of the first name in Roster is referenced
or selected by either of the two forms:

        Roster [1] [1]

        Roster [1,1]

The last character of the last name would then be selected by Roster
[100] [20] or Roster [100, 20]. The later form is commonly used.

Processing Multidimensional Arrays

    We can visualize the data in Roster arranged in a
two-dimensional format of 100 rows, each row containing one name
that occupies 20 columns. Convention dictates that the first index
is associated with a row and the second with a column.

    To write the fifteenth name in the Roster, we may use:

        FOR Position := 1 TO 20 DO
           Write (Roster [15, Position]);
        Writeln

To write the first character of the first 65 names, we may use:

        FOR NameIndex := 1 TO 65 DO
           Write (Roster [NameIndex, 1])

To initially set each name to twenty blanks, we may use

        FOR NameIndex := 1 TO 100 DO
           FOR Position := 1 TO 20 DO
              Roster [NameIndex, Position] := ' '

    The order of nesting of the two FOR-DO statements above could
be described by the pseudo code:

        FOR NameIndex := 1 TO 100 DO
           Blank out a name

Alternatively, filling each of the 2000 characters in Roster with the blank character may be organized by columns using:

        FOR Position := 1 TO 20 DO
           Blank out a column

The phrase "Blank out a column" may be expanded to a Pascal FOR-DO
statement, yielding:

        FOR Position := 1 TO 20 DO
           FOR NameIndex := 1 To 100 DO
              Roster [NameIndex, Position] := ' '

Sample Program, InterestTable

    Information presented in the form of a table is often stored in
a two-dimensional array. Consider a table illustrating the future
value of an initial investment compounded at various rates of
interest. In a table with a fixed initial investment, there are two
indices, the interest rate and the number of years. How we decide
to print the information then determines which index refers to a row
and which to a column.

    We shall use $100 as the initial investment, four interest
rates--6, 9, 12, and 15 percent--and 5 years. We shall display the
information using the interest rate as the column index and the year
as the row index. Although it is not necessary, we shall include a
row with index 0 for the initial amount. We shall use 1..4 as the
indices for the four interest rates. The two-dimensional array in
which the computations will be stored is:

        Amount : ARRAY [0..5, 1..4] OF Real

    This declaration appears on line 7 of the program in listing
9.4 below. We have used the technique of computing each new balance
by first calculating the new interest, then adding that to the
current balance, and finally storing the result in the proper
position in the array Amount.

```
1     PROGRAM InterestTable (Input, Output);
2
3     { Print table of amounts accumulated at various
4         compound interest rates }
5
6     VAR
7         Amount : ARRAY [0..5, 1..4] OF Real;
8         RateIndex, Year, Rate : Integer;
```

```
 9          Balance, Interest : Real;
10
11     BEGIN
12     { Compute the amount for each interest rate }
13     FOR RateIndex := 1 TO 4 DO
14        BEGIN
15        { Set rate and initial balance }
16        Rate := 3 + RateIndex * 3;   { Rate = 6, 9, 12, 15 }
17        Balance := 100.0;
18        Amount [0, RateIndex] := Balance;
19        { Compute amount for each year }
20        FOR Year := 1 TO 5 DO
21           BEGIN
22           Interest := Balance * (Rate / 100.0);
23           Balance := Balance + Interest;
24           Amount [Year, RateIndex] := Balance
25           END
26        END;
27     { Print table }
28     { Print Heading of table }
29     Writeln ('Table of interest, compounded annually'); Writeln;
30     Writeln ('        Rate         6         9         12         15')

31     Writeln ('  Year');
32     { Print body of table }
33     FOR Year := 0 TO 5 DO
34        { Print a row }
35        BEGIN
36        Write (Year : 6, '      ');
37        FOR RateIndex := 1 TO 4 DO
38           Write (Amount [Year, RateIndex] : 10 : 2);
39        Writeln
40        END
41     END.
```

Run:

Table of interest, compounded annually

Rate	6	9	12	15
Year				
0	100.00	100.00	100.00	100.00
1	106.00	109.00	112.00	115.00
2	112.36	118.81	125.44	132.25
3	119.10	129.50	140.49	152.09
4	126.25	141.16	157.35	174.90
5	133.82	153.86	176.23	201.14

Listing 9.4

The program may be outlined by comments included in the listing above. Here is a separate listing of the comments alone:

```
{ Print table of amounts accumulated at various
    compound interest rates }
{ Compute the amount for each interest rate }
  { Set rate and initial balance }
  { Compute amount for each year }
{ Print table }
{ Print Heading of table }
{ Print body of table }
  { Print a row }
```

In Chapter 10, we shall introduce user-defined procedures which will enable us to construct major portions of a program as separate units. This will also permit us to avoid presenting long program listings by concentrating on what amounts to the expansion of the comment or pseudo code which describes a portion of a program.

The number of indices of an array need not be restricted to one or two. Consider a book of 100 pages, each page containing 50 lines, and each line containing 70 characters. We can create a three-dimensional array to hold all of this information by declaring:

```
Book : ARRAY [1..100, 1..50, 1..70] OF Char;
```

The amount of memory required to store Book is 350,000 cells, each containing a character. Note that, when creating multidimensional arrays, one can easily run out of memory space.

An interesting use of a three-dimensional array would be a tabulation of the number of occurrences of the 17,576 (26 cubed) distinct letter triplets. Assuming only uppercase alphabetic characters for simplicity, the frequencies would be stored in an array declared by:

```
Frequency : ARRAY ['A'..'Z', 'A'..'Z', 'A'..'Z'] OF Integer
```

All the values of this array need to be set initially to zero by the nested statements:

```
FOR First := 'A' TO 'Z' DO
   FOR Second := 'A' TO 'Z' DO
      FOR Third := 'A' TO 'Z' DO
         Frequency [First, Second, Third] := 0
```

A textfile could be read character by character, and, for each
occurrence of three consecutive alphabetic characters in the file,
an appropriate array element of Frequency would be incremented. If
the three consecutive characters are stored in W [1], W [2], and
W [3], the incrementation would take the form:

Frequency [W [1], W [2], W[3]] :=
            1 + Frequency [W [1], W [2], W[3]]

This table could then be used to develop an estimate of the relative
frequency of various combinations of letters. Since different
authors' writing styles involve usage of words at characteristic
frequencies, such a table could be used as a coarse technique for
identifying the author of an anonymous work.

Chapter 4, "Language, in Scientific and Engineering
Problem-Solving with Computers" by William Bennett, is an
interesting source for an introduction to the statistical analysis
of language and its relationship to codes and cryptanalysis.

9.3 Summary

Structured data types, such as arrays, may be declared as
PACKED, in which case a compact form of storage is used. Character
strings are packed arrays of characters. Literal strings are stored
as character strings. Individual components of packed arrays may be
accessed by index in the same fashion as unpacked arrays. If an
entire character string is to be accessed character by character, it
is more efficient to use an Unpack procedure. There is a
corresponding Pack procedure.

Strings may be compared using the relational operators <, =,
and >. The comparison is lexicographic, i.e., as in a dictionary,
provided all alphabetic characters are either uppercase or
lowercase. Using the transfer functions Ord and Chr, a lowercase
alphabetic character can be converted to the corresponding uppercase
character.

The base type of a structured data type may itself be a
structured data type. This permits us to declare arrays of arrays,
or two-dimensional arrays. Examples of two forms of the declaration
are:

```
        Roster : ARRAY [1..100] OF [1..20] OF Char;
        Roster : ARRAY [1..100, 1..20] OF Char;
```

A pair of indices R and C are used to reference a specific component
such as Roster [R, C]. The first index is often thought of as the
row and the second the column, though we may print the array column
by column or row by row.

     The number of indices or dimensions of an array may be two or
more. Tabular data is frequently stored in a two-dimensional array.

Exercises for Chapter 9

1. The twelve signs of the Zodiac are Aries, Taurus, Gemini,
Cancer, Leo, Virgo, Libra, Scorpio, Sagittarius, Capricorn,
Aquarius, and Pisces. The longest, Sagittarius, has twelve
characters. Therefore, each of them can be stored in a string,
PACKED ARRAY [1..12] OF Char, with trailing blanks if necessary.
One can declare an array:

        Zodiac : ARRAY [1..12] OF PACKED ARRAY [1..12] OF Char

and assign values such as:

        Zodiac := 'Gemini   ';

Create a program which prints the names of the twelve signs which
have been stored in an array such as Zodiac.

2. Look up twelve birthstones, one for each month of the year.
Write a program which permits the user to enter the month of the
year in which he or she was born. Have the program print the
corresponding birthstone.

3. Can people generate numbers in a random-like fashion? Throw
some light on this question by writing a program which asks the user
to enter 30 or more five digit numbers. Have the program count the
number of times that Q has followed P, for each pair of digits P and
Q. Are there any patterns? Perhaps you may need to obtain a larger
sample than 30 to answer the question.

4.   Some graphics systems use a two-dimensional array with a
component for each region of the screen that can be independently
illuminated. These regions or dots are often called "pixels". Each
component of the array determines whether or not the corresponding
pixel is on or off. How would such a data structure be declared?
How might a program turn on the pixels in alternate lines? Or in
alternate columns?

5.   A satellite black and white picture is received as a series of
digitized signals. For each of many small regions on the map, an
integer in a range, called the gray scale for that satellite, is
received. Suppose the gray scale is 0..7. Describe an efficient
data structure for storing this information in a computer. How many
bits are needed to store the data on each small region?

6.   An array Height is declared by:

        Height : ARRAY [-10..10, -10..10] OF Integer

and values are computed for each component by:

        FOR X := 10 DOWNTO -10 DO
           FOR Y := 10 DOWNTO -10 DO
              Height [X, Y] := X * X + Y * Y -25

Write a program which finds the indices, or X- and Y-coordinates,
for which Height [X, Y] = 0.

7.   The surface area of a certain rectangular region has been
divided into a grid of small squares. Each small square region may
be characterized as essentially clear, swampy, forested, watery,
rocky, or paved. The map can be displayed by these features coded
as characters. An example might be:

        W   S   F   R   W
        S   C   P   R   W
        S   C   F   C   W

Write a program which permits a user to establish or change the
terrain features of a grid of reasonable size and then prints the
map. Have the program find the grid coordinates of all regions that
are clear or paved.

8.   If r and n are positive integers such that r is less than or
equal to n, the number of distinct ways that r objects can be chosen
from n distinguishable objects is an integer which is often denoted
by C(n,r). For example, if n = 3, C(3,1) = 3, C(3,2) = 3, C(3,3) =
1. It is customary, and also convenient, to include C(3,0) = 1 as
indicating that 0 objects can be chosen in one way. Extending the
notation to include C(n,0) = 1, these numbers have the property
that:

$$C(n+1,r+1) = C(n,r) + C(n,r+1)$$

These numbers are called binomial coefficients. Writing the numbers
C(i,j) in the ith row, a table of these coefficients appears as:

```
1  1
1  2  1
1  3  3  1
1  4  6  4  1
```

Write a program which prints this table for a user-supplied value of
n of 20 or less.

    If C(0,0) = 1 is also included, the coefficients can be
displayed in a triangular form, such as:

```
          1
       1     1
    1     2     1
 1     3     3     1
```

This is called Pascal's triangle. Modify the program so the output
is produced in this form.

9.   A two-dimensional array is called a matrix. Write a program
which, for a matrix of reals, finds the sum of the rows, the sum of
the columns, and the sum of all the entries.

10.   Students have ranked a course on a questionnaire by responding
with an integer in the range 1..5. The responses have been
tabulated separately for seniors, juniors, sophomores, and freshmen.
Write a program which will use this tabulation as input and produce
a table showing, by class of student, the percent who chose each
ranking.

CHAPTER 10

User-Enumerated Data Types

Sections

10.0   Introduction

Many types of data are specific to particular problems:
examining a map may require the directions on a compass; designing
a menu may require the categories of various foods; collecting
time-dependent data may be done according to the days of the week or
months of the year. Pascal provides the facility to create data
types appropriate for these and other problems.

New data types may be created by enumerating the constants that a variable of the newly defined data type may have. The enumeration establishes an ordering between constants of the same type. Two constants of the same type can be used to specify a subrange.

Selection of one of several alternatives may be made using the CASE statement. The constants of a newly defined enumerated data type may be used as the labels for the case selected. To ensure that one of the labeled cases is selected, a test using the construct of SET may precede the CASE statement.

The declaration part of a program may include a type section, between the constant and variables sections. The description or template for new types may be declared in this type section. These types are then available to the remainder of the program.

10.1   User-Enumerated Data Types

There are four points on the compass. In a program in which a certain variable might have as one of its values a compass point and in which some action might depend on which compass point it is, we could use the constant declaration section to create four constants such as the following:

```
CONST
    North = 0;
    East  = 1;
    South = 2;
    West  = 3;
```

If we then declared a variable by:

```
VAR
    NextDirection : North..West;
```

it would be appropriate to make an assignment such as:

```
NextDirection := South;
```

Pascal also permits a more terse declaration than the above, one in which a variable is declared by following the identifier and colon with a list in parentheses of the constant values that the variable may take.

Declaring an Enumerated Type

     The declaration described in figure 10.1 allows the specified
variable to be assigned any one of these four values. As also
indicated in figure 10.1, the data space of the program then
contains a memory cell which can hold one of the four constants
enumerated in the definition. We shall refer to the data types
introduced in this fashion as user-enumerated.

NextDirection | East | VAR
                                 NextDirection: (North, East, South, West);

Figure 10.1 Data Space and Declaration of User-Enumerated Type

     The variable that is defined and the constant values it may
take on are named by identifiers. The general form of the
declaration is:

     < variable > : (< constant 1 >, ..., < constant M >) ;

More than one variable capable of having as its value one of the
enumerated constants can be declared by separating the names of the
variables by commas.

     Here are several other possible examples:

     Rating : (Blockbuster, Hit, SoSo, Fizzle, Bomb);
     PrimaryColor : (Blue, Yellow, Red);
     SoupDuJour : (Onion, SplitPea, Chicken, Chowder, Borscht);
     Bone : (Ankle, Knee, Hip, Neck);
     Today, ArborDay, Meeting : (Sunday, Monday, Tuesday,
               Wednesday, Thursday, Friday, Saturday);
     Class, Status : (Freshman, Sophomore, Junior, Senior)

     The identifiers used for the names of the constants must be
distinct from other identifiers. (This rule is qualified when
procedures are used.) Thus, the above declaration of SoupduJour
cannot appear in the same declaration as

          Entree : (Steak, Liver, Chicken, Shrimp)

because the identifier Chicken appears in both lists.

Scalars

     Jensen and Wirth use the term scalar type for the basic data
types integer, character, real, Boolean, and user-enumerated.
Scalar, in this context, means simple or indivisible as opposed to
structured and therefore divisible into components. When dealing
with subranges, the applicability of Successor and Predecessor, and
use with the CASE statement, they must exclude the type Real from
the scalar types mentioned. We shall more often use the term
enumerated to refer to integer, character, Boolean, and
user-enumerated types, rather than to refer to scalar with the
exception of real. The term discrete has also been used to refer to
the simple types, excluding reals.

Ordering

     Each of these types is given by enumerating the identifiers
which constitute the values of that type. This creates an ordered
set of values, ordered by their appearance in the list. Given the
above declarations, each of the following expressions has the value
True:

          Sunday < Saturday,
          Blockbuster < SoSo,
          Blue < Red,
          Knee < Hip

Relational operators may be used with each of the five simple data
types--integer, real, character, Boolean, and user-enumerated.

Iteration

     The standard functions Succ, for successor, Pred, for
predecessor, and Ord, for ordinal, are defined for user-enumerated
types. The value of Ord is determined by assigning zero to the
first constant in the enumeration and increasing Ord by one for each
position in the list. Pred is not defined for the initial
constants--such as Sunday, Blockbuster, Blue, Onion, and
Ankle--while Succ is not defined for the final constants--such as
Saturday, Bomb, Red, Borscht, and Neck.

     To perform some action for each of the last four days of the
week, we may use:

```
        FOR Today := Thursday TO Saturday DO
           Perform some action
```

The number of repetitions may not be fixed. If an action is to be
repeated for each value in a certain range of values until some
condition B becomes True or the range is exhausted, a form of
iteration such as the one given below is appropriate:

```
        Finished := False;
        Today := Thursday;   { initial value }
        REPEAT
           Perform some action
           IF B OR (Today = Saturday)
              THEN
                  Finished := True
              ELSE
                  Today := Succ (Today)   { next value }
        UNTIL Finished
```

Note how the IF-THEN-ELSE statement guards against the error of
attempting to evaluate Succ (Saturday).

Subrange

     Enumerated types may be used to create subranges. After the
above declaration for Today has appeared, we could include:

        WeekDay : Monday..Friday

WeekDay would now be a variable of the same associated simple type
as Today, but an attempt in the program to make the assignment:

        WeekDay := Sunday

would result in a run-time error message indicating an out of range
assignment.

     Subranges may be used as the indices of arrays. To record the
average daily temperature for each day of a week, we may (again
after Day has been declared) include:

        Temperature : ARRAY [Sunday..Saturday] OF Real;

Similarly, the following are acceptable:

```
WaveLength : ARRAY [Blue..Red] OF Real;
Calories : ARRAY [Onion..Borscht] OF Integer;
BoneLength : ARRAY [Ankle..Neck] OF Real
```

as are references in the executable portion, such as:

```
Difference := WaveLength [Blue] - WaveLength [Red];
Read (BoneLength [Hip]);
Calories [Borscht] := 55
```

10.2 CASE Statement

Suppose that we have the definitions:

```
VAR
    Menu : (Franks, Spaghetti, MeatLoaf, Spam,
            Ratatouille);
    Day : (Monday, Tuesday, Wednesday, Thursday, Friday)
```

The following chain of IF-THEN statements will determine a value of menu for each value of Day:

```
IF Day = Monday
    THEN
        Menu := Franks;
IF Day = Tuesday
    THEN
        Menu := MeatLoaf;
IF Day = Wednesday
    THEN
        Menu := Spaghetti;
IF Day = Thursday
    THEN
        Menu := Ratatouille;
IF Day = Friday
    THEN
        BEGIN
        Menu := Spam
        Writeln ('TGIF')
        END
```

The coding of this chain of alternatives is tedious. It is also

inefficient from the point of view of execution since, if Day has
the value Monday, each of the succeeding IF-THEN statements is
executed, although the Boolean condition tested will in all four
instances be False. (This inefficiency could be removed by using a
chain of IF-THEN-ELSE statements.)

Form of the CASE Statement

        A more convenient and efficient form than the above chain of
IF-THEN-ELSE statements is the CASE statement. This alternative
will also more likely lead to the correct specification of the
actions to be taken for each of the possible values of a controlling
variable. Using the CASE statement, we may replace the previous
sequence of five IF-THEN statements with:

```
        CASE Day OF
            Monday    : Menu := Franks;
            Tuesday   : Menu := MeatLoaf;
            Wednesday : Menu := Spaghetti;
            Thursday  : Menu := Ratatouille;
            Friday    : BEGIN
                        Menu := Spam;
                        Writeln ('TGIF')
                        END
            END { Case of Day }
```

        The general form is

```
        CASE < expression > OF
            < case label list > : < statement >;
                  ...
            < case label list > : < statement >
            END
```

Figure 10.2 gives a flowchart and the form of a CASE statement with
selector E, N case label lists, L1, ..., LN, and corresponding
statements S1, ..., SN. The selector E must be an expression whose
value is an enumerated type. A case label list is one or more
constants of the same type as the selector. No constant may appear
in more than one list. If the constants are integers, there may be
an implementation dependent restriction on the difference between
the maximum and minimum value.

        If there is more than one constant in a given case label list,
they are separated by commas. As an example, suppose that
Thursday's menu proves to be extremely unpopular and it is decided

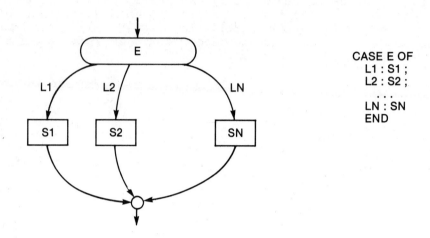

Figure 10.2   Flowchart and Form of the CASE Statement

to serve Franks instead.   The menu selection for Monday and Thursday could then be combined in:

Monday, Thursday : Menu := Franks;

As indicated in the selection for Friday, the statement executed when Day has this value may be a compound statement.   In more complicated situations, the statement selected may contain compound statements, repetitions, and even other CASE statements.

Note that the CASE statement is delimited by the pair CASE, END.   We recommend that the END so paired with CASE be followed by a comment indicating the CASE that is being closed.   The CASE statement is used to select one of several mutually exclusive possibilities.   Standard Pascal places the burden on the programmer of insuring that every possible value that the selector may take on be present in the various case label lists.   Some extensions of the language will have an ELSE or OTHERWISE label which can be used as the last case label list to select "none of the above".   We prefer to precede a CASE statement in which the labels are not exhaustive by a test to insure that the selector has as its current value one of the labels.   To make the labels all-inclusive, at least for user-enumerated types, one might consider including a "none of the preceding" or miscellaneous value in the list of values and perhaps initially assign this value to a variable.

Reading User-Enumerated Types

Now that we have the case statement available, we can outline a
method for reading a user-defined type. Remember that we can only
read numbers and characters from the Input file. What we shall do
is read sufficiently many characters to decide which scalar value is
intended. If a list such as:

          Animal : (Aardvark, Beaver, Coyote, Dolphin)

is given, then, since the first character determines the intended
value for Animal, the following fragment will assign an appropriate
value to Animal:

```
    { Prompt for input of first letter of name of animal }
    Readln (Choice)           { Choice : Char }
    IF (('A' <= Choice) AND (Choice <= 'D') OR
        ('a' <= Choice) AND (Choice <= 'd'))
       THEN
          CASE Choice OF
              'A', 'a' : Animal := Aardvark;
              'B', 'b' : Animal := Beaver;
              'C', 'c' : Animal := Coyote;
              'D', 'd' : Animal := Dolphin
              END   { Case of Choice }
       ELSE
          { Output error message }
```

Sets

The manner in which the IF statement guards the integrity of
the above input is probably more easily handled by testing Choice
for membership in a set of acceptable characters. Sets are
discussed in more detail in Chapter 12. Due to the convenience of
the concept, we shall anticipate a full discussion of sets.

A set of characters can be created by bracketing a list of
members of the set. The list consists of either individual
constants or subranges separated by commas. The set of characters
which would be first letters of the above four animals may be
denoted by ['A'..'D', 'a'..'d']. If a variable, such as Choice, is
of type character, then

          Choice IN ['A'..'D', 'a'..'d']

is a Boolean expression which will have the value True if Choice has

one of the eight values and False otherwise. This expression can
then replace the longer parenthesized expression following IF.

     Consider asking a user to specify a day of the week. The names
'Tuesday' and 'Thursday' have the same first letter, as do the names
'Saturday' and 'Sunday'. Therefore, we must prompt the user for at
least the first two letters. An appropriate fragment would be:

```
{ Prompt for input of first two letters of name of
     the day of the week }
Readln (FirstLetter, SecondLetter);
IF FirstLetter IN ['F', 'M', 'S', 'T', 'W',
                   'f', 'm', 's', 't', 'w']
    THEN
       Case FirstLetter OF
          'F', 'f' : Today := Friday;
          'M', 'm' : Today := Monday;
          'S', 's' :
             BEGIN { Examine second letter }
             IF SecondLetter IN ['A', 'a', 'U', 'u']
                THEN
                   Case SecondLetter OF
                      'A', 'a' : Today := Saturday;
                      'U', 'u' : Today := Sunday
                      END  { Case of SecondLetter }
                ELSE
                   { Output error message }
             END;
          'T', 't' :
             BEGIN { Examine second letter }
             IF SecondLetter IN ['H', 'h', 'U', 'u']
                THEN
                   Case SecondLetter OF
                      'H', 'h' : Today := Thursday;
                      'U', 'u' : Today := Tuesday
                      END  { Case of SecondLetter }
                ELSE
                   { Output error message }
             END;
          'W', 'w' : Today := Wednesday
          END  { Case of FirstLetter }
    ELSE
       { Output error message }
```

Writing Enumerated Types

     If the above fragment is part of some document handling
program, the program might include a fragment in which the value
supplied to Today determines an appropriate output string. Remember
that the value of Today is not a string of characters but a constant
of an enumerated data type. To place the appropriate string of
characters in the document being prepared, the following might be
used:

```
     CASE Today OF
        Sunday    : Write (Document, 'Sunday');
        Monday    : Write (Document, 'Monday');
        Tuesday   : Write (Document, 'Tuesday');
        Wednesday : Write (Document, 'Wednesday');
        Thursday  : Write (Document, 'Thursday');
        Friday    : Write (Document, 'Friday');
        Saturday  : Write (Document, 'Saturday')
     END { Case of Today }
```

     Here is an alternate scheme. 'Wednesday' is the longest of
these strings. It has length 9. If we declare an array by:

```
     DayName : ARRAY [Sunday..Saturday] OF
                         PACKED ARRAY [1..9] OF Char
```

we could then establish initial values for the components of this
array by seven assignments:

```
        DayName [Sunday]   := 'Sunday   ';
        DayName [Monday]   := 'Monday   ';
               ...
        DayName [Saturday] := 'Saturday ';
```

Having done this, we could then place the appropriate string in the
document by the simple statement:

```
        Write (Document, DayName [Today])
```

     This latter method has the defect of leaving several blanks
after the shorter names.

Alternate Form of IF-THEN-ELSE

    Occasionally, a choice which can be described by the
IF-THEN-ELSE statement is more readable if presented in the form of
a CASE statement. The statement:

```
        IF  < Boolean expression >
            THEN
                < Then statement >
            ELSE
                < Else statement >
```

is equivalent to the CASE statement:

```
        CASE < Boolean expression > OF
            True  : < Then statement >
            False : < Else statement >
```


10.3 Defining New Data Types

    Up to this point, we have introduced a number of data types:
some are called simple; others are referred to as structured. Here
is a tabulation:

```
    Simple Types
        Predefined
            Integer, Real, Char, Boolean
        User-enumerated
        Subrange (of Integer, Char, Boolean, or user-enumerated)
    Structured Types
        Textfiles
        Array
        Packed Array
```

    One strength of the Pascal language lies in its data
structuring facilities. Additional structured types will be
introduced shortly. (They are FILE of arbitrary type, SET, and
RECORD.)

Type Identifier

The declaration part of the body of a program may contain a
Type section, introduced by the reserved word TYPE. In this
section, identifiers, called type identifiers may be specified as
being synonymous with specified data types. These type identifiers
may then function as simple types in subsequent declarations. Since
constants may be used in the description of new types, the CONST
section precedes the TYPE section. Since newly defined types may be
used to specify the type of a variable in the VAR section, the VAR
section follows the TYPE section.

Suppose that a line in a certain document consists of 80
characters, and that, at any moment in the processing of the
document, it is desired to retain the last two lines being read.
This part of the processing could be done using the following
fragments:

```
CONST
    LineSize = 80;

TYPE
    LineRange = 1..LineSize;
    LineType = ARRAY [LineRange] OF Char;

VAR
    CurrentLine, PreviousLine : LineType;
    Index : LineRange;
...
BEGIN
...
{ Save old CurrentLine before reading new one }
PreviousLine := CurrentLine;
For Index := 1 TO LineSize DO
    Read (CurrentLine [Index])
...
```

The TYPE section is a list of entries of the form

    < type identifier > = < type > ;

Each definition in this list defines a new type with the specified
identifier as its name. Once a new type has been defined, it may
appear as a simple type in subsequent definitions. The type that
appears to the right of the equality sign is either a simple type,
predefined or defined by an earlier definition, or a structured
type. The structured types may also draw on types defined in
previous definitions. For example, if one wished to retain a page

consisting of 65 lines in the data space of a program, then one could append the following declarations to the above TYPE and VAR sections, respectively:

        PageType = ARRAY [1..65] OF LineType;

        CurrentPage : PageType;

Note that an equal sign is used to define a new type whereas a colon is used in the creation of a variable.

        A type is a template or an outline of the shape of a data object in terms of previously defined data objects. The identifier, such as PageType, which we have called a type identifier, cannot be assigned a value; rather it is used to describe variables of that type.

        New data types may be created by enumerating the set of constant values in the TYPE section. The following represents an alternate method of creating variables, such as Today and NextDirection:

        TYPE
            DirectionType = (North, East, South, West);
            DayofWeekType = (Sunday, Monday, Tuesday, Wednesday,
                                Thursday, Friday, Saturday);
        VAR
            NextDirection : DirectionType;
            Today : DayofWeekType;

        The suffix Type on the type identifiers is an optional practice which we recommend. It is a reminder that the identifier is a type identifier. Therefore, it is to be used to define variables or other types but is not itself an identifier of a variable and cannot be assigned a value.

10.4 Summary

        The constant values of a user-enumerated data type are specified by providing a list of the names of the constants. The names are separated by commas and the list is enclosed in parentheses. A variable of that type can be declared directly in the VAR section by the form:

        < identifier > : (< enumeration of constants >) ;

An example would be:

        Direction : (North, East, South, West, Up, Down);

This allows assignments to be made, such as:

        Direction := East

    The successor function and the predecessor function are
available for use with these types. The values are determined by
the ordering in the enumeration. In the previous example, Succ
(West) = Up. The ordinal function, Ord, is also available. Ord of
the initial constant is 0. In the previous example, Ord (North) = 0
and Ord (Up) = 4. Subranges may be created and used in
declarations, such as:

        PlanarDirection : North..West

    A TYPE section, appearing between the CONST and VAR sections,
permits names to be given to these types and allows types to be
referred to in subsequent declarations. These names function in the
same way as the predeclared names such as Integer. The newly
introduced types can be referred to in subsequent type definitions
and following VAR sections. The form of a type declaration is:

        < type identifier > = < type definition > ;

where the type definition can be a previously defined data type, an
enumeration of a new data type, a specification of a subrange, a
structured data type, or a pointer (see Chapter 17).

    A selection of the next action to be executed in a program may
be accomplished by a CASE statement. For each value that the
controlling expression may have, a statement is chosen for
execution. The general form of the CASE statement is:

        CASE < expression > OF
          < case label list > : < statement >;
                      ...
          < case label list > : < statement >;
          END;

where each case label list is one or more constants separated by
commas. Each such constant must be of the same type as the value of
the expression used to select the next action. The constants should

exhaust the possible execution-time values of the expression. This
can be enforced by the use of the SET construct in the program. The
possible constants or subranges are listed within square brackets,
creating a set, and the selection expression is tested for
membership in that set. As an example:

```
        IF Day IN [Monday..Wednesday, Friday]
            THEN
                CASE Day OF
                    Monday, Friday : < statement >;
                    Tuesday        : < statement >;
                    Wednesday      : < statement >
                    END; { Case of Day }
```

ensures that Day will have one of the four values appearing in the
case label list whenever the CASE statement is executed.

Exercises for Chapter 10

1. Define a type which has vocations as its list of various values.
If, for each vocation, there is an average yearly salary, how should
a data object which contains this information be declared?

2. The weather for a given day of the week has been classified as
sunny, cloudy, rainy, or snowy. The data for the weather for a
certain week has been stored in the data space of a program and is
printed out by the statement:

```
        FOR Day := Sunday TO Saturday DO
            Writeln (DayofWeekName [Day],
                    WeatherName [Weather [Day]])
```

Supply the necessary declarations. How might one store and print
the weather for a year using the month and day of the month as
indices?

3. A picture or screen is determined by giving for the row and
column of each dot (or pixel) on the screen one of six colors.
Assuming some reasonable number of rows and columns, how might one
declare a data object that would determine the state of the screen?

4. A Board, defined as ARRAY [-10..10, -10..10] OF Char, is initially set to all blanks. A pair of integer variables, CurrentRow and CurrentColumn, are initially set to 0. Write a program which allows the user to choose any one of the three actions Move, Print, or Quit, until Quit is chosen. If the user chooses Move, the user is then allowed to choose a direction from Up, Right, Down, Left. The current position is changed accordingly, provided it remains on the board. If the user chooses Print, the current position is marked with an X, positions that were previously occupied are marked with an 0, and unvisited positions are printed with a blank.

5. A survey has questioned respondents about their attitudes toward a certain policy. 1000 responses have been obtained, and they have been characterized as strongly favorable, mildly favorable, neutral, mildly opposed, strongly opposed, and no opinion. Each response has been stored in the component of an array. Write the portion of a program which will count the number of responses of each of the six kinds.

   Suppose that each respondent has also been characterized as high, middle, or low income, and the value of this attribute is stored in another corresponding 1000 element array. Write a portion of a program which counts the number of respondents, first grouping them by income and then by attitude toward the policy.

6. A form letter will be sent to a number of people. In order to make the letters seem individualized, the letter contains positions for the insertion of the recipient's first name, college, and home state. These positions are marked by < first name >, < college >, and < home state >, respectively, in a textfile named Form. This is the only appearance of angle brackets in this file. A second textfile, named Mailing, is arranged in units of three lines: the first line in a unit is a first name; the second line a college; and the third line a state. Write a program which will produce, for each of these units of three lines in Mailing, a copy of Form with appropriate substitutions for < first name >, < college >, and < home state >.

CHAPTER 11

Procedures

Sections

11.0   Introduction

We have occasionally described programs or algorithms by pseudo code, that is, combinations of Pascal and English phrases. This creates a short general description of a program free from obscuring detail. It also provides a technique for following a widely practiced methodology called Top-Down Design, in which the design of

the algorithm is carried from the general to the specific. At each
level in this subdivision process, several components or modules of
the algorithm may be specified. The process is then continued by
characterizing, for each of these modules, what are its inputs and
how its output is specified. The module can then be treated as a
procedure with specified input and output and developed further in a
similar manner, as if it were the program.

Pascal allows the inclusion of program fragments, called
procedures, which serve to break a long and complex program into
these manageable units. New functions may also be included in a
program and used when needed. Procedures and functions can be
thought of as techniques for enlarging the programming language,
thereby bringing the text of the program closer to pseudo code.

11.1   Top-Down Design

In several of the programs that we have constructed, we have
included comments to describe the major sections. Comments used in
this way may be considered as English language statements to be
further refined either into more detailed comments, or as the
ultimate goal, into statements in a programming language. This
technique has proven to be very successful in designing large and
complex programs. It is one aspect of what is called top-down
design. The technique is very similar to constructing an outline in
English except that, here, the aim is to use programming language
statements at the lowest level. Some of the intermediate level
statements may combine both English-like phrases and the control
structures such as WHILE-DO and IF-THEN.

With some care in the design, many programs can be constructed
in stages so that portions of the program can be run (and tested)
before other stages are developed. A well-conceived design will
isolate portions of the program and make explicit the data that a
given portion expects to find available. The design should also
make clear how a section processes the data, and what it may pass on
to a subsequent section. The use of parameters with procedures,
which can be used to specify this passage of data to and from
procedures, has been postponed to Chapter 15. Students who wish to
use parameters with procedures should read Chapter 15 after this
chapter.

Program BarGraph

     We shall try to illustrate this process in the development of a
program which displays the magnitude of a sequence of numbers by
printing a row of asterisks for each number. Such a display is
often called a bar graph. A typical run of the final program might
be given by:

     Run:
          Enter at most 20 integers in range 0..60
          Input terminated by a negative number
     5 29 0 11 -1   !Input
          5   *****
         29   *****************************
          0
         11   **********

     The first version of the program, shown below in listing 11.1,
consists of the heading, a general description of the program, and
the major portions.

     PROGRAM BarGraph (Input, Output);

     { User enters a sequence of at most 20 integers in the
          range 0..60.
       Program produces a bar graph containing for each integer
          entered a row with a corresponding number of asterisks }

     { Version 1 }

     BEGIN
     { Prompt for input }
     { Obtain input }
     { Produce bar graph }
     END.

                         Listing 11.1

     We expect the obtain input section to supply to the produce
bargraph section the list of numbers stored in an array as well as
an integer variable giving the length of the list. Therefore, the
declarations will include:

     CONST
          ArraySize = 20;

```
VAR
    List : ARRAY [1..ArraySize] OF 0..60;
    Length : 0..ArraySize;
```

Let us ignore the problem of obtaining the input from the user and, in a sense, "fudge" some data by temporarily inserting in the obtain input section:

```
Length := 5;
FOR Index := 1 TO Length DO
    List [Index] := Index
```

The result of executing this code will be List [1] = 1, ..., List [5] = 5. We may now concentrate on writing the bar graph section.

Creation of the Bar Graph

The creation of the bar graph is an iteration, for each entry in the array, of the printing of a row of asterisks. We will also include on each line the decimal representation of each number. A description of this process is:

```
{ Produce bar graph }
For each row
      Write number
      Write corresponding number of asterisks
      Furnish NewLine character
```

This can be translated into:

```
FOR Row := 1 TO Length DO
    Write List [Row]
    Write List [Row] asterisks
    Furnish NewLine character
```

In turn, Write List [Row] asterisks is:

```
FOR Position := 1 TO List [Row] DO
    Write ('*')
```

Listing 11.2 is the second version:

```
PROGRAM BarGraph (Input, Output);

{ User enters a sequence of at most 20 integers in the
     range 0..60.
  Program produces a bar graph containing for each integer
     entered a row with a corresponding number of asterisks }

{ Version 2, Produce bar graph developed }

CONST
   ArraySize = 20
VAR
   List : ARRAY [1..ArraySize] OF 0..60;
   Length : 0..ArraySize;
   Row, Index : 1..ArraySize;
   Position : 1..60;

BEGIN
{ Prompt for input - to be developed }
{ Obtain input - to be developed - temporary listing }
Length := 5;
FOR Index := 1 TO Length DO
   List [Index] := Index;
{ Produce bar graph }
{ For each row }
FOR Row := 1 TO Length DO
   BEGIN
   { Write number }
   Write (List [Row] : 6, '      ');
   { Write List [Row] asterisks }
   FOR Position := 1 TO List [Row] DO
      Write ('*');
   { Furnish NewLine character }
   Writeln
   END
END.

Run:
         1      *
         2      **
         3      ***
         4      ****
         5      *****
```

Listing 11.2

11.2   Procedures

   After one has developed several computer programs, it becomes
clear that a particular portion of a program, if it performs a task
that is required in other programs, may be useful as a subprogram in
these other programs. Often, one would like to retain the essential
features of the subprogram but vary the specific data item the
subprogram manipulates.

   Most programming languages permit the creation of what are
called subprograms, subroutines, or procedures. In this section, we
shall consider a simple form of the procedure, one which does not
include parameters. (Parameters are part of a mechanism that
permits flexibility in the specification of the variables used by a
procedure.)

   The use of procedures permits the programmer to call for the
performance of the actions described in the definition of the
procedure by using the procedure name in what is called the
procedure statement. An example of this is the use of the standard
procedure Writeln by including its name in the executable part of a
program.

Declaration of Procedure

   The declaration of a procedure is much like a program within a
program. It has a heading, introduced by the reserved word
PROCEDURE and followed by an identifier that is the name of the
procedure. The procedure heading may include a parameter list (see
Chapter 15). The declaration of the procedure may itself have a
declaration part. It must have an executable part delimited by
BEGIN-END. More formally, a procedure declaration is of the form:

        < procedure heading > < block > ;

where this block has its own declaration and executable part. As an
example, here is the declaration of a procedure called BlankOut.

```
        PROCEDURE BlankOut;
        { Inputs   Line : Array of Char;
                   LineSize : Integer
          Output   Line [1] to Line [LineSize] are set to ' ' }
        VAR
           Column : Integer;
```

```
     BEGIN
     FOR Column := 1 TO LineSize DO
        Line [Column] := ' '
     END;   { BlankOut }
```

The particular procedure BlankOut requires that preceding
declarations include an integer variable or constant LineSize and an
array of characters Line.

Once a procedure has been declared, the name is then available
in the body of the enveloping program, and the name is a statement
which commands the execution of the body of the procedure. This
appearance of the procedure name is said to invoke or call the
procedure. (In FORTRAN, the invocation of a subroutine is
accomplished by preceding the name with the command CALL.)

In the context of this section, you may consider the appearance
of a procedure name as replaceable by the body of the procedure.

Program BarGraph Again

Listing 11.3 is a version of the bar graph program that
utilizes procedures for the two main parts of the program. The
procedures are listed after the VAR sections of what we shall now
call the main program and before the executable part of the main
program. Lines 18 through 35 comprise the listing of ObtainInput
and lines 37 through 53 the listing of ProduceBarGraph.

```
  1    PROGRAM BarGraph (Input, Output);
  2
  3    { User enters a sequence of at most 20 integers
  4         in the range 0..60.
  5      Program produces a bar graph containing for each
  6         integer entered a row with a corresponding
  7         number of asterisks }
  8
  9    { Version 4, Rewritten with procedures }
 10
 11    CONST
 12       ArraySize = 20;
 13
 14    VAR
 15       List : ARRAY [1..ArraySize] OF 0..60;
 16       Length : 0..ArraySize;
 17
 18    PROCEDURE ObtainInput;
```

```
19    VAR
20       Number, Size : Integer;
21    BEGIN
22    { Prompt }
23    Writeln ('Enter at most 20 integers in range 0..60');
24    Writeln ('Input terminated by a negative number');
25    { Get List }
26    Read (Number);
27    Size := 0;
28    WHILE Number >= 0 DO
29       BEGIN
30       Size := Size + 1;
31       List [Size] := Number;
32       Read (Number)
33       END;
34    Length := Size
35    END;   { ObtainInput }
36
37    PROCEDURE ProduceBarGraph;
38    VAR
39       Row : 1..ArraySize;
40       Position : 1..60;
41    BEGIN
42    { For each row }
43    FOR Row := 1 TO Length DO
44       BEGIN
45       { Write number }
46       Write (List [Row] : 6, '      ');
47       { Write List [Row] asterisks }
48       FOR Position := 1 TO List [Row] DO
49          Write ('*');
50       { Furnish NewLine character }
51       Writeln
52       END
53    END;   { ProduceBarGraph }
54
55    BEGIN { Main }
56    ObtainInput;
57    ProduceBarGraph
58    END.
```

Listing 11.3

The executable part of the program, lines 55 through 58 (beginning with the line with the comment { Main }), consists of two procedure statements. The effect of the first procedure call, ObtainInput, is to execute lines 21 through 35. The effect of the second procedure call, ProduceBarGraph, is to execute lines 41

through 53.   In terms of line numbers, the resultant order of
execution is:

     56, 21 through 35, 57, 41 through 53

Data Spaces

     Figure 11.1 describes the data spaces created by program
BarGraph, and it also indicates how the procedures are nested within
the main program. Each procedure can access and modify all global
variables, i.e., variables defined in the declaratory part of the
main program. Each procedure may also access all global constants
and make use of all global types. A procedure may also access and
modify its own local variables, i.e., variables defined in the
declaratory part of the procedure definition.

Clash of Identifiers

     There is one exception to the above access rule: if the same
identifier is used to name both a global variable and a local
variable, a reference to this identifier in the body of the
procedure will be understood by the compiler as a reference to the
local variable. Thus, the presence of the local variable with the
same name prevents the global variable from being referenced in the
body of the procedure. This is referred to as the "most closely
nested rule".

     Since procedures may be nested within other procedures, this
rule must also apply to a situation in which Procedure A is nested
within Procedure W. If the same identifier is used to name a global
variable and a variable local to W, so that two different variables
are named by the same identifier, then reference to that identifier
in A is to the variable in W because the procedure A is more closely
nested within W.

Scope of Identifiers

     One advantage of this hierarchy of global and local data is
that the global definitions may be restricted to the most
significant data objects, namely, those which are shared by various
procedures. In the above example, the variables used to index
positions in the array or to store temporarily some information can

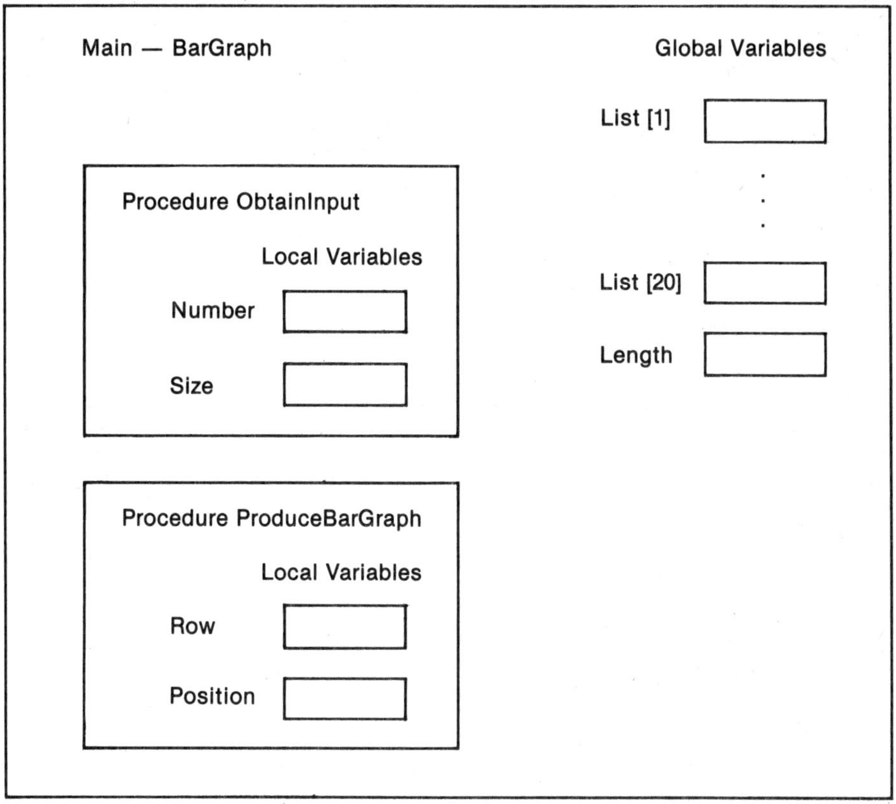

Figure 11.1   Data Space of Program BarGraph

be relegated to subsidiary parts of the program, leaving the
designer and the reader with an uncluttered view of the global data
objects.

Variables local to a procedure cannot be referenced in the main
part of a program. The portion of the text of the program in which
a given identifier can be referenced is called the scope of the
identifier. Thus, the identifiers associated with local variables
have a more limited scope than the global identifiers. As indicated
in the next paragraph, these local variables literally do not exist
in the main part since their life span is the duration of the

execution of the procedure in which they are declared.

In large programs, it is an advantage that local variables have
a short life span. A memory cell for a local variable is created
upon entry to the procedure, that is, at the instant it is called,
and the memory cell is released upon exit from the procedure, that
is, when execution returns to the next instruction after the
procedure call. In fact, the actual physical location of data in
BarGraph might be such that the data space of ProduceBarGraph
coincides with (or overlays) the data space for ObtainInput. It is
a consequence of this method of memory allocation, that, if a
certain procedure is invoked a second (or subsequent) time, the
value of a local variable at the instant of the previous exit from
the procedure has been lost. If the value of a variable must be
saved through several calls to the same procedure, then the variable
should not be local to the procedure.

As an example in which the two procedures in BarGraph might be
called several times, we may permit the user the option of repeating
the previous program. We need a global variable Response of type
character, and we can modify the main part to be the following:

```
BEGIN { Main }
REPEAT
   ObtainInput;
   ProduceBarGraph;
   Writeln ('Do you wish to produce another Bar Graph');
   Writeln ('Enter Y for Yes, N for No');
   Readln (Response)
   UNTIL (Response = 'N') OR (Response = 'n')
END.
```

Alternatively, we could create another procedure to obtain
Response.

Sections of the Declaratory Part

A declaratory part may contain up to six sections which appear
in the order LABEL, CONST, TYPE, VAR, PROCEDURE, FUNCTION. (The
FUNCTION section will be the subject of the next section in this
chapter. The LABEL section is used in conjunction with the
unconditional branch or GOTO statement.) The fact that a procedure
definition has a declaratory part implies that a procedure
definition may include the definition of subsidiary or nested
procedures. We shall refer to procedures declared in the
declaratory part of the main program as first-level procedures.

Procedures declared in the declaratory part of first-level procedures are then referred to as second-level procedures, and so on.

Nested Procedures

We might decide to enhance our BarGraph program by allowing the user the choice of the character used. We would need a global variable, say SpecialSymbol, to hold this value, since two first-level procedures will refer to this character. Furthermore, we could decide to subdivide the procedure ObtainInput into two second-level procedures: GetSpecialSymbol and GetList. The general form of the code for ObtainInput would now appear as:

```
PROCEDURE ObtainInput;

    PROCEDURE GetSpecialSymbol;
    BEGIN
    { Executable part of GetSpecialSymbol }
    END; { GetSpecialSymbol }

    PROCEDURE GetList;
    VAR  Number, Size : Integer;
    BEGIN
    { Executable part of GetList }
    END; { GetList }

BEGIN { ObtainInput }
GetSpecialSymbol;
GetList
END; { ObtainInput }
```

The structure of the program BarGraph with its procedures and their nesting and levels would be described by figure 11.2:

The nesting or containment relation among procedures that is indicated in figure 11.2 shows procedures at the same level listed left to right in their order of appearance in the text of the program. For large programs, this structure can become deep and wide.

The level and nesting of a procedure defines a sequence of integers which can be used to determine what other procedures are callable from a given procedure. In a simple case, there will be N first-level procedures. Each procedure can have one of the N one element sequences 1., 2., ..., N. assigned to it corresponding to

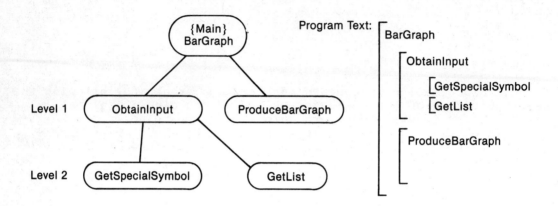

Figure 11.2   Procedure Nesting of Program BarGraph

its order of appearance in the source program. In the following
skeleton of a program each of the three first-level procedures has
been annotated with the corresponding sequence:

```
PROGRAM Skeleton (   );
...
PROCEDURE First;                    { 1. }
...
PROCEDURE Second;                   { 2. }
...
PROCEDURE Third;                    { 3. }
...
BEGIN { Main }
...
END.
```

An identifier cannot be used before it is declared and the
appearance of the procedure heading constitutes a declaration of the
procedure name. This rule permits First to be invoked in the body
of the procedure Second and both First and Second to be invoked in
the body of the procedure Third. First, Second, and Third can

appear in the body of the main program. The rule also permits recursion, whereby a procedure may invoke itself. Therefore both First and Second may be invoked in the body of Second.

The procedures directly nested within a given procedure are ordered by the order of their appearance in the source program. The integer corresponding to this order can be appended to the sequence of the "parent" procedure (followed by a dot to separate the integer from other integers that may be appended to its "children" procedures). The sequence obtained in this manner is the sequence corresponding to the procedure. The following skeleton is annotated in this fashion.

```
        PROGRAM Skeleton (  );
        ...
        PROCEDURE First;                      { 1. }
        ...
           PROCEDURE Golly;                   { 1.1. }
           < body of Golly >;
           PROCEDURE Gee;                     { 1.2. }
           < body of Gee >;
        BEGIN { First }
        ...
        END; { First }

        PROCEDURE Second;                     { 2. }
        ...
           PROCEDURE DoSomething;             { 2.1. }
           ...
              PROCEDURE Hot;                  { 2.1.1. }
              < body of Hot >;
              PROCEDURE Tepid;               { 2.1.2. }
              < body of Tepid >;
              PROCEDURE Cold;                { 2.1.3. }
              < body of Cold >;
           BEGIN { DoSomething }
           ...
           END; { DoSomething }

           PROCEDURE DoAnything;             { 2.2. }
           < body of DoAnything >;

           PROCEDURE DoNothing;              { 2.3. }
           < body of DoNothing >;

        PROCEDURE Third;                      { 3. }

        BEGIN { Main }
```

```
...
END.
```

A procedure such as Tepid, with sequence 2.1.2. may invoke the
procedures Hot (sequence: 2.1.1.) and Tepid (sequence: 2.1.2.),
but not Cold (sequence: 2.1.3.). DoSomething (2.1.), Second (2.),
and First (1.) may also be called by Tepid. In each of these
instances, the procedure with sequence A.B.C. may invoke any
procedure with sequence A.B.K., where K <= C; any procedure with
sequence A.L., where L <= B; and any procedure with sequence M.,
where M <= A.

Using nested within as the parent relation and, among
procedures with a common parent, using the order of appearance in
the source program as corresponding to earlier birth, a procedure
may call all its earlier siblings, all the earlier siblings of its
parent, all the earlier siblings of the parent of its parent, and so
on. (Also, a procedure may call its children.)

As another example, if the nesting structure of procedures
appears as in figure 11.3, then each procedure may call the
procedures listed to its right in the following table:

Procedure	may call these procedures
M	F, G, H, M
F	S, T, F,
G	U, F, G
H	V, W, F, G, H
S	S
T	S, T
U	A, B, F, U
V	F, G, V
W	V, F, G, W
A	F, A
B	A, F, B

11.3 User-Defined Functions

Normal usage of the word "function" carries with it the meaning
that one quantity depends on, or is determined by, another set of
quantities or conditions. We might say that the weather is a
function of the season, meaning that, if we know what season it is,

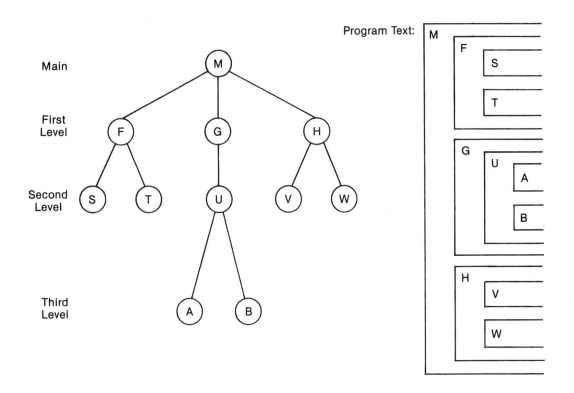

Figure 11.3   Nested Procedures

we can then decide what the weather will be.   Normal usage is fairly
imprecise, since the weather clearly depends on a complicated set of
circumstances.

Presentation of Functions

There are two ways of representing a function or indicating a
functional dependence.   One is to present a table in which on each
row there is in one column the quantity or set of quantities whose
value determines the value in the final column.   The table may
include several columns before the final column, but the value in
the final column is the value of the function and must be
unambiguously determined by the initial set of quantities.   An

example of daily maximum temperatures such as:

Date	Maximum Temperature
Feb. 1,1981	40.6
Feb. 2,1981	35.3
Feb. 3,1981	27.0
Feb. 4,1981	22.7
Feb. 5,1981	27.0

displays the quantity Maximum Temperature as a function of Date.
There is not necessarily an implication of causality in this more
abstract notion of function. It simply indicates that we may
unambiguously determine the Maximum Temperature on a given day by
looking for the given day in a certain row of the column labeled
Date and then finding the corresponding maximum temperature in the
same row in the column labeled Maximum Temperature.

The second way of presenting a function is to supply an
expression for the dependent value in terms of the quantities which
determine its value. For example, the Boolean expression:

Index > 100

is an expression which determines a Boolean value. It would be
unreasonable to enumerate all of the rows of the tabulation of this
function, though one could give a sample of them, such as:

Index	Index > 100
-100	False
0	False
50	False
100	False
101	True
2,147,483,647	True

Many functions are presented in the form of tables consisting
of samples of the determining or independent values and of the
determined or dependent values. If you have had trigonometry and
examined a trig table, what you have seen is a sample of the values
for various angles of some of the trigonometric functions. If you
have applied for a loan, you have probably seen someone look up the
value of a function which gives a repayment figure based on
variables such as the amount of the loan, the interest rate, the
length of the loan, and the frequency of repayment. If you have
considered planting seeds, you may have obtained a planting date as
a function of a geographic zone by looking at planting dates

superimposed on a map.

Sometimes a function is defined by a rule or procedure for computing the value of the determined quantity instead of by an expression. You may not have realized it, but a function such as First letter of last name is such a rule. If LastName were a string variable, that is, a PACKED ARRAY [1..N] OF Char, then LastName [1] would furnish the function which extracted the first letter of the string and therefore of the name.

Standard Functions

Most programming languages supply the user with predeclared or standard functions. These are chosen for their usefulness and universality. Some of them are numerical, in the sense that if we think of them in tabular form, all of the entries on a given row would be numbers, either integers or reals. Others are useful in relating characters to integers and vice versa, or in obtaining input, or in dealing with other common situations.

A useful analogy to illustrate how a function behaves in a programming language is to think of a function as a machine which has an input hopper and an output slot. We input the determining quantities into the input hopper, and the machine or function supplies us with the output or determined value. The name domain is frequently used for the set of permissible input values, while range is used for the set of possible output values. The input to a function is also referred to as its argument or arguments.

We have already encountered the predeclared or standard function Ord, which takes a character as its input parameter and produces a numeric value giving a relative position of the character in the collating sequence. As in mathematical notation, the input variable or expression is written in parentheses after the function name, so that in the above case we have written expressions such as Ord (Ch). A function with or without parameter values may be used in the same way as any expression of the same type as the function's output. For example, since both Ord ('a') and Ord ('A') are integers, it makes sense to write the expression:

Ord ('a') - Ord ('A')

Defining a Function

    In addition to the predeclared functions, Pascal, like many
other programming languages, allows the user to define functions.
Here is an example of a program containing a user-defined function:

```
1    PROGRAM Cube (Input, Output);
2
3    { Example of a user defined function
4      Function returns the cube of its argument
5      Argument and function value are both integers }
6
7    VAR  Number : Integer;
8
9    FUNCTION Cube (Dummy : Integer) : Integer;
10   BEGIN
11       Cube := Dummy * Dummy * Dummy
12   END; { Cube }
13
14   BEGIN { Main }
15       Writeln ('Enter integers, terminate with -999');
16       Writeln ('Program will calculate cubes');
17       Read (Number);
18       WHILE Number <> -999 DO
19           BEGIN
20           Writeln (Number : 6, Cube( Number ) : 12);
21           Read (Number)
22           END
23   END.
```

```
  Run:
       Enter integers, terminate with -999
       Program will calculate cubes
  3  5  11  25  -999                                    !Input
           3              27
           5             125
          11            1331
          25           15625
```

Listing 11.3

    The syntax of the function statement which declares the
function is:

        < function heading > < block > ;

where block has an optional declaration part and an executable part
of the form BEGIN < statement > END.

Parameters

The function heading is of the form:

    FUNCTION < function name > (< parameter list >) : < data type > ;

The function name is an identifier. The variables in the parameter
list are called formal or dummy variables. When a function is
invoked--by the appearance of its name in the body of the invoking
program or procedure--the formal parameters are given the values of
the corresponding variables in the function call statement. The
variables in the function call statement are referred to as actual
parameters. In this particular example, the actual parameter is
Number and the formal parameter is Dummy.

The data type of the value that the function returns or
computes must be a simple data type. The value that the function
returns is established within the body of the function definition,
by the last execution of an assignment statement of the form

    < function name > := < expression >

A function need not take arguments of a single data type and
may return a value which is different in type from its arguments.
For example, listing 11.4 is a function definition which returns
true if the real variable X is within 0.5 of the integer variable N:

```
FUNCTION Close (X : Real, N : Integer) : Boolean;
CONST
   Tolerance = 0.5;
BEGIN
IF (-Tolerance < (X - N)) AND ((X - N) < Tolerance)
   { Absolute value of X-N < Tolerance }
   THEN Close := True
   ELSE Close := False
END; { Close }
```

Listing 11.4

Close (2.8, 3) will evaluate to true. Close (5.4, -1) will
evaluate to false. Close (3, 3.3) will generate an error message
because the data types of the actual and formal parameters are not
in agreement. Note that position in the argument list is crucial
since each element in the formal parameter list includes the
specification of data type.

We may also use one function in the body of another function.
The function Close may be written using the function Abs, which
returns the absolute value of its argument. The appropriate code is
below:

```
FUNCTION Close (X : Real, N : Integer) : Boolean;
CONST
    Tolerance = 0.5;
BEGIN
IF Abs (X-N) < Tolerance
    THEN Close := True
    ELSE Close := False
END; { Close }
```

Listing 11.5 is another example of a function definition which
makes use of the order of characters established by the collating
sequence. The function returns true if the argument is an
alphabetic character.

```
FUNCTION IsAlphabetic (C : Char) : Boolean;
BEGIN
IF ('A' <= C) AND (C <= 'Z')
    THEN { upper case }
        IsAlphabetic := True                        { * }
    ELSE
IF ('a' <= C) AND (C <= 'z')
    THEN { lower case }
        IsAlphabetic := True                        { * }
    ELSE { not alphabetic }
        IsAlphabetic := False                       { * }
END; { IsAlphabetic }
```

                          Listing 11.5

An asterisk has been placed as a comment on each of the three
lines containing the assignment statements which potentially
determines the value that the function will have.

In indenting the code of this function definition, we have
violated the usual indentation rule by bringing the first ELSE
clause out to line up with the initial IF. The reason for this is
that we wish to line up the two possible tests, the first for
uppercase and the second for lowercase. In the event that the
character is uppercase and the first test results in true, the
second test will not be performed, because the second IF statement
is the statement following the first ELSE. When writing future
chains of tests of this type, we shall line up the IF statements in
this fashion.

A function may return any enumerated data type. For example, if we have available the type definitions:

```
HueType = (Violet, Blue, Green, Yellow, Orange, Red);
ColorClassType = (Primary, NonPrimary)
```

the function ColorClass, declared below, will return the value Primary or NonPrimary depending on the value supplied to the dummy argument Color.

```
FUNCTION ColorClass (Color : HueType) : ColorClassType;
BEGIN
IF Color IN [Blue, Yellow, Red]
   THEN
      ColorClass := Primary
   ELSE
      ColorClass := NonPrimary
END; { ColorClass }
```

11.4 Summary

The technique of top-down design consists of establishing a general outline, first with only the major details and most likely containing pseudo code, and then refining this outline into a sequence of more and more detailed problem solutions. Eventually, the refinement is at the level of statements in a programming language. Previously detailed schemes may be incorporated as procedures or functions or new procedures, and functions may be developed as needed.

The declaration of a procedure within the main program, or in another procedure, appears in the declaratory part, after the VAR section. The declaration is of the form:

```
< procedure heading >  < block > ;
```

The block has a declaratory part (which may include the declaration of other nested procedures) and an executable part of the form BEGIN < statement > END. The appearance of the procedure name invokes the procedure: that is, the executable part of the procedure is executed.

The declaratory part of a procedure creates a temporary data
space of the locally declared data, whose lifetime is the lifetime
of the execution of a single invocation of the procedure. If a
procedure is invoked several times, previous values of local data
are not retained or restored. Procedures may access global data,
provided no local data item is named by the same identifier.

Functions may also be declared after the PROCEDURE section. A
function may take arguments or parameters which determine the value
that the function returns. The form of a function declaration is:

    < function heading > < block > ;

where function heading is of the form:

   FUNCTION < function name > (< parameter list >) : < data type > ;

The parameter list contains the dummy arguments which receive actual
values when the function is invoked. The particular form of the
parameter list is a repetition of lists of the form:

     < identifier >, ..., < identifier > : < data type >

where these lists in turn are separated by semicolons. The
identifiers correspond by position to the actual arguments used when
the function name and actual arguments enclosed in parentheses
appear in an expression. The value that the function returns is
determined by the last execution in the executable part of the
function of a statement of the form:

     < function name > := < expression >

The data type returned by a function must be a simple type
although the arguments may be of structured type.

Exercises for Chapter 11

1. Write and test a procedure which finds the maximum of an array
of integers. Design the procedure so that it finds the maximum of a
specified initial segment as well as returns the index of the
maximum component.

2. Write and test a procedure which finds the string which comes

first in the dictionary order in an array of strings of a certain
length. For simplicity, you might want initially to assume that all
alphabetic characters are uppercase.

3. The bar graph program is severely limited in its usefulness
because of constraints on the input. Here are some modifications
that could be made to this program:

   A. Scale the output so that one asterisk may represent several
   units. Have the program determine the scale so that
   effectively Maxint is the upper limit on the largest integer
   that may be entered.

   B. Have the program obtain its input from an external file.

   C. Have the program depict negative numbers and positive
   numbers. Move the zero axis to the center of the output line,
   and print asterisks to the right of this axis for positive
   entries and asterisks to the left for negative entries.

   D. Print the bars vertically. (This will limit the number of
   entries by the number of columns that can be used.)

4. At the end of Chapter 9, Section 1, a technique for converting
lowercase aphabetic characters to uppercase alphabetic characters
was given. Using this technique, create a function which performs
the conversion. Be precise about what you intend the function to do
if the argument is not a lowercase alphabetic character.

5. Write a procedure which supplies a 20-character string by
prompting for a line of input and packing into the character string
the first 20 characters of an input line, padded with trailing
blanks if fewer than 20 characters were in the input line.

6. Suppose that CharacterType has been defined by:

          CharacterType = (UpperCaseAlphabetic,
               LowerCaseAlphabetic, Digit, Blank, Other);

Define a function which is given a character and returns its
CharacterType. Embed this function in a program that tests the
function.

CHAPTER 12

Sets

Sections

12.0 Introduction

The construction of a set with specified members chosen from an enumerated data type was introduced earlier. The set was used to guard the selection of alternatives preceding a CASE statement. A structured data object is available to permit the typing and declaration of variables which are subsets of a subrange of an

enumerated data type. Certain operations are defined for these
structures: there is a test for membership; there are set
operations--union, intersection, and difference; there are
relational operators--equals, not equals, is contained in, and
contains.

Sets may be used to model many relations. Algorithms can be
designed to manipulate the information encoded in sets and to
compute the consequences of the relations among members of a set.
In cases where implementation constraints prevent the creation of
large sets, models of large sets can be created using Boolean
arrays. An example is given using this latter technique to compute
prime integers.

12.1 Sets

Base Type

We have already used a set of characters, such as ['A'..'Z',
'a'..'z'], for the set of alphabetic characters. Any enumerated
type--i.e., the three predeclared types; integer, character, and
Boolean, or a scalar type defined by enumerating the values of that
type--may be used to construct sets. The enumerated type is called
the base type, and a set of a given base type has as its potential
members, none, some, or all of the values of that base type.

Declarations and Assignments

Let ColorType be enumerated by:

```
TYPE
    ColorType = (Violet, Blue, Green, Yellow, Orange, Red);
```

Variables whose type is SET OF ColorType may then be declared.
Such a variable has as its data type or set of values any subset of
the six constants of ColorType. For example, the following
declarations and assignments could be made:

```
VAR
    CoolColor, WarmColor, PrimaryColor : SET OF ColorType;
    SomeColor : ColorType;
    ...
```

```
        CoolColor := [Violet..Green];
        WarmColor := [Orange, Red];
        PrimaryColor := [Blue, Yellow, Red];
        SomeColor := Yellow;
```

The variable SomeColor of ColorType can have any one of six possible
values. The three variables--CoolColor, WarmColor, and
PrimaryColor--can have any one of the 64 different subsets as its
value, although the choice of the identifiers suggests the
particular subsets assigned above.

     Specific sets are created by enclosing in brackets a list of
the members. Particular constants or subranges may be used in the
list. These set values are then assigned to a set variable. Since
SomeColor is of type Color, it must be assigned a specific value of
the base type, while variables of type ColorSet may be assigned
subsets of type Color.

     Structured types of the form SET OF some enumerated type may be
created in the TYPE section. For example:

```
    TYPE
        WeatherType = (Sunny, Cloudy, Rainy, Snowy, Windy);
        WeatherSetType = SET OF WeatherType;
    VAR
        SimpleWeather : WeatherType;
        RealWeather : WeatherSetType;
    ...
        SimpleWeather := Windy;
        RealWeather := [Cloudy, Rainy, Windy];
```

     In either the TYPE or VAR section, the creation of this data
type is by the form:

```
        SET OF < base type >
```

This creates a structured data type. In the TYPE section, this form
follows an equality sign. In the VAR section, it follows the colon.

     The assigment SomeColor := [Yellow] would create an error
because SomeColor and [Yellow] are incompatible types. Similarly,
WarmColor := Red would create an error.

Membership

Constants, variables, and, in general, expressions of the base type are related to sets of the base type by the relation of membership. The expression:

< base type > IN < set of base type >

will be either True or False depending on the two operands. Given the previous assignments, the following are True:

    Blue IN CoolColor
    Yellow IN [Yellow]
    NOT (Violet IN PrimaryColor)

The following are False:

    Violet IN PrimaryColor
    Yellow IN []
    NOT (Red IN WarmColor)

The empty set is denoted by []. Note that in order to test if an element is not in a set, one must construct a somewhat awkward phrase by placing the NOT first.

Set Operations

Three operations are available for combining two sets to obtain a resultant set. The operators are + for union or join, * for intersection, and - for difference. Given the declarations:

    UpperCase, LowerCase, Digit, Terminator, Vowel,
    Consonant, Alphabetic, Alphanumeric,
    LowerCaseConsonant : SET OF Char

the following assignments will give these set variables their intended values:

    UpperCase := ['A'..'Z'];
    LowerCase := ['a'..'z'];
    Digit := ['0'..'9'];
    Terminator := ['.', ' ', '!', '?', ':', ';'];
    Vowel := ['A', 'E', 'I', 'O', 'U',
              'a', 'e', 'i', 'o', 'u'];
    Alphabetic := UpperCase + LowerCase;
    Consonant := Alphabetic - Vowel;

```
        LowerCaseConsonant := Consonant * LowerCase;
        Alphanumeric := Alphabetic + Digit
```

Set Relations

Sets may be tested for equality, inequality, inclusion, and
containment, using the relational operators =, <>, <=, and >=,
respectively. With the above assignments, the following are True:

```
        Vowel <= Alphabetic
        Alphabetic <= Alphanumeric
        Alphanumeric >= Digit
        Alphanumeric = (Alphabetic + Digit)
        Vowel <> Consonant
```

The following are False:

```
        WarmColor = PrimaryColor
        CoolColor <= PrimaryColor
        LowerCase >= Alphabetic
        Red <> (WarmColor * PrimaryColor)
```

The members of a set may be listed in any order, e.g., [Red,
Yellow, Blue] = [Blue, Red, Yellow].

Processing Each Element of a Set

Frequently a set is assigned a value and then something must be
done for each base type which is a member of the set. One way to
accomplish this is to run through each possible value of the base
type, test for membership, and, if membership is True, perform the
appropriate action. For example, to count the number of elements in
a set S, we can use:

```
        Cardinality := 0;
        FOR Element := InitialValue TO FinalValue DO
            IF Element IN S
                THEN
                    Cardinality := Cardinality + 1
```

As another example, suppose that a base type called
Participants has been defined with initial value Alice and final
value Zod. In addition, suppose we have the following variables:

```
    Anyone : Alice..Zod;
    LuckySet : SET OF Alice..Zod;
    PayOff : ARRAY [Alice..Zod] OF Integer
```

Then, to increment by 200 the Payoff for each member of the
LuckySet, we would use:

```
    FOR Anyone := Alice TO Zod DO
        IF Anyone IN LuckySet
            THEN
                PayOff [Anyone] := PayOff [Anyone] + 200
```

A booking agency, or perhaps a local of the musicians union,
might wish to maintain a list of performers and the instruments on
which they are proficient. In all likelihood, this information
would be structured using the RECORD construct (to be introduced in
the next chapter); nevertheless, we may illustrate some of the
features here using sets. Some of the declarations might be:

```
    TYPE
        MusicalInstrument = (DoubleBase, Cello, Viola, Violin,
            Piano, Harp, Clarinet, Oboe, Bassoon, Flute, Tuba,
            FrenchHorn, Saxophone, Trombone, Trumpet, Tympani);
        Proficiency = SET OF MusicalInstrument;

    VAR
        Winds, Reeds, Strings, Symphonic, Jazz : Proficiency;
        Performers : ARRAY [1..100] OF Proficiency;
```

The sets could be initialized by:

```
    Winds := [Clarinet, Oboe, Bassoon, Flute, Tuba,
            FrenchHorn, Saxophone, Trombone, Trumpet];
    Strings := [DoubleBase, Cello, Viola, Violin,
            Piano, Harp];
    Symphonic := [DoubleBase..Tympani] - [Saxophone];
    Jazz := [Clarinet, Piano, Flute, Saxophone, Trombone,
            Trumpet];
```

It would be permissible to assign the instruments that performers
are proficient on by statements such as:

```
    Performer [1] := [Clarinet, Saxophone, Flute];
    Performer [2] := [Piano, Trumpet, Violin, Clarinet]
```

Performers [1] and [2] would have an instrument in common--namely,
the clarinet. Consequently, the following expression will have the

value True:

    (Performer [1] * Performer [2]) <> []

    The portion of the program which permitted the entry of the
instruments that a given performer could play might first determine
a value of the integer variable Index corresponding to the given
performer, and then for each instrument query the user of the
program. If, for a given instrument, the response is positive, then
that instrument would be adjoined to the set Performer [Index] of
instruments. This could be written as:

```
Performer [Index] := [];
FOR Instrument := DoubleBase TO Tympani DO
   BEGIN
   { Determine if Performer plays Instrument }
   IF Yes
      THEN
          Performer [Index] :=
               Performer [Index] + [Instrument]
```

12.2 Applications of Sets

Finding the Follows Relation

    In figure 12.1, we have diagrammed six tasks that might be
considered in creating a garden. (A seventh task, resting, has not
been included.) The tasks are connected by directed edges. An edge
from task A to task B indicates that task B immediately follows task
A. In a simple diagram such as this one, it is easy to see that a
consequence of the relationships is that the task plant seeds
follows the task plow ground. Our aim will be to describe an
algorithm for determining the tasks that follow a given task.

Representation of the Immediately Follows Relation

    Figure 12.1 is not a suitable data object for a computer
program. We shall assume that there is given for each task a set of
immediately following tasks. This could be in the form of an array
of sets, so that ImmFollow [PlowGround] would be the set of tasks
immediately following plow ground.

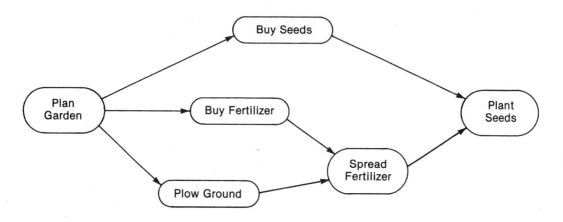

Figure 12.1   Create a Garden

    The relationship diagrammed in figure 12.1 is an example of a
graph in which the tasks are the nodes or vertices of the graph and
the immediately follows relation is represented by directed edges.
Let us say that task F follows task B if either task F immediately
follows task B or there is some sequence of intermediate tasks T1,
..., TK, such that T1 follows B, T2 follows T1, and so on,
terminating with F follows TK. The algorithm that we wish to
describe computes, for a given task B, those tasks which follow B in
this extended sense.

    A hydraulic analogy is appropriate. View the edges as carrying
a fluid in a given direction, perhaps with some color (or
contaminator). Suppose that the fluid moves from one node to the
next in one clock pulse. Then, for each clock pulse, there is a set
of nodes that have just been colored. Our aim is to find the set of
nodes which are eventually colored.

Accumulating all Following Tasks

    We can think of each clock pulse as starting with two sets, the
most recently colored nodes and all the currently colored nodes.
Each clock pulse, or iteration, must re-establish appropriate values
of these two sets. Let the set of most recently colored nodes be
called NewlyAdjoined and the current set of colored nodes be called
Follow. (The set Follow is the set of nodes which have been reached

so far by following the immediately follows relation.)

During each clock pulse, we examine all of the nodes that
immediately follow nodes in NewlyAdjoined. Any such node that has
not already been colored is to appear in the next version of
NewlyAdjoined. These nodes must also be added to Follow.
Eventually, for some clock pulse, the next version of NewlyAdjoined
will be empty. This indicates that the set Follow has reached its
final size.

Initially the node that we start at, in this case PlowGround,
is placed in both Follow and NewlyAdjoined.

An outline of the algorithm is given in listing 12.1:

```
Let NewlyAdjoined and Follow be ImmFollow [PlowGround]
WHILE NewlyAdjoined is not empty DO
    FOR Each Task T in NewlyAdjoined DO
        FOR Each Task U in ImmFollow [Task T] DO
            IF Task U not in Follow
                THEN
                    Adjoin Task U to Follow
                    Adjoin Task U to NextNewlyAdjoined
    Update NewlyAdjoined
```

Determine Follow for Task PlowGround
Version 1

Listing 12.1

The iteration in the WHILE-DO loop accumulates the set Follow.
Follow must be initially set to ImmFollow [PlowGround] prior to
entering the loop. Each iteration of the WHILE-DO loop develops a
next value of NewlyAdjoined, which we have referred to as
NextNewlyAdjoined. This is essentially an update type of process.
Inside the loop, at its head, a set NextNewlyAdjoined should be
initialized to the empty set. New tasks in the Follow set are
adjoined to NextNewlyAdjoined. At the tail of the loop, the set
NewlyAdjoined is given the value of NextNewlyAdjoined.

Listing 12.2 is a fully developed version of the algorithm:

```
NewlyAdjoined := ImmFollow [PlowGround];
Follow := ImmFollow [PlowGround];
WHILE NewlyAdjoined <> [] DO
    BEGIN
    NextNewlyAdjoined := [];
    { FOR Each Task T in Newly Adjoined DO }
```

```
        FOR TaskT := FirstTask TO LastTask DO
            IF TaskT IN NewlyAdjoined
                THEN
                    { FOR Each Task U in ImmFollow [Task T] DO }
                    FOR TaskU := FirstTask TO LastTask DO
                        { IF Task U not in Follow }
                        IF NOT (TaskU IN Follow)
                            THEN
                                BEGIN
                                { Adjoin Task U to Follow }
                                Follow := Follow + [TaskU];
                                { Adjoin Task U to Next Newly Adjoined }
                                NextNewlyAdjoined :=
                                        NextNewlyAdjoined + [TaskU]
                                END;
        NewlyAdjoined := NextNewlyAdjoined
        END

            Determine Follow for Task Plow Ground
                       Version 2

                    Listing 12.2
```

The inclusion of the task PlowGround in this example is not essential; it could be replaced by any given task.

12.3   Large Sets

Again using the creation of a garden as an example, it is possible to record the immediately follows relation in tabular form. The table would consist of rows and columns both labeled with the tasks or nodes and with a T entered in a given row and column if the task in the column immediately follows the task in the row. The other entries may be left blank, or, because we wish to suggest that the entries can be viewed as True or False, the remaining entries will be F.

Table 12.1 contains precisely the same information as figure 12.1:

	Plan Garden	Buy Seeds	Buy Fert.	Plow Ground	Spread Fert.	Plant Seeds
Plan Gard.	F	T	T	T	F	F
Buy Seeds	F	F	F	F	F	T
Buy Fert.	F	F	F	F	T	F
Plow Grd.	F	F	F	F	T	F
Spread Fert.	F	F	F	F	F	T
Plant Seeds	F	F	F	F	F	F

Immediately Follows Relation

Table 12.1

The information contained in this table may be stored in the data object ImmRelation defined by:

```
TYPE
    TaskType = (PlanGarden, BuySeeds, BuyFertilizer,
                PlowGround, SpreadFertilizer, PlantSeeds);
    TaskRange = PlanGarden..PlantSeeds;

VAR
    ImmRelation : ARRAY [TaskRange, TaskRange] OF Boolean;
```

where ImmRelation is given the value described in either figure 12.1 or table 12.1.

Boolean Arrays as Subsets

The set of tasks immediately following a task such as PlowGround is obtained by taking those tasks which have a T in their columns for the row PlowGround. In fact, if we consider any row, the T's mark the columns of immediate followers. This suggests that any row of Booleans is capable of representing a subset of a set.

Implementation dependent restriction on the size of the base type of a set may prevent one from creating large sets by the methods of Section 1, that is, by declaring a SET OF the given base type. Let Large be a positive integer larger than this allowable size. Define the following:

```
Subset : ARRAY [1..Large] OF Boolean;
```

A value of Subset corresponds to a subset of the integers in the

range 1..Large. An integer N is in the subset if and only if Subset
[N] = True. One can think of Subset as a row of T's and F's such
as:

```
                    [1]   [2]   ...   [Large]
         Subset      F     T             F
```

One can pick off the elements of Subset by finding the positions in
which a T appears. In particular, the empty set would contain all
F's and the whole set all T's.

     Let A, B, C, D also be ARRAY [1..Large] OF Boolean. C would be
the complement of D if C were constructed using the following:

```
     FOR Element := 1 TO Large DO
         C [Element] := NOT (D [Element])
```

To give A the value representing the union of B and C, and to give D
the value representing the intersection of B and C, we would use:

```
     FOR Element := 1 TO Large DO
         BEGIN
         A [Element] := B [Element] AND C [Element];
         D [Element] := B [Element] OR C [Element]
         END
```

Prime Integers

     As an application of large sets, consider the problem of
finding the prime positive integers less than or equal to some large
number. A positive integer is prime if it is divisible only by
itself and by 1. This is equivalent to saying that it is not a
multiple of a smaller positive integer other than 1. A consequence
of this is that a positive integer is prime if and only if it is not
a multiple of a smaller prime.

     An algorithm for finding primes based on this property is
called the sieve of Eratosthenes, a method developed about 250 B.C.
A large set, which we shall call Sieve, is created. It initially
contains all the integers from 2 to Large. The initial prime 2 is
selected. While there is a next prime to be discovered, the
following steps are repeated: first, all the multiples of the prime
currently being considered are removed from Sieve; then, the next
larger number which is still in Sieve is established as a prime.
Listing 12.3 is a first version of this algorithm:

```
Set all elements of Sieve to True
Set Number to 2
{ Number is now the first prime }
WHILE there are still numbers to consider DO
    Remove all multiples of Number from the Sieve
    Seek the next larger number still in the Sieve
```

Sieve of Eratosthenes
Version 1

Listing 12.3

Final Version of the Sieve of Eratosthenes

In the expanded version, we have created a variable State which can take on three values: Working, Seeking, and Finished. Working indicates that there are still numbers to consider; Seeking indicates that we are searching for a next larger number which has not been deleted from the sieve. Sieve is declared as an array [2..Large] of Boolean. Listing 12.4 is an expanded version:

```
{ Set all entries in Sieve to True }
FOR Element := 2 TO Large DO
    Sieve [Element] := True;
{ Set number to first prime }
Number := 2;
State := Working;
WHILE State = Working DO
    BEGIN
    { Remove all multiples of Number from Sieve }
    FOR Multiplier := 2 TO (Large DIV Number) DO
        Sieve [Multiplier * Number] := False;
    { Seek next Number still in Sieve if there is one,
        otherwise terminate search }
    State := Seeking;
    WHILE State = Seeking DO
        IF Number < Large
            THEN { Test next Number }
                BEGIN
                Number := Number + 1;
                IF Sieve [Number]
                    THEN
                        State := Working
                END
            ELSE { No more numbers to test }
```

```
                    State := Finished
        END

                    Sieve of Eratosthenes
                         Version 2

                     Listing 12.4
```

12.4   Summary

   The data type whose values are subsets of a given set of
elements is created by the declaration:

     SET OF < base type >

where the elements of the set are taken from the enumerated data
type that has been specified as the base type.   The size of the base
type is implementation dependent.

   An element of the base type may be tested for membership in a
subset by the relation IN.   The result of the test is given by the
Boolean value of the expression:

     < element > IN < subset >

If the test is for an element not belonging to a set, the result of
the test is given by the Boolean value of the expression:

     NOT (< element > IN < subset >)

   Two sets may be combined to obtain their union, intersection,
or difference.   They may also be compared with respect to either
equality or containment.   A table of the symbols for the appropriate
operators is:

Operator	Symbol
Union	+
Intersection	*
Difference	−
Equality	=
Not Equal	<>
Is Contained In	<=
Contains	>=

In particular, a set S is not empty if and only if S <> [] is True, where [] denotes the empty set.

If First and Last are the initial and final constants in the enumeration of the base type, the processing of each element in a subset can be accomplished by:

```
FOR Element := First TO Last DO
    IF Element IN S
        THEN
            Perform the appropriate action
```

Boolean arrays may be substituted for subsets if the size of the set exceeds the implementation dependent maximum size for sets. An array S declared as ARRAY [First..Last] OF Boolean may be used, where S [Element] = True indicates that Element was in the subset determined by S.

Exercises for Chapter 12

1. Given the following declarations and assignments:

```
TYPE
    MenuType = (Soup, Appetizer, Vegetable, Meat,
        Sandwich, Fish, Cheese, Sweets, Beverage, Nuts);
VAR
    Choice : MenuType;
    Bite, Feast, Meal, Snack, Taste : SET OF MenuType;

Feast := [Soup..Nuts];
Snack := [Sandwich..Sweets] − [Fish];
Bite := [Cheese, Nuts, Beverage];
Meal := [Soup..Meat, Sweets, Beverage]
```

What is the value of each of the following expressions?

        Snack + Bite
        Bite * Meal
        Cheese IN Snack
        Feast - Snack
        (Snack * Meal) <> []
        Bite <= Meal
        Meal + [Vegetable]
        Meal + (Snack + Bite)

What is the value of Taste after the following fragment is executed?

        Taste := [];
        FOR Choice := Soup TO Nuts DO
            IF Ord (Choice) IN [0, 2, 5, 6]
                THEN
                    Taste := Taste + [Choice]

2.   Consider the declarations below:

        TYPE
            ResponseType = (Lightening, Speedy, Quick, Fast,
                Normal, Slow, Glacial);
        VAR
            Adjective, AResponse : ResponseType;
            FasterResponses : SET OF ResponseType;

The enumeration of the constants of ResponseType has preserved an
ordering based on intended meaning. Supply a program fragment so
that, for each possible value of AResponse, after the fragment is
executed, FasterResponses will have as its value the set of all
ResponseTypes faster than AResponse. For example, if AResponse =
Quick, then FasterResponses must be assigned the value [Lightening,
Speedy].

3.   Indicate the context in which a variable OysterMonth could be
assigned the set of months whose names contain an r.

4.   The algorithm for finding the tasks that follow a given task
when the immediately following tasks are known is an example of a
general search procedure in a graph called breadth first search.
The examination and accumulation of nodes procedes on a broad front,
testing all closer nodes before moving further away from the

starting node. Modify this algorithm so that each node that follows
the starting node is put in a set consisting of those nodes which
make their appearance in the Follow set during the same clock pulse,
and these sets are retained by the program. Thus, the set of nodes
that are NewlyAdjoined for clock pulses 1, 2, 3, etc., could be
printed along with the pulse. This number of clock pulses is the
minimum number of edges of the graph that must be traversed in order
to go from the starting node to the node that has just made its
appearance.

CHAPTER 13

Records

Sections

13.0   Introduction

An elegant and extremely useful data structure permits the collection of several different data types into an aggregate called a RECORD. Each component of a record may be selected by using the name of that component. Entire records may be accessed and a record may be assigned the value of a similar record.

Records may be defined in fixed format; that is, each record
of a given type has exactly the same components, or records may
differ in so-called variant parts.

A collection of records of the same type may be grouped
together by creating an array of records. Such a structure, often
referred to as a table, provides access to any record by specifying
the index of the record. Some of the changes that might be made in
a table, such as insertion and deletion, are illustrated by
examples.

13.1   Records

An Array is a structured data type, indexed by a simple
enumerated data type, in which each indexed component is of the same
data type. A File is a structured data type consisting of a
sequence of components, where again each component is of the same
data type. Both arrays and files are homogeneous structures. Most
structured data is, however, in a nonhomogeneous form; that is, the
components are of different data types. For example, a
Massachusetts driver's license contains the following information:
License Number (same as social security number); Date of
expiration; Name; Address; Height; Class; Restrictions; and
Date of Birth. An individual license is a structured piece of
information consisting of a number of fields, each field containing
data of a specific type quite different from the data in other
fields. One can think of countless other examples of nonhomogeneous
collections of data. A date consists of three fields: month of the
year, day of the month, and year. A piece of structured data, such
as a date, may in turn be part of another type of structured data,
such as a record of a driver's license.

Many significant programs maintain large collections of records
of nonhomogeneous data. Lists of reservations, subscriptions,
inventory, accounts payable and receivable, personnel records,
patient records, and tax records are some possible examples.

Declaring Records

     Pascal permits the declaration of data types and variables
which have components or fields, each field having its own data
type. The list of components and data types is delimited by the
reserved words RECORD and END. The name of the component is an
identifier which is referred to as the field identifier and which is
used to select the component.

     To create a data type PersonIDType with two components, Name
and Age, we declare the following in the Type section:

```
     PersonIDType =
       RECORD
       Name : PACKED ARRAY [1..20] OF Char;
       Age  : 0..999
       END; { PersonIDType }
```

The field identifier Name selects a component which is a string
variable. If this were part of a student record, we might be
inclined to include other information (and also predeclare a
NameType since it would undoubtedly be used in other parts of the
program). We might use this:

```
   TYPE
     NameType = Packed Array [1..20] of Char;
     ClassType = (Freshman, Sophomore, Junior, Senior);
     PersonIdType =
       RECORD
       Name  : NameType;
       Age   : 0..999;
       Class : ClassType
       END; { PersonIdType }
```

     The part of the declaration which we have indented the deepest
and which is delimited by the reserved words RECORD and END is
called the field list. A field list is a succession of entries of
the form:

     < list of identifiers > : < data type >

separated by semicolons. The identifiers in the field list are the
field identifiers of the record. The field list is enclosed by
RECORD and END. The entire declaration of the data type
PersonIDType is of the form:

     < identifier > = RECORD < field list > END;

The entire declaration could have been written on one line, but we
have adopted an indentation style to improve readability.

Assigning Values to Components

Using the above declaration of PersonIDType, we can create
several variables of this type, and also indicate how components of
these variables can be assigned values.

```
VAR
    Someone, SomeoneElse : PersonIDType;
    .
    .   { Executable part }
    .
    Someone.Name := 'Methuselah          ';
    Someone.Age   := 969;
    SomeoneElse.Name := 'Juliet Capulet        ';
    SomeoneElse.Age   := 14;
    SomeoneElse.Class := Freshman
```

A specific component of the record is selected by appending to
the variable name a period followed by the field identifier. Blanks
may be used before or after the period to improve readability. A
record can be diagrammed as a row which has been divided into
columns labeled with the field identifiers. Figure 13.1 indicates
how we might visualize the data space containing the previous two
records and the assignments that have been made to them:

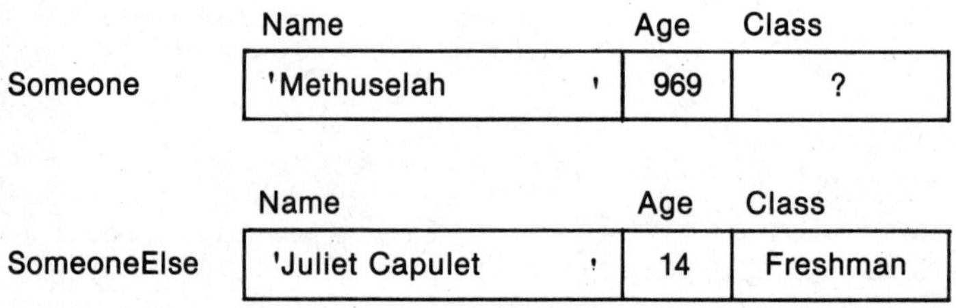

	Name	Age	Class
Someone	'Methuselah '	969	?

	Name	Age	Class
SomeoneElse	'Juliet Capulet '	14	Freshman

Figure 13.1 Data Space Containing Records

Examples

We can combine user-defined data types with the record construct to create an unlimited variety of new data types. Here is an example:

```
TYPE
    SoupType = (ClamChowder, Noodle, MockTurtle, Tomato);
    VegetableType = (Broccoli, Carrot, Bean, Corn, Squash);
    MeatType = (Beef, Chicken, Lamb, Pork);
    DessertType = (Fruit, Jello, Custard, BakedAlaska, Mousse);
    Weekday = (Monday, Tuesday, Wednesday, Thursday, Friday);
    MealType =
        RECORD
        Soup : SoupType;
        Vegetable : VegetableType;
        Meat : MeatType;
        Sweets : DessertType;
        Price : Real;
        Calories : Integer
        END; { MealType }
    WeeksMenuType = Array [Weekday] of MealType;

VAR
    ThisWeeksMenu : WeeksMenuType;
```

It would be appropriate to make the following assignments in a program containing the above declarations:

```
ThisWeeksMenu[Monday].Soup := Noodle;
```

One may introduce blanks between the various identifiers to improve readability, and write instead:

```
ThisWeeksMenu [Monday] . Soup := Noodle;
```

Additional assignments might include:

```
ThisWeeksMenu [Monday] . Vegetable := Squash;
ThisWeeksMenu [Monday] . Meat := Beef;
ThisWeeksMenu [Monday] . Sweets := Custard;
ThisWeeksMenu [Monday] . Price := 6.50;
ThisWeeksMenu [Monday] . Calories := 1200;
```

The WITH Statement

The previous six assignment statements each contain the phrase:

ThisWeeksMenu [Monday] .

Instead of repeating the phrase in each individual assignment
statement, the entire group of statements can be qualified by the
WITH statement. An equivalent form of these six statements is then:

```
WITH ThisWeeksMenu [Monday] DO
   BEGIN
   Soup := Noodle;
   Vegetable := Squash;
   Meat := Beef;
   Sweets := Custard;
   Price := 6.50;
   Calories := 1200
   END;
```

Note that the form is:

WITH < prefix > DO < statement >

where the prefix is the record being addressed, and that, in order
to make the WITH statement apply to the six following assignment
statements, we must build a compound statement using BEGIN and END
as delimiters.

Another appropriate assignment would be:

ThisWeeksMenu [Thursday] := ThisWeeksMenu [Monday]

Both sides of this assignment statement are of data type MealType.
Here is another example:

```
TYPE
   Movie =
      RECORD
      Title : PACKED ARRAY [1..20] OF Char;
      Category : (Scifi, Musical, Comedy, Drama,
                                 Horror, Costume);
      Rating : (Rave, Warm, Tepid, Deplorable)
      END; { Movie }
```

```
VAR
   Flick : Movie
      .
      .   { Executable part }
      .
   Flick . Title := '2001
   Flick . Category := Scifi;
   Flick . Rating := Rave;
```

More than one identifier may appear in the WITH statement.
Suppose there is an array of customer records which includes a debit
balance field and an array of invoices which includes a total field.
To debit Customer [Index] the amount of Invoice [Number], we may use
either of the two statements:

```
Customer [Index] . DebitBalance := Invoice [Number] . Total
     + Customer [Index] . DebitBalance

WITH Customer [Index], Invoice [Number] DO
     DebitBalance := Total + DebitBalance
```

Records may be nested within records, so that there are
identifiers which provide a chain of fields into a given record. If
these identifiers are listed in the WITH statement, they must be
written in the order in which they appear in a compound selector.
An example of this would be an array of cars which has a component
Model which, in turn, has components such as Cylinders,
Manufacturer, and Color. The WITH statement could be used to govern
the assignment of values to these three nested components by the
statement:

```
WITH Car [Index], Model DO
   BEGIN
   Cylinder := 4;
   Manufacturer := Chevrolet;
   Color := Puce
   END
```

The first assignment has given Car [Index] . Model . Cylinder the
value 4.

13.2 Variant Records

Many records exhibit an internal dependency in which, depending
on the values of certain components determine whether or not other
components are present. It would be wasteful to create components
for all possible fields. Pascal allows for the creation of records
with variant fields.

As an example, consider a simplified record of a performer as
it might be maintained by a booking agency. Let us try to structure
two variations of a record for a performer, one for actors and one
for singers (for the moment, assume that no actor is a singer and
that no singer is an actor).

For an actor, include age, sex, and a component called casting.
For a singer, include age and voice. Each record, whether it is for
an actor or for a singer, contains a component age. Depending on
whether the performer's metier is actor or singer, the record
contains either sex and casting or voice, respectively.

Tag Field

The form of two possible records of a performer might have one
of the two following structures:

```
Age     | Metier   | Sex     | Casting
--------+----------+---------+-------------------
31      | Actor    | Female  | [Comic, Satiric]

Age     | Metier   | Voice
--------+----------+-------
26      | Singer   | Alto
```

The field component with field identifier Metier is called the Tag
field. The value of the tag field is used to determine the variant
of the record.

These two variations may be combined in one declaration. For
the above example, this would be done by the declaration:

```
PerformerType =
   RECORD
   { fixed part }
   Age : 0..100;
```

```
          { Variant part }
          CASE Metier : MetierType OF
             Actor  : (Sex      : SexType;
                       Casting : CastingType);
             Singer : (Voice : VoiceType)
          END; { PerformerType }
```

The variant part of the record must always come last. The
reason is that, for a variable of this type, the compiler will
create a memory cell which is large enough to contain the largest
variant (in the above case this would be one with tag field actor),
and the initial segments of this cell will be interpreted as
components of the fixed part. Only one variant part is allowed in
any record, but a variant part may itself contain a variant part.

Form of the Variant Part

     The form of the variant part is:

```
     CASE < tag field >  < type identifier > OF
          < one or more variants separated by semicolons >
```

     In our example, there are two variants. They are:

```
        Actor  : (Sex      : SexType;
                  Casting : CastingType);
        Singer : (Voice : VoiceType)
```

Following the colon, after the case label, is a field list for the
components for that particular variant. This variant field list
must be enclosed in parentheses.

     The tag field is optional, but the type of the tag is not. If
the tag field is omitted, there is no component in the record with
the tag field as its name, though the constants of the tag field
type still label the variant components. In general, it is
advisable to include the tag field since the value of the tag field
can be used to choose which variant is selected.

     Here the tag field is:

     Metier :

It creates a component with the field identifier Metier of type
MetierType. The variant has a list of the constants of the given
type identifier in its case label lists, here one list with Actor

and the other with Singer. Following the colon and enclosed by
parentheses is a field list such as the field list defined for
records in the preceding section. Perhaps, it may be that for some
value or values of the tag field, there are no dependent fields.
The appropriate form is then:

        < case label list > : ( );

     In the example given above, several types were referenced. A
complete declaration for PerformerType would include something like
the following:

```
TYPE
    MetierType = (Actor, Singer);
    SexType = (Male, Female);
    CastingTypes = SET OF (Comic, Dramatic, Romantic,
                            Satiric);
    VoiceType = (Soprano, Alto, Tenor, Bass);
    PerformerType =
        RECORD
        Age : 0..100;
        CASE Metier : MetierType OF
            Actor  : (Sex      : SexType;
                        Casting : CastingTypes);
            Singer : (Voice : VoiceType)
        END; { PerformerType }
```

```
VAR
    APerformer : PerformerType;
    PerformerNumber : ARRAY [1..100] OF PerformerType;
```

     Using the variable APerformer, we can assign values to the four
components:

```
WITH APerformer DO
    BEGIN
    Age := 31;
    Metier := Actor;
    Sex := Female;
    Casting := [Comic, Romantic, Dramatic]
    END;
```

     This record can be assigned to the record PerformerNumber [1],
and another set of values may be assigned to APerformer before it is
assigned to PerformerNumber [2]. The code for this is:

```
   PerformerNumber [1] := APerformer;
   WITH APerformer DO
      BEGIN
      Metier := Singer;
      Voice := Alto
      END;
   PerformerNumber [2] := APerformer;
```

These instructions cause PerformerNumber [2] to inherit the age, 31, of the earlier value of APerformer, but, since Metier is singer, Performer [2] is now a variant with three components--Age, Metier, and Voice.

Writing Variant Records

     To output a description of one of these records, say PerformerNumber [1], a number of nested case statements may be used. Here is the code to print this information:

```
   WITH PerformerNumber [1] DO
      BEGIN
      Writeln ('Age ', Age : 3);
      CASE Metier OF
         Actor  : BEGIN
                  Writeln ('Metier Actor');
                  CASE Sex OF
                     Male   : Writeln ('Sex Male');
                     Female : Writeln ('Sex Female')
                     END; { Case of Sex }
                  Writeln ('Casting');
                  FOR CastingIndex := Comic TO Satiric DO
                     IF CastingIndex IN Casting
                        THEN
                           CASE CastingIndex OF
                              Comic    : Writeln ('  Comic');
                              Dramatic : Writeln ('  Dramatic');
                              Romantic : Writeln ('  Romantic');
                              Satiric  : Writeln ('  Satiric')
                              END { Case of CastingIndex }
                  END;
         Singer : BEGIN
                  Writeln ('Metier Singer');
                  CASE Voice OF
                     Soprano : Writeln ('Soprano');
                     Alto    : Writeln ('Alto');
```

```
                    Tenor    : Writeln ('Tenor');
                    Bass     : Writeln ('Bass')
                    END { Case of Voice }
               END
          END { Case of Metier }
     END { WITH PerformerNumber [1] DO }
```

The above code requires the declaration of a local variable:

          CastingIndex : (Comic, Dramatic, Romantic, Satiric)

In this particular instance, the output would be:

```
     Age  31
     Metier Actor
     Sex Female
     Casting
        Comic
        Dramatic
        Romantic
```

13.3 A Menu Program

     In this section, we shall develop a number of steps in the
design of a program to maintain a class list, while attempting to
illustrate a number of programming techniques, using top-down
design. The choice of data structures and declaration of variables
will be postponed until they are necessary. We will attempt to make
each version of the program a running program so that the currently
defined procedures can be tested. To do the latter, we shall
frequently create stubs, or program segments, that temporarily
replace complex portions of a program with simpler segments, often
of the form BEGIN < comment describing the segment > END. These
stubs will be used for many of the operations to be included in the
final program version.

     Many programs assume that the user will choose one of a number
of alternative operations. They present the user with a menu,
prompt for a choice among these menu items, obtain the user's
choice, perform the chosen operation, and then return to prompt
again for another choice of operation. The program continues in
this fashion until the user chooses to terminate the program. Here
is version 1 of the program:

```
PROGRAM ClassList (Input, Output);

   { Maintain a class list

   Programmer: CS115
   Version 1, August 30, 1980 }

VAR
   Finished : Boolean;

PROCEDURE PresentMenu;
BEGIN
Writeln ('Procedure PresentMenu Executing')
END; { PresentMenu }

PROCEDURE RequestOperation;
{ Prompt for and Obtain the Operation Requested }
BEGIN
Writeln ('Procedure RequestOperation Executing');
{ temporary assignment } Finished := True
END; { RequestOperation }

PROCEDURE PerformOperation;
BEGIN
Writeln('Procedure PerformOperation Executing')
END; { PerformOperation }

BEGIN { Main }
Finished := False;
PresentMenu;
WHILE NOT Finished DO
   BEGIN
   RequestOperation;
   PerformOperation
   END
END.
```

Listing 13.1

Each of the stubs has included an output statement with a literal string of the form 'Procedure < name > Executing'. This version was compiled and the expected output appeared, that is:

```
Procedure PresentMenu Executing
Procedure RequestOperation Executing
Procedure PerformOperation Executing
```

Except for the introduction of global data types and variables, the main program is complete. In version 2, we shall develop PresentMenu and RequestOperation. As we do this, we shall introduce output in both of these procedures so that the temporary Writeln statements may be deleted.

Presenting the Menu

To design PresentMenu, we must make a decision as to what operations will be allowed. The class list will be read from and written to an external file, while allowing insertion and deletion in the current list. This list will be stored in the program data space as an array, permitting easy access to the individual records. Since the user may have made several changes in the list, we shall allow a printout of the current list. Since the menu may no longer be on the CRT screen after several operations have been performed, we shall allow the menu to be printed again. Instead of requiring the user to enter an entire word as a description of the operations to be performed, we shall ask for a single character. An appropriate explanation will be included in the menu presentation. (We are therefore assuming that each operation will correspond to a unique character.)

Procedure RequestOperation prompts for and obtains a character which we call Operation. This identifier will be declared globally so that the procedure PerformOperation can have access to it. The procedure RequestOperation uses the Input file and makes the assumption that, upon its invocation, the input file pointer is at the beginning of a new and empty line.

In listing 13.2, we have included the details of RequestOperation and PresentMenu:

```
PROCEDURE PresentMenu;
BEGIN
Writeln ('Enter a Single Uppercase Character to Choose');
Writeln ('One of the Following Operations:');
Writeln (' D    Delete a Student');
Writeln (' E    End the Program');
Writeln (' I    Insert a Student');
Writeln (' M    Print this Menu');
Writeln (' P    Print Current Class List');
Writeln (' R    Read Old Class List from File OldClass');
Writeln (' W    Write Current Class List to File NewClass')
END; { PresentMenu }
```

```
PROCEDURE RequestOperation;
{ Prompt for and Obtain the Operation Requested by supplying
    a value to the global variable Operation : Char.
  Input file is assumed to be found with pointer pointing
    to beginning of empty line.  Input file is left
    pointing to beginning of empty line }
BEGIN
Writeln ('Enter Operation Chosen.');
Readln (Operation);
{ temporary echo } Writeln ('Operation is: ', Operation);
{ temporary assignment } Finished := True
END; { RequestOperation }
```

Listing 13.2

We have been very explicit about the interaction of the
procedure RequestOperation with the Input file. In our experience,
improper handling of the Input file is a source of errors that is
very difficult to catch when writing interactive programs that read
characters. In a sense, the procedure can only make an assumption
that it will find the Input file in a certain state, but it can
ensure that it leaves the Input file with the file pointer pointing
to the beginning of a new line.

Menu as a CASE Statement

In the next version of the program, version 3, we shall develop
the procedure PerformOperation. This procedure is easily described
using the CASE statement. Two of the cases can be coded
immediately. If the value of Operation is 'M', meaning that the
user has chosen to see the menu again, we already have available the
procedure PresentMenu. If the value of Operation is 'E', meaning
that the user has chosen to end the program, we need only set
Finished to True.

The remaining menu selections will be encoded as five
procedures: Delete, Insert, PrintList, ReadFile, and WriteFile.
Each of these procedures could be declared prior to the appearance
of the procedure PerformOperation, or they can be nested inside
PerformOperation. Since they are only invoked within
PerformOperation, we shall nest them inside this procedure. In
order to depict this nesting, we shall enlarge the indentation
scheme, indenting each of these procedures with respect to
PerformOperation.

The prompt in RequestOperation asks for uppercase characters.
We shall adopt our usual lenient attitude toward the user (for it
may be ourselves) and include in the set of constants that label the
various alternatives in the case statement the corresponding
lowercase characters.

Listing 13.3 contains the development of the procedure
PerformOperation and the nested procedures that it has spawned:

```
PROCEDURE PerformOperation;

    PROCEDURE Delete;
    BEGIN
    Writeln ('Procedure Delete Executing')
    END; { Delete }

    PROCEDURE Insert;
    BEGIN
    Writeln ('Procedure Insert Executing')
    END; { Insert }

    PROCEDURE PrintList;
    BEGIN
    Writeln ('Procedure PrintList Executing')
    END; { PrintList }

    PROCEDURE ReadFile;
    BEGIN
    Writeln ('Procedure ReadFile Executing')
    END; { ReadFile }

    PROCEDURE WriteFile;
    BEGIN
    Writeln ('Procedure WriteFile Executing')
    END; { WriteFile }

    { End of Procedures nested inside PerformOperation }

BEGIN { PerformOperation }
    CASE Operation OF
        'D', 'd' : Delete;
        'E', 'e' : Finished := True;
        'I', 'i' : Insert;
        'M', 'm' : PresentMenu;
        'P', 'p' : PrintList;
        'R', 'r' : ReadFile;
        'W', 'w' : WriteFile
        END { Case of Operation }
```

```
END; { PerformOperation }
```

Listing 13.3

Again, version 3 is a program which can be compiled and run.
It allows us to enter the various characters that select each
alternative. In this fashion, we can "exercise" each of the
possible paths through the program (at this stage of refinement).
If one is testing a program, this is an important property that the
test data should have--namely, that every portion of the code be
executed at least once.

In the refinement process that we have been following, the
development of the procedure PerformOperation has spawned a set of
five procedures which must in turn be developed. The one that
logically should be expanded first is the procedure Insert.

Insertion

Expanding the procedure Insert will force us to make some
decisions about the nature of the data with which we are dealing.
The class list itself will be an array of a certain maximum size of
records, each of which identifies a student. A description of a
student would normally contain more information. Since this is a
sample program, we will restrict the amount of information. We
shall include only an array of characters giving the last name and
an array of characters giving the first name. This forces us to
decide on the maximum number of characters that we will allow in a
name.

Once insertion in the list is possible, we will need a variable
whose value will be the current size of the class list.

The class list itself, and its size, will be declared globally
since their values should be retained during the entire lifetime of
the program. If they were declared locally inside PerformOperation,
they would exist only during the execution of the procedure and
would not retain their values from one invocation to the next.

The algorithmic form of procedure Insert will be:

Obtain the position of the new entry
    The position should be requested repeatedly until
    it has a value between 1 and 1 more than the current
    size of the class.
The block of entries extending from this position to

      the end of the class list must be moved one place
      towards the end. This has to be done from the rear
      down to the position in which the new entry is made
      so that no entry is lost.
   Obtain the new entry
   Increment the size of the class list

An alternate description of the algorithm, organized according to
the control statements that might appear at this level of
refinement, is given next:

   Prompt for position
   REPEAT
      Obtain position
      IF position is not acceptable
         THEN
            request reentry
      UNTIL position is acceptable
   For each entry from the rear down to this position
      Move entry up one position
   Obtain and insert the new entry
   Increment the size of the class list

We must also remember to initially set the size of the class to 0.

   Here are the new global declarations in version 4:

   CONST
      MaxClassSize = 4;
      MaxLastNameSize = 15;
      MaxFirstNameSize = 10;

   TYPE
      StudentType =
         RECORD
         LastName : ARRAY [1..MaxLastNameSize] OF Char;
         FirstName : ARRAY [1..MaxFirstNameSize] OF Char;
         END; { StudentType }

   VAR
      ClassList : ARRAY [1..MaxClassSize] OF StudentType;
      SizeofClass : 0..MaxClassSize;

   In developing the procedure Insert, we have chosen to delay the
writing of the portion of the program in which the information
relating to a new student is actually entered. We have simply
created a nested procedure ObtainNewEntry. Listing 13.4 contains
the procedure Insert:

```
PROCEDURE Insert;
VAR
    Place : 1..MaxClassSize;
    Position : Integer;
    Acceptable : Boolean;

    PROCEDURE ObtainNewEntry;
    BEGIN
    Writeln ('Procedure ObtainNewEntry Executing')
    END; { ObtainNewEntry }

BEGIN
{ Obtain Position of new entry }
Writeln ('Current Size of Class List is ', SizeofClass : 5);
Writeln('Enter Position of New Entry');
REPEAT { until a position in 1..(SizeofClass + 1) is given }
    Readln (Position);
    Acceptable := (1 <= Position) AND
                        (Position <= SizeofClass + 1);
    IF NOT acceptable
       THEN
           BEGIN
           Writeln ('Position not in range 1..',
                   SizeofClass+1 : 3);
           Writeln ('Please reenter position of new entry')
           END
    UNTIL Acceptable;
{ Move students at tail of list to open up Position }
FOR Place := SizeofClass DOWNTO Position DO
    ClassList [Place + 1] := ClassList [Place];
ObtainNewEntry;
SizeofClass := SizeofClass + 1
END; { Insert }
```

Listing 13.4

Having introduced a constant for the maximum size of the class, we can alter the manner in which the case statement in PerformOperation deals with 'I'. If the size of the class is already equal to the maximum class size, then we will not permit the user to insert another entry, but rather will inform the user that the class is full. (This is why we have temporarily set MaxClassSize to 4--we can easily check that we have indeed prevented the user from making an entry in an already full class.) The new alternative in the CASE statement is:

```
'I', 'i' : IF SizeofClass < MaxClassSize
                THEN Insert
                ELSE Writeln ('Class is full.');
```

Having chosen a small maximum class size in version 4, we can quickly test the insertion procedure by entering positions outside the appropriate range, and then attempting to insert in an already full class. We will not be able to fully test insertion, however, until we complete the designs of ObtainNewEntry and of the procedure which prints the current class list.

Printing the List

Using only the standard features, we must output an array of characters, character by character. Here is the procedure PrintList:

```
PROCEDURE PrintList;
    VAR
        Index : 1..MaxClassSize;
        LN : 1..MaxLastNameSize;
        FN : 1..MaxFirstNameSize;
    BEGIN
    FOR Index := 1 TO SizeofClass DO
        { Print a student }
        WITH ClassList [Index] DO
            BEGIN
            Write (Index : 3, '  ');
            FOR LN := 1 To MaxLastNameSize DO
                Write (LastName [LN]);
            Write ('    ');
            FOR FN := 1 TO MaxFirstNameSize DO
                Write (FirstName [FN]);
            Writeln
            END
        END; { PrintList }
```

This same technique of accessing the input character by character is necessary in procedure ObtainNewEntry. Recall that this procedure is nested within procedure Insert and that the user has established an appropriate value for the variable Position as the place in the class list where the new entry is to be placed. Here are some of the details of ObtainNewEntry:

```
PROCEDURE ObtainNewEntry;
VAR
    LN, LNPadding : 1..MaxLastNameSize;
    FN, FNPadding : 1..MaxFirstNameSize;
BEGIN
    WITH ClassList [Position] DO
        BEGIN
        Writeln ('Enter last name, at most ',
                 MaxLastNameSize : 3, ' characters');
        LN := 0;
        WHILE NOT Eoln DO
            BEGIN
            LN := LN + 1;
            Read (LastName [LN]);
            END;
        FOR LNPadding := (LN + 1) TO MaxLastNameSize DO
            LastName [LNPadding] := ' ';
        Readln;
        Similar code for FirstName
        End
End; { ObtainNewEntry }
```

With these procedures in place, the insertion procedure can be fully tested. The reading and writing to external files is best postponed until the next chapter, in which we consider files of any data type. We will then be in a position to define a file of StudentType and read the file in units of the record StudentType.

The remaining procedure is Delete. This is left as an exercise.

Documentation

We are NOT DONE. The program documentation should be reviewed and improved. For example, a comment similar to the following should introduce the program:

```
{ Maintain a class list consisting of student records
  Each student record is of the form
     Last Name  : 20 characters
     First Name : 15 characters

User may choose program function by menu
     See procedure PresentMenu
```

    Permanent record created by 'W' option in file OldClass
It is assumed that there is a system procedure to copy an
   updated class list in OldClass to an input file NewClass
NewClass can be read into the program data space for update
   purposes by the 'R' option

    Programmer: CS115
    Version 6, September 4, 1980 }

    Perhaps another warning ought to be included. When using this
program--and using other programs like it (such as a text editor)
which allow one to make permanent records of some of the data--it is
an excellent idea to write to files frequently. Consider the
frustration of the user of this program, who has just spent the
better part of an hour creating a list of students. The user is
about to enter the 43rd student, gets the prompt for the position,
and, instead of entering the digits 43, enters the student's last
name and hits return before realizing it was a mistake. The system
now issues an error message and aborts the program. The work of the
previous hour is lost. Had the user, after entering every fifth
student, taken advantage of the 'W' option to write the current
class list to a permanent file, only the work of entering the last
three students would have been lost.

    An even better method, which requires more effort on the part
of the programmer, would be to read all input as characters. The
program then converts digits to their corresponding numerical value
when digits are expected, and, if a digit is expected, but some
other character is read, the program prompts the user for the proper
input.

13.4 Summary

    A RECORD is a data type consisting of several components, where
each component has its own data type and a field identifier that is
used to select a specific component. A typical record is of the
form:

```
            RECORD
            < field identifier 1 > : < data type 1 >;
            < field identifier 2 > : < data type 2 >;
                .
                .
                .
            < field identifier N > : < data type N >
            END
```

If several components were of the same data type, the field
identifiers could be listed together, as in this record:

```
            RECORD
            Cost, SellingPrice : Real;
            OnHand : Integer;
            Supplier : PACKED ARRAY [1..20] OF Char
            END
```

    A particular component of a record is selected by following the
name of the variable with a period and the field identifier. Thus,
if Item were declared to be a record of the above type, a value
could be assigned to the component SellingPrice and the quantity
OnHand of Item could be printed by:

```
            Item . SellingPrice := 1.99;

            Writeln ('On hand : ', Item . OnHand : 6)
```

Thus, individual components may be selected. If two records are of
the same type, one record may be assigned to another, thereby
copying the value of each component of the first record into the
corresponding component of the second record.

    In reading and writing information from or to the terminal (or
textfiles in general), remember that only integers, characters, and
reals can be read, and only these three types along with Booleans
and literal strings may be written when the standard procedures are
used.

    Instead of including the variable and period as a prefix when
selecting several components of a record, the WITH statement may be
used to specify the variable whose components are being selected.
An example using Item would be:

```
WITH Item DO
    Writeln (Cost : 10 : 2, SellingPrice : 10 : 2,
                  OnHand : 10, '        ', Supplier)
```

Records may contain variant parts. This is desirable if the
presence or absence of certain components is determined by the value
of another component in a field called the Tag field. The variant
part of a record must be declared last. A typical declaration with
variant part would be of the form:

```
RECORD
< fixed part >
< variant part >
END
```

The variant part would be of the form

```
CASE < field identifier > : < tag field data type > OF
```

followed by a list of variants, each given by:

```
    < constant of tag field data type > :
        ( < list of variant components in the usual form
             field identifier : data type > )
```

Several constants may select the same variant. In this case, they
are separated by commas. Note that a single appearance of END
closes the variant part and the RECORD.

An application of record is contained in a menu type program
giving the user the choice of performing a variety of actions on an
array of records. The development of the procedures to perform
these actions can be postponed by creating stubs or procedures which
perform no processing. This is a technique for incrementally
developing and testing a program step by step.

Exercises for Chapter 13

1. Develop the Delete procedure for the Class List program. Try to
protect the user.

2. If the Delete procedure is included in the Class List program, a

user can replace an entry by deletion followed by insertion. It
would be more efficient to create a separate procedure to replace or
substitute an entry, thus avoiding the unnecessary rearrangement of
the tail of the array. Modify the Class List program so that it
includes this option. Another option that could be added is the
option of extending the list by several entries. How might this
option be included?

3. Give appropriate declarations and assignments to create the
following data objects:

	Month	Day	Year
Today	|'September '| 30	1983 |

Name	Hospital	Disease

	Name	Hospital	Disease
Patient	|'Kildare '| Flower	| TyphoidFever |

	Source	Destination	Flight [1] Leave	Arrive	[2] Leave	Arrive
Route	|Bangor	|Rockport |	905 |	1030 |	1500 |	1625 |

4. A business has disbursements for which a daily total is
accumulated. The disbursements are classified as Salaries,
Shipping, Postage, GoodsPurchased, Insurance, Commissions,
Telephone, Taxes, Miscellaneous. Write a program which will store
and update the disbursements of the current month and will print the
current totals for each classification.

5. Given a record type such as:

```
ItemType = RECORD
           IDNumber : 0..9999;
           Cost : Real;
           Color : (Red, Yellow, Green, Blue)
           END
```

If Item is declared as a variable of ItemType, the information in a variable is organized in a hierarchical fashion. This is displayed in a graph of the form:

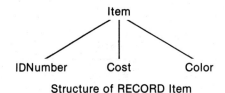

Structure of Record Item

The components of a record may themselves be records, in which case the lower nodes of the graph may have nodes hanging from them. Draw a graph corresponding to the hierarchical organization of information in a variable declared by:

```
SomeFlight : RECORD
             Number : 0..999;
             Origin, Destination : CityType
             Capacity, Reserved :
                RECORD
                FirstClass : 0..50;
                Economy : 0..250
                END
             Craft : PlaneType
             END
```

Suppose that an assignment is to be made to reserve two more Economy tickets on this Flight. Supply a Pascal fragment to perform this action.

6. A complex number is a pair of real numbers, the first called the
RealPart and the second called the ImaginaryPart. If (a, b) and
(c, d) are two complex numbers, the sum is defined as (a + c, b + d)
and the product as ((a * c) − (b * d), (a * d) + (b * c)). Define a
complex number as a record, and write a program which obtains the
real and imaginary parts of two complex numbers and computes and
prints their sum and product.

7. A company is interested in maintaining the inventory records on
a computer so that, as goods are received and shipped, the amount on
hand can be readily accessed. Write a pilot program to show how
this maintenance program might appear to the user and what functions
it might perform.

CHAPTER 14

Files

Sections

14.0   Introduction

     A file is typically a large amount of information which is
retained in auxiliary memory, such as disks and tapes. The
information is usually a sequence of records. To permit processing
of such files, Pascal allows the declaration of a file of any data
type, simple or structured (other than data types which are
themselves composed of files).

     The unit of information, or component of a file, is accessed by
several standard procedures which take the place of the Read and
Write procedures used for textfiles. In addition to the Rewrite and

Reset procedures, a procedure Get is used for reading, a procedure Put for writing, and a file buffer variable is used to hold the value of the file component which is being read or being written.

14.1 Files of Arbitrary Data Types

In Chapter 7, we confined ourselves to files of characters or textfiles. These files were of the same type as the Input and Output files. All of the information stored in these files was in the form of a sequence of characters, including a control character which we have denoted by <EOL>. In a well-designed system, these files will be the same as those that can be created by a text editor. For example, when the value of an integer variable is written to this type of file, the value of the integer is represented (with leading blanks) by a string of digits preceded by a sign, if necessary.

Declaration of a File

Data may be stored in files in the form in which it is normally stored in the data space of a program, so that conversion to and from characters is unnecessary and information is stored efficiently. The general form of the declaration of a file is:

        < identifier > : FILE OF < data type >

Textfiles are a special case, namely FILE OF Char.

The data type that appears in this definition can be given by enumeration, by a subrange, by one of the packed or unpacked structured types array, or by a previously declared type. A previously declared type is referred to as simple in this context since only its name appears, even though the name may refer back to a structured type. (We have not yet introduced the data type pointer. One may create a file of pointers, but it would not be a useful object since pointers are essentially addresses which do not retain their applicability from one execution of a program to the next.)

Let the following types be defined:

```
MatrixType = ARRAY [1..10, 1..10] OF Real;
ScaleTone = (C, DFlat, D, EFlat, E, F, FSharp, G, AFlat,
             A, BFlat, B);
```

Then the following would be definitions of files in which the data types are simple:

```
Tables : FILE OF MatrixType;
Opus : PACKED FILE OF ScaleTone;
DataFile : FILE OF Integer;
Grades : FILE OF 0..100;
Chapter : Text  { FILE OF Char }
```

Other examples of definitions of files using structured types are:

```
Votes : FILE OF PACKED ARRAY [1..200] OF Boolean;
Page : FILE OF ARRAY [1..70] OF Char;
```

SET and RECORD may also be used, but FILE OF FILE is not usually permitted. Files may be packed, instructing the compiler to adopt a compact representation of the items in the file.

Reset, Rewrite

If a file is external, then the file identifier must be included in the list of files in the program heading. Prior to reading from a file, the file must be Reset; prior to writing into a file, an empty file must be created with the Rewrite procedure (except that the standard files Input and Output must not be reset or rewritten).

Only FILE OF Char or Text has available the Read and Write procedures, and the Boolean function Eoln. These files may also be accessed by the Put and Get procedures which we will describe below.

Window, Buffer Variable

The definition of a file creates a pointer or window which, during reading, points to a position in the file. The value of the item at this position in the file is available during reading as the value of a buffer variable, which is denoted by the file identifier followed by an up-arrow (if it is in the character set) or by the circumflex, ^. We shall use the circumflex. The buffer variable is given the value to be entered, and then the Put procedure places that value at the end of the file and moves the window.

The relation of the file buffer variable X^ to the file X is depicted in figure 14.1:

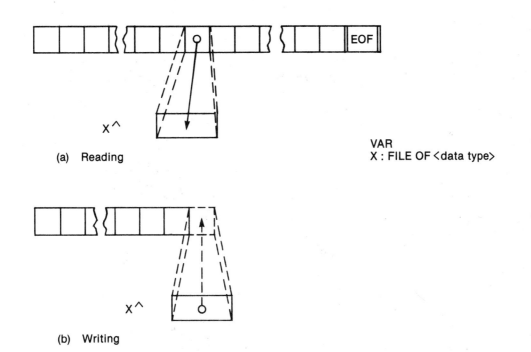

(a) Reading

VAR
X : FILE OF <data type>

(b) Writing

Figure 14.1   Diagram and Declaration of FILE OF < data type >

Using the procedures mentioned above, the following fragment will write all twelve tones in chromatic order into the file Opus:

```
Rewrite (Opus)
FOR Tone := C TO B DO
   BEGIN
   Opus^ := Tone;
   Put (Opus)
   END
```

The combination of the two instructions, assigning the file buffer
variable a new value and appending the new value to the file, can be
achieved using the Write procedure. The above fragment is
equivalent to:

```
Rewrite (Opus);
FOR Tone := C TO B DO
   Write (Opus, Tone)
```

The file variable, in this case Opus, must be listed as the first
parameter for the Write procedure.

Using a File

        Suppose that a file of these scale tones has been created and
it is desired to count the number of times each of the twelve tones
appears in the file. The technique is to examine the current value
of the file buffer, and then to move the window (thereby changing
the value of the file buffer) using the procedure Get. When the
window points to the end-of-file mark, the function Eof will become
True and the controlling WHILE-DO loop will be terminated. Assume
that appropriate definitions have been made, including:

```
Frequency : ARRAY [C..B] OF 0..Maxint
```

Then, the following fragment will count the number of times each
tone appears in the file:

```
Reset (Opus);
FOR Tone := C TO B DO
   Frequency [Tone] := 0;
WHILE NOT Eof (Opus) DO
   BEGIN
   Frequency [Opus^] := Frequency [Opus^] + 1;
   Get (Opus)
   END
```

The combination of the two instructions, assigning the file buffer

variable a new value and appending the new value to the file, can be
achieved by using the Read procedure. The above fragment is
equivalent to:

```
Reset (Opus);
FOR Tone := C TO B DO
   Frequency [Tone] := 0;
WHILE NOT Eof (Opus) DO
   BEGIN
   Read (Opus, Tone);
   Frequency [Tone] := Frequency [Tone] + 1
   END
```

The file variable is listed as the first parameter for the Read
procedure. When Eof (Opus) becomes True, the value of Tone should
be considered to be undefined.

   Both the buffer variable Opus^ and Tone will be of the
enumerated type (C, ..., B). The creation of the variable Opus^ is
implicit in the definition of the file Opus.

A detailed set of snapshots of the effect of several statements used in writing to a file Data of Integer is given in figure 14.2.

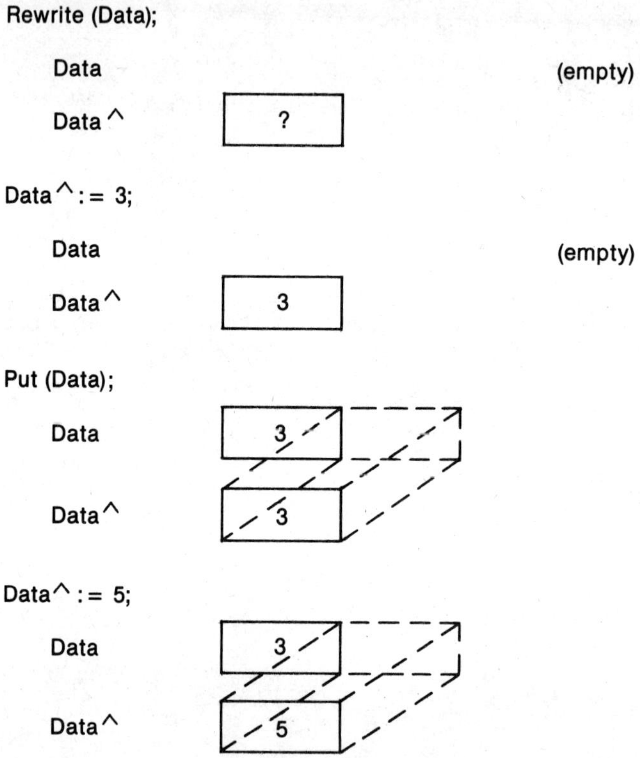

Rewrite (Data);

Data   (empty)

Data^   [?]

Data^ := 3;

Data   (empty)

Data^   [3]

Put (Data);

Data   [3]

Data^   [3]

Data^ := 5;

Data   [3]

Data^   [5]

Figure 14.2 Writing to a File

Assuming that the file has been written and is now to be read, figure 14.3 gives a set of snapshots of the effect of reading from the file Data. The values of Eof (Data) and of an auxiliary variable Number into which values of the file are read have been included.

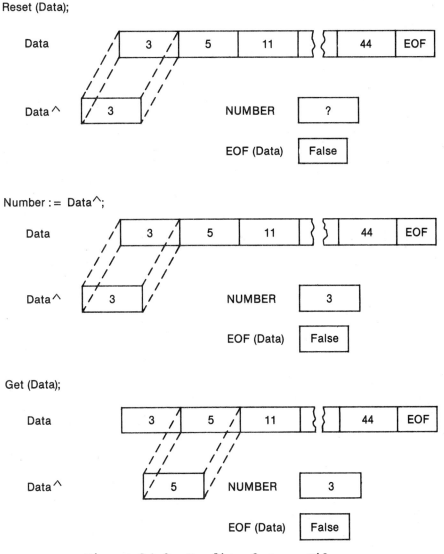

Figure 14.3   Reading from a File

Figure 14.4 depicts the reading of a file at the point where the last component of the file has been read and shows the effect of executing the Get procedure.

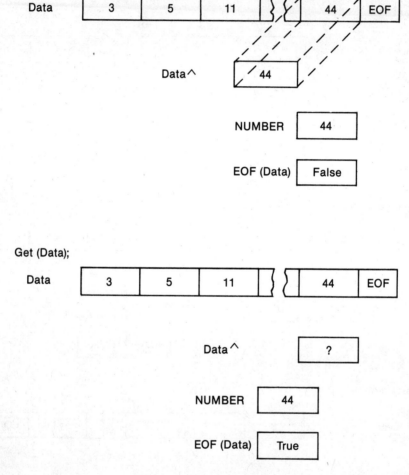

Figure 14.4   Reading a File with the Window at the Last Component

14.2   Applications

Files are used for two reasons: to make data permanent and to
process large amounts of data.   Typically, a program which uses
files produces new or updated versions of those files.

Mailing List

A simple update function on a file might be eliminating all
records that fail to satisfy a certain condition.   As an example,
consider a mailing list of subscribers to some monthly publication.
Possible type declarations are:

```
TYPE
    NameType = PACKED ARRAY [1..30] OF Char;
    AddressType = PACKED ARRAY [1..60] OF Char;
    AccountType =
        RECORD
        Name : NameType;
        Address : AddressType;
        ExpirationDate : RECORD
                          Month : 1..12;
                          Year : 81..99
                          END { Expiration Date }
        END; { AccountType }
```

Removing a Record

Each month, prior to the use of the file to prepare mailing
labels, the records of those individuals whose subscriptions have
expired are removed from the file.   This means that a new file is
created.   Declarations for the old and new files and variables to
hold the next current year and month are:

```
VAR
    MailingList, NewMailingList : FILE OF AccountType;
    GivenYear : 81..99;
    GivenMonth : 1..12;
```

Assuming that GivenYear and GivenMonth have been assigned
values, the code for preparing the NewMailList is:

```
      Reset (MailingList);
      Rewrite .(NewMailingList);
      WHILE NOT Eof (MailingList) DO
          BEGIN
          WITH MailingList^ DO
              IF (ExpirationDate . Year > GivenYear) OR
                  ((ExpirationDate . Year = GivenYear) AND
                   (ExpirationDate . Month >= GivenMonth))
                  THEN
                      BEGIN
                      NewMailingList^ := MailingList^;
                      Put (NewMailingList)
                      END;
          Get (MailingList)
          END;
      Writeln ('Expired subscribers dropped');
```

Note that the file buffer variables MailingList^ and
NewMailingList" are handled in the same fashion as any other
variable of type AccountType. A long Boolean expression determines
whether the current MailingList^ is copied into NewMailingList^ and
placed in the new file, or whether it is not copied and thereby
dropped from the subscription list.

Perhaps one would choose to put these records that are being
dropped in a separate file in order to send the individuals another
reminder (or a free issue in hopes of keeping their subscription).
This would be accomplished by including an ELSE clause and an
appropriate action.

Reading a File

When writing to a file in this fashion, the assignment of a
value to the file buffer variable is usually followed by a call to
the procedure Put. Reading from a file will usually be done by the
form:

```
      WHILE NOT Eof (< file variable >) DO
          BEGIN
          Use the file buffer variable in some way
          Get (< file variable >)
          END
```

In the Class List program of the previous chapter, the reading of the file OldClass into the array ClassList would be coded as follows:

```
PROCEDURE ReadFile;
{ Read File OldClass into Array ClassList
    from Index = 1 to SizeofClass
  Establish the value of SizeofClass }
VAR   Index : 0..Maxint;
BEGIN
Reset (OldClass);
Index := 0;
WHILE (NOT Eof (OldClass)) AND (Index < MaxClassSize) DO
    BEGIN
    Index := Index + 1;
    IF Index = MaxClassSize
        THEN
            Writeln ('Not all file components may have ',
                'been read, increased array size advised')
    ClassList [Index] := OldClass^;
    Get (OldClass)
    END;
SizeofClass := Index
END; { ReadFile }
```

In the above fragment, the pair of statements:

```
ClassList [Index] := OldClass^;
Get (OldClass)
```

can be replaced by:

```
Read (OldClass, ClassList [Index])
```

Do not confuse this with the general form for processing a text file, which is usually done line by line. In this case, the general form is:

```
WHILE NOT Eof (<file variable>) DO
    BEGIN
    Process a line
    WHILE NOT Eoln (<file variable>) DO
        BEGIN
        Read (<file variable>, Ch);
        Process a character
        END;
    Readln (<file variable>)      { Move past EOL }
    END
```

Writing to a File

      The general form for writing to a file is:

```
Rewrite (< file variable >);
WHILE There is a next unit to write DO
   BEGIN
   Assign file buffer variable the value of next unit
   Put (< file variable >);
   Prepare to obtain next unit
   END
```

In the case of the Class List program of the previous chapter, this
would be the following:

```
PROCEDURE WriteFile;
{ Write the array of records, ClassList [1] to
    ClassList [SizeofClass] to file NewClass }
VAR  Index := 1..Maxint;
BEGIN
Rewrite (NewClass);
Index := 1;
WHILE Index <= SizeofClass DO
   BEGIN
   NewClass^ := ClassList [Index];
   Put (NewClass);
   Index := Index + 1
   END
END; { WriteFile }
```

In the above fragment, the pair of statements:

```
NewClass^ := ClassList [Index];
Put (NewClass);
```

can be replaced by:

```
Write (NewClass, ClassList [Index])
```


Using Put and Get with Textfiles

      Text files may be processed using the file buffer variable
instead of the Read and Write procedures. Suppose Book is declared
as Text. Then, to process Book, one may use either the previous
form or equivalently the form below:

```
WHILE NOT Eof (Book) DO
    BEGIN
    { Process a line }
    WHILE NOT Eoln (Book) DO
        BEGIN
        Do something with Book¨
        Get (Book)
        END;
    Get (Book)    { Move past EOL }
    END
```

Read (Book, Ch) is equivalent to the two instructions:

```
Ch := Book¨;
Get (Book)
```

Similarly, Write (Book, Ch) would be equivalent to the two instructions:

```
Book¨ := Ch;
Put (Book)
```

Under certain circumstances one might wish to make a verbatim record of the input to a program. A text file LogFile could be created and the input could be placed in this file as each character from the input file is processed. A scheme for doing this would be:

```
WHILE NOT Finished DO
    BEGIN
    WHILE NOT Eoln DO
        BEGIN
        { Save Input^ }
        LogFile¨ := Input¨;
        Put (LogFile);
        Use Input^ in some way
        END;
    Writeln (LogFile);
    Readln { Get (Input) would have the same effect here }
    END
```

If a file is not too large, it may be read into an array. We have illustrated this technique with the file OldClass and the array ClassList in the Class List program.

14.3   Summary

A file of any data type may be declared by:

> < identifier > : FILE OF < data type >;

The identifier is called the file variable. A file buffer variable
is established which provides a window into the file component by
component. This variable is denoted by the file variable followed
by an up-arrow or circumflex. To write to a file, an empty file is
opened for writing by Rewrite (< file variable >). As long as there
are unwritten components left to write to the file, they are
appended to the file by iterating the statements:

> < file variable >¨ := < next component > ;
> Put (< file variable >)

This is equivalent to:

> Write (< file variable >, < next component >)

A file is read by first using Reset (< file variable >) to
position the file window or buffer variable at the beginning of the
file. The Boolean expression Eoln (< file variable >) is available
to control the reading. The actual reading is accomplished by the
combination of the following:

> < some variable > := < file variable >¨ ;
> Get (< file variable >)

The assignment captures the current value of the file buffer
variable, and the procedure Get moves the window to the next
component, if there is one; otherwise, it sets Eof (< file
variable >) to True. These two instructions are equivalent to:

> Read (< file variable >, < some variable >)

Exercises for Chapter 14

1. Given the declarations:

```
CustomerType =
   RECORD
   Name : PACKED ARRAY [1..30] OF Char;
   Address : RECORD
                Street : PACKED ARRAY [1..50] OF Char;
                CityState : PACKED ARRAY [1..20] OF Char;
                Zip : ARRAY [1..5] OF '0'..'9'
             END
   END

   Customers : FILE OF CustomerType;
```

Write a program which places every component of Customers whose Zip
code begins with 012 in a file Special.

2. Assume that two files, call them LeftFile and RightFile, are
both files of the same data type and that this data type contains a
component:

```
LastName : PACKED ARRAY [1..20] OF Char
```

Assume that each file is sorted by the field LastName; that is, for
each pair of consecutive entries in either file, LastName of the
first precedes LastName of the second. (If the last names are
distinct, LastName is called the sort key.)

    Write a program which produces a file MergeFile, containing the
components of both LeftFile and RightFile and which is also sorted
on LastName. As a first version, you might assume that the same
LastName does not appear in both LeftFile and RightFile. Decide
what action to take in the event that the same LastName does appear
in both files. One possibility is to assume that the two records
with the same LastName are identical and discard one of them; this,
however, is not very realistic. Consider the presence of another
component, FirstName, and in this case use FirstName to determine
equality or precedence.

3. A simple inventory file contained records consisting of a
description of the item, the quantity on hand, and the current cost.
It has been decided to maintain a more complex record with a
quantity for each item such that, if the quantity on hand falls

below this amount, the item should be reordered. The record will
also contain the index of the name of the principal supplier in an
array of suppliers. Write a program which reformats the old
inventory file into a new inventory file capable of containing the
additional information.

CHAPTER 15

Procedures, Using Parameters

15.0   Introduction

   Many times in describing a set of instructions we use the
phrase "Let X be the input". The use of a placeholder such as X
permits the person following the instructions to substitute an
appropriate name for X in the text of the instructions.

   Procedures with parameters that play the role of X allow us to
create program fragments which may not only be invoked at several
places in the calling program but also may vary the "actual" objects
that take the place of parameters such as X.

A procedure will usually require certain values. It
manipulates these input values and possibly other variables to which
it has access. It then makes available appropriate values of
certain variables as its output to the calling program or procedure.

Pascal, like several other programming languages, permits
recursion. The run-time execution of procedures is implemented in
such a way that a procedure may invoke itself. In effect, a new
copy of the procedure is created and execution of the old copy is
suspended while the new copy is executed. Recursion will be used in
the chapter on pointers.

15.1 Passing Parameters

Three significant advantages of using procedures are:

1. The program is better organized conceptually;

2. Previously tested modules may be included;

3. A given algorithm may be invoked several times, each
time acting on different data.

The third function is achieved by passing parameters to the
procedure. Parameters appear in two places in the program: they
are listed, enclosed in parentheses, after the procedure name
invoking the procedure; a corresponding set of parameters, along
with additional information, appears in the procedure heading.

Procedure Sum

As a simple example, suppose we create a procedure Sum designed
to accept two integers as input and return a third integer whose
value is the sum of the first two. We would write:

```
VAR
    A, B, C, X, Y, Z : Integer;
...
PROCEDURE Sum (First, Second : Integer;
                    VAR Total : Integer);
BEGIN
```

```
      Total := First + Second
      END; { Sum }
      ...
      Sum (A, B, C)
      ...
      Sum (X, Y, Z);
      ...
```

Actual and Dummy (Formal) Parameters

In both of the procedure calls, Sum (A, B, C) and Sum (X, Y, Z), the six variables A, B, C, X, Y, Z are called actual parameters. They have all been previously declared. The corresponding variables in the procedure heading are First, Second, and Total. They are called the formal or dummy variables or parameters.

The procedure heading contains the data types of the parameters and amounts to an implicit declaration of the parameters. The procedure heading may also contain additional information describing the method that is to be used in passing parameters. Pascal permits two methods of passing variables as parameters.

Value Parameter

In one method, the formal variable is given a copy of the value of the actual parameter. (We used this method exclusively in an earlier section for functions.) This is the default mechanism, meaning that, in the absence of any further specification, this is the method used. The formal parameters are then called value parameters. In the above example, First and Second are value parameters. Each time the procedure is invoked, the variables First and Second are given copies of the values of the variables which occupy the corresponding positions in the procedure call. Consequently, they get the current values of A and B as a result of the procedure call Sum (A, B, C) and then get the current values of X and Y as a result of the procedure call Sum (X , Y, Z). Changes that the procedure Sum might have made to the formal variables First and Second would not affect the values of the actual variables.

Reference Parameters

To allow a procedure to change the value of an actual parameter, one needs to declare explicitly this intention in the procedure heading. This is accomplished by prefixing the appropriate variables with the reserved word VAR. Parameters declared in this fashion are called reference parameters. Changes made to the value of a formal variable by a procedure are changes made to the value of the actual variable. In fact, for the duration of the procedure call, the reference parameter and the actual parameter in the call are identical.

Thus, in the call Sum (A, B, C), the reference parameter Total refers to the actual parameter C. In the call Sum (X, Y, Z), the reference parameter Total refers to the actual parameter Z. With respect to a reference parameter, you may consider that, at each activation of the procedure, each occurrence of the formal parameter in the body of the procedure is replaced by the actual parameter.

The two procedure calls establish a flow of information according to the arrowheads in the diagram below:

```
        Call                          Procedure Sum

        Sum (                         Sum (
           A,        ------>             First,
           B,        ------>             Second : Integer;
           C)        <------>            VAR Total : Integer)

        Sum (                         Sum (
           X,        ------>             First,
           Y,        ------>             Second : Integer;
           Z)        <------>            VAR Total : Integer)
```

The value parameters, such as First and Second above, are given as their initial value the values of their corresponding actual parameters; on the other hand, a reference parameter, such as Total above, shares the value of the corresponding actual parameter.

Figure 15.1 is a diagram of the data space of a program containing the procedure Sum and the direction in which information is sent.

In the procedure call, a value parameter may be specified by an expression. Using the previous declarations,

        Sum (10, A - 3, C)

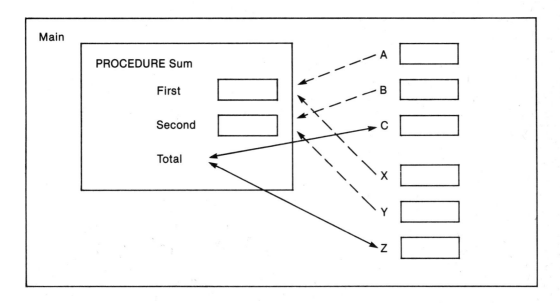

Figure 15.1   Parameter Passing

is acceptable. Upon execution of this statement, the two
expressions 10 and A - 3 are evaluated, and their values are
assigned to First and Second in the data space of the procedure.
Subsequent execution of Total := First + Second in the procedure
body assigns the value of Total to C.

On the other hand, an actual parameter in a procedure call
which corresponds to a reference parameter must be specified by a
variable. A variable must be available to receive any value the
procedure assigns to the reference parameter.

The type of example we have used, namely, a procedure returning
a single, simple data type as its value may alternatively be coded
as a function. We would write:

```
VAR
    A, B, C, X, Y, Z : Integer;
...
FUNCTION Total (First, Second : Integer) : Integer;
BEGIN
Total := First + Second
```

```
      END; { Total }
      ...
         C := Total (A, B);
      ...
         Z := Total (X, Y);
      ...
```

If we intend to return more than a single, simple value, we
must use a procedure. As an example, consider the problem of
calculating the average and normalizing an array of real numbers.
(By normalizing an array we mean replacing each element by its value
minus the average.) Here are fragments of a program, including the
desired procedure:

```
      CONST
         MaxListSize = 100;
      TYPE
         MaxRange = 1..MaxListSize;
         ListType = Array [MaxRange] of Real;
      VAR
         ThisList, ThatList : ListType;
         ThisAverage, ThatAverage : Real;
         ThisLength, ThatLength : MaxRange;
      ...
      PROCEDURE Normalize (VAR List : ListType,
                           VAR Average : Real;
                              Length : Integer);
      VAR
         Total : Real;
         Index : Integer;

      BEGIN
      Total := 0.0;
      FOR Index := 1 To Length DO
         Total := Total + List [Index];
      Average := Total / Length;
      FOR Index := 1 To Length DO
         List [Index] := List [Index] - Average
      END; { Normalize }
      ...
        Normalize (ThisList, ThisAverage, ThisLength);
      ...
        Normalize (ThatList, ThatAverage, ThatLength);
```

                        Listing 15.1

Side Effects

        Value parameters protect the programmer from unwittingly using
procedures that modify the values of variables which should not be
changed.   FORTRAN allows only reference parameters, and one source
of programming errors in FORTRAN is the unwanted change by a
subroutine (similar to a procedure) of the value of a variable in
the main or calling program. If a procedure or function changes the
value of a variable which has not been passed as a reference
parameter, and which is not local to the procedure or function, it
is said to have a side effect. Side effects should be avoided.
They make programs difficult to understand and to maintain.

        A large structured data object passed as a parameter may be
declared as a reference parameter even if the procedure does not
alter its value. This saves both program data space and execution
time.

        File variables may be passed to procedures, but they must be
passed as reference parameters. This restriction is necessary
because a procedure cannot have a file as a local variable.

FUNCTION, PROCEDURE Parameters

        Sometimes it is desirable to pass the name of a function or
procedure as a parameter. As an example, consider the integration
of a function. If the values of a numerical function are
nonnegative for arguments in a certain range, then integration
computes the area under the graph of the function and above the
X-axis and between two vertical lines. A numerical technique for
computing the integral consists of dividing the range or interval
into a large number of small subintervals, then taking the sum for
all these subintervals of the product of a value of the function in
the subinterval with the length of the subinterval. (This
approximates the area by the sum of the areas of thin rectangular
slices.)

        The data objects that need to be known by this function,
Integrate, are the function to be integrated, the initial and final
range values, and the number of subintervals. Listing 15.2 contains
the definition of the function:

```
FUNCTION Integrate (FUNCTION F : Real;
                    LowerLimit, UpperLimit : Real;
                    NumberofSubintervals : Integer) : Real;
```

```
{ Function calculates the integral of the function F
     from LowerLimit to UpperLimit, using
     NumberofSubintervals rectangles and calculating the
     function value at the midpoint of each subinterval }

VAR    Sum, SubLength, AreaofSlice, Midpoint : Real;
       SliceNumber : Integer;

BEGIN
SubLength := (UpperLimit - LowerLimit) /
                                        NumberofSubintervals;
Sum := 0.0;
FOR SliceNumber := 1 TO NumberofSubintervals DO
   BEGIN
   Midpoint := LowerLimit + (SliceNumber - 1) * SubLength
                              + (SubLength / 2.0);
   AreaofSlice := F (Midpoint) * SubLength;
   Sum := Sum + AreaofSlice
   END;
Integrate := Sum
END; { Integrate }
```

Listing 15.2

This listing can be included in any program and used to
evaluate the integral of a function that is available to the
program. The function might be a standard function, as in:

    Writeln (Integrate (Sin, 0.0, 3.1416, 500) : 8 : 2)

This will produce the output 2.00. Alternatively, the function
could be one defined in the body of the program.

The name of a procedure may also be passed by preceding the
dummy variable with the reserved word PROCEDURE. In both these
instances, all of the parameters for the function or procedure that
is being passed must be value parameters.

15.2   Recursion

In Pascal, and a number of other languages, the invocation of a
procedure suspends the current processing. Furthermore, the
position of suspension and the values of variables local to the

currently active data space are retained in such a fashion that the
processing can, after the called procedure has been completed,
resume at the point of suspension. Upon resumption, the values of
variables local to the data space are restored. (Those that have
been passed as reference parameters may be restored with modified
values, while those not referenced in that way will be inviolate for
the duration of the suspension.) The points of suspension and the
local environments are retained by being stacked one on top of other
so that when a called procedure completes its processing the
previously suspended processing may be resumed by unstacking its
point of suspension and local environment. This stacking of the
units necessary to resume processing permits a procedure to call
upon itself and in effect suspend one copy of the procedure to
process another. A procedure which calls itself is said to be
directly recursive.

Recursion has a similarity to a hall of mirrors scene or the
appearance of the old cereal box which contains a picture of someone
holding the cereal box, which in turn contains a picture of someone
..., and so on. Just as iteration presents the possiblity of
creating endless loops, recursion presents the possibility of
creating an endless sequence of procedure calls, which can only be
terminated by the intervention of an outside agent, such as the
operating system informing the user that there is no more space to
retain the memory of suspended procedures.

Program MacDonald

A simple example may make recursion clearer. Many nursery
rhymes are based on a recursive-like scheme in which, after a new
stanza or verse is added, all of the previous song is repeated. One
such song is "Old MacDonald's Farm". Listing 15.3 contains a
procedure Play, which calls itself recursively to produce an
abbreviated version of "Old MacDonald's Farm":

```
 1     PROGRAM MacDonald (Input, Output);
 2
 3     { Example of recursion using Old MacDonald's Farm }
 4
 5     TYPE AnimalType = 1..6;
 6
 7     VAR Stanzas,
 8         AnimalNumber : AnimalType;
 9
10     PROCEDURE Play (Animal : AnimalType);
11     BEGIN
```

```
12    Case Animal of
13       1  : Writeln ('With a chick, chick here',
14                        ' and a chick, chick there');
15       2  : BEGIN
16            Writeln ('With a quack, quack here',
17                        ' and a quack, quack there');
18            Play (Animal - 1)
19            END;
20       3  : BEGIN
21            Writeln ('With a gobble, gobble here',
22                        ' and a gobble, gobble there');
23            Play (Animal - 1)
24            END;
25       4  : BEGIN
26            Writeln ('With an oink, oink here',
27                        ' and an oink, oink there');
28            Play (Animal - 1)
29            END;
30       5  : BEGIN
31            Writeln ('With a moo, moo here',
32                        ' and a moo, moo there');
33            Play (Animal - 1)
34            END;
35       6  : BEGIN
36            Writeln ('With a hee, haw here',
37                        ' and a hee, haw there');
38            Play (Animal - 1)
39            END
40       END { Case of Animal }
41    END; { Play }
42
43    BEGIN
44    Writeln ('How many stanzas?');
45    Readln (Stanzas);
46    FOR AnimalNumber := 1 to Stanzas DO
47       BEGIN
48       Writeln ('Old MacDonald had a farm');
49       Play (AnimalNumber);
50       Writeln
51       END
52    END.
```

Run:

How many stanzas?
3   !Input

Old MacDonald had a farm
With a chick, chick here and a chick, chick there

```
Old MacDonald had a farm
With a quack, quack here and a quack, quack there
With a chick, chick here and a chick, chick there

Old MacDonald had a farm
With a gobble, gobble here and a gobble, gobble there
With a quack, quack here and a quack, quack there
With a chick, chick here and a chick, chick there
```

Listing 15.3

We shall trace the way in which the last four lines of output
are produced. Consider the last time the procedure Play is called,
on line 49, when AnimalNumber has the value 3. The procedure Play
has one local variable, Animal. This variable gets 3 as its value,
and execution of a copy of Play commences. Since Animal is equal to
3, the case statement selects the statement labeled 3 on line 20.
This prints some gobbles and then (at line 23) suspends execution to
call another copy of Play with the actual parameter 3 - 1. When
this copy of Play begins life, its local variable Animal has the
value 2. Consequently, the case chosen starts at the statement
labeled 2 on line 15. This prints some quacks and invokes a third
copy of Play (at line 18) with actual parameter 2 - 1. When this
third copy of Play starts its life, its local variable Animal has
the value 1. This case breaks the growing chain of recursive calls.
It writes some chicks and then completes its processing. The second
copy of Play now resumes its processing at line 19 and completes its
processing without producing any further output. Finally, the first
copy of Play resumes its processing at line 24 and completes its
processing. The next instruction executed is the instruction to
skip a line on line 50, which completes the third iteration of the
FOR-DO loop.

The general form of direct recursion can be outlined as
follows:

```
PROCEDURE P;
...
BEGIN { P }
   ...
   P
   ...
END; { P }
```

Indirect Recursion, FORWARD Directive

     In addition to direct recursion, indirect recursion is also
permitted. Here, through a chain of procedure calls, a procedure
eventually calls itself. An example would be where procedure P
calls procedure Q and, in turn, procedure Q calls procedure P.

     One of the aims of Pascal is to provide a compact and efficient
language. To this end, the compiler is a one-pass compiler; that
is, it scans the source program only once, and never returns to an
earlier portion of the text. With respect to indirect recursion,
this may seem to create a dilemma similar to the dilemma of which
came first, the chicken or the egg. To compile P, it would seem
that the compiler needs to know the details of Q, and to compile Q,
the compiler needs to know the details of P.

     However, to include a procedure call in any part of a program,
all that must be known about the procedure is the information
contained in the procedure heading. The compiler can be given a
directive stating that the body of the procedure appears at a later
point in the source text. This directive is supplied by following
the procedure heading with the reserved word FORWARD and then a
semicolon to separate it from subsequent text. Here is an outline
of the scheme for indirect recursion:

```
    PROCEDURE P; FORWARD; { directive to the compiler that the
                   body of the PROCEDURE appears later in the
                   source program.  If the PROCEDURE heading
                   includes a parameter list it must be
                   included as part of the heading. }

    PROCEDURE Q;
    ...
    BEGIN { Q }
      ...
      P
      ...
    END; { Q }

    PROCEDURE P;   { Only the identifier appears here, not the
                   parameter list although it is recommended
                   that the parameter list be repeated inside
                   a comment }

    BEGIN { P }
      ...
      Q
      ...
```

END; { P }

   In order to avoid generation of an endless chain of calls, every recursive procedure must have some test which eventually does not initiate further recursive calls. In the previous example, since each recursive call to Play used Animal - 1, the most deeply nested copy of Play received the value 1 and did not initiate another recursive call.

   There are a number of general situations in which recursion supplies an elegant means of solution. One situation is: where the problem can be formulated in terms of some positive integer and the solution for any positive integer can be formulated using a hypothesized solution to the problem for a smaller positive integer. In this case, there must be an explicit solution for some sufficiently small integer such as the integer 1.

   Another general situation where it is frequently more reasonable to present a recursive solution, i.e., a solution by means of a recursive procedure or procedures, is where the problem involves a data structure that is defined recursively. This method will be illustrated in Chapter 17 in printing a family tree.

15.3   Summary

   Procedures may be defined with parameters. The invocation of a procedure P is then of the form:

     P (< list of actual parameters >)

The list of actual parameters or arguments consists of variable identifiers, or of expressions separated by commas, which agree in type with the corresponding parameters listed in the procedure heading.

   The procedure heading is of the form:

     PROCEDURE < procedure name >
       (< formal parameter section list >)

The formal parameter section list is a list of segments containing the formal or dummy parameters and including their data type. Each segment may start with VAR, in which case the qualified formal parameters are replaced by references to the actual parameter and changes to the formal parameters are changes to the actual parameters. The parameters qualified in this way are called reference parameters.

The default, in the absence of VAR, is to give the formal parameter a value which is a copy of the value of the actual parameter. The formal parameter now functions as a local variable, and any change to the formal parameter does not change the actual parameter. Such formal parameters are called value parameters. Expressions other than variables may be used as actual parameters corresponding to value parameters, but not to reference parameters.

Each time a procedure is invoked, the variables and expressions listed in the procedure call are matched with corresponding formal parameters in the procedure heading. Normal passage of information into a procedure is by value parameters, while passage of information from a procedure to the calling program must be by reference parameters. For large structured data objects, input to a procedure may use a reference parameter to avoid the cost in time and space necessary to copy the value of the object. Information may also be passed using variables not local to the procedure by having the procedure modify such variables. This is called a side effect and should be avoided since it makes programs difficult to understand.

Procedures may call themselves or they may call other procedures which eventually create calls to the first procedure. A program using this feature is called recursive. The heading of a procedure followed by the directive FORWARD postpones the declaration of the body of the procedure. In this way, the procedure may be used recursively prior to its full declaration.

Exercises for Chapter 15

1. Write a procedure which takes a textfile as input and produces as output the textfile modified so that, between every two nonblank lines of the original file, there is a blank line.

2. Write a procedure which takes as input a textfile and a positive integer N and which produces as output the textfile modified so that every nonblank line has been prefixed with N blanks.

3. Write a procedure which accepts as input an array of characters
(perhaps thought of as representing a line of text) and converts all
lowercase alphabetic characters to corresponding uppercase
alphabetic characters.

4. Write a procedure which accepts as input an array of characters
(perhaps thought of as representing a line of text) and counts the
number of words on the line. You must make certain assumptions
about how to recognize the beginning and ending of a word. For
example, the beginning of a word could be recognized either as the
first position in the line or as a position in which an alphabetic
character follows a blank.

5. Define a data type by

        AnswerType = (Yes, No, Unacceptable);

Write a procedure which prints the message, 'Do you wish to
continue?', reads a line of input, and returns a value of a variable
Response such that, if the first nonblank character is Y or y,
Response = Yes; if N or n, Response = No; otherwise, Response =
Unacceptable.

6. Given a sequence of N real numbers stored in an array X in
positions 1..N, the variance of this sequence, which is a measure of
how the values cluster about the average, is given by the sum of the
squares:

        (X [J] - Avg) ** 2 / N

with J going from 1 to N, where Avg is the average and ** is the
symbol used for exponentiation. The square root of the variance,
called the standard deviation, is a more common measure of
dispersion. Write a procedure which returns the standard deviation
of a sequence.

7. Simpson's rule for evaluating the integral of a function F
divides the interval of integration into slices and, for each slice
or subinterval, approximates the area of the slice by the area of a
region bounded by a parabola and the X-axis. The formula for the
area of a slice is

        ((F (LEP)) + (4 * F (MP)) + F (REP)) / 6

where LEP is the lefthand endpoint of the subinterval, MP is the
midpoint of the subinterval, and REP is the righthand endpoint of
the subinterval. Write a procedure which will integrate an
arbitrary function over an interval using a specified number of
subintervals.

8. Given the following program, determine which variables are
actual parameters, formal parameters, value parameters, and
reference parameters. Also determine what the output is (without
compiling and running the program).

```
PROGRAM Mood (Output);

TYPE  MoodType = (Happy, Sad, Droopy, Mad);

VAR  ThisMood, ThatMood : MoodType;

PROCEDURE WriteMood (AMood : MoodType);
BEGIN
CASE AMood OF
   Happy  : Writeln ('Happy');
   Sad    : Writeln ('Sad');
   Droopy : Writeln ('Droopy');
   Mad    : Writeln ('Mad')
   END { Case of AMood }
END; { WriteMood }

PROCEDURE NewMood (XMood : MoodType;
                   VAR YMood : MoodType);
BEGIN
WriteMood (XMood);
WriteMood (YMood);
XMood := Droopy;
YMood := Happy;
WriteMood (XMood);
WriteMood (YMood)
END; { NewMood }

BEGIN { Main }
ThisMood := Mad;
ThatMood := Sad;
NewMood (ThisMood, ThatMood);
WriteMood (ThisMood);
WriteMood (ThatMood)
END.
```

CHAPTER 16

Using Labels and GoTos

Sections

16.0   Introduction

The language Pascal is named after Blaise Pascal (1623-1662).
At the age of 19, Blaise built a computing machine to perform
arithmetic calculations. (He built it for his father who was a tax
collector.) The British inventor Charles Babbage (1791-1871) was
probably the first person to design a general purpose computing
machine capable of performing lengthy and complex computations
controlled by instructions stored in the machine itself. (It is
possible that the concept of a stored program machine was the
contribution of his associate, Countess Ada Lovelace (1815-1852).)
Babbage's machine, called the Analytic Engine, was never completed,
because the current technology was not capable of machining the
moving parts to the required tolerances.

During the period of the second World War, electronic
technology began to replace mechanical technology in computing
machines. Many outstanding scientists were involved in the
development of these computers. John von Neumann (1903-1954) and
Alan Turing (1912-1954) are often mentioned as having made
significant contributions, including the rediscovery of the concept
of storing both instructions and data in the memory of a computer.
In such machines, a memory cell contains a pattern of bits. The

machine may treat the contents as either data or instructions.

Many early computers were laboriously programmed by entering
the codes for the instructions and for the data into the various
memory cells. In the 1950's, programming languages were developed
to avoid this tedious and error-prone activity.

The first programming language which went beyond a language
that substituted mnemonic codes for the instructions and symbolic
names for the data was FORTRAN. Nevertheless, FORTRAN still tended
to pattern the control statements that were made available to the
programmer after comparable machine instructions. One of the
typical machine instructions which interrupted the normal sequence
of executing instructions stored in contiguous storage locations was
a jump instruction, which caused the machine to seek its next
instruction at a location determined by the jump instruction.

The situation is very similar to a set of instructions labeled
Step 1, Step 2, and so on. The agent who executes the instructions
starts by executing Step 1, and, in the absence of any
countermanding command, when Step K is completed, the agent executes
Step K + 1. In some instances, however, Step K may contain the
instruction, perform Step M next.

A model for such a set of instructions might be

Step 1 : ...

Step 2 : IF light is green THEN perform Step 4 next

Step 3 : Do several things. Perform Step 1 next.

Step 4 : ...

These instructions will result in a repetition of a number of steps
until the light is green, whereupon the agent goes to Step 4. A
computer mimics this type of control by using a special register or
storage location, frequently called the program counter in which the
location of the next instruction is kept.

During normal sequential processing, the program counter is
incremented by an amount which makes it point to--that is, contain
the location of--the next instruction. However, the execution of a
jump instruction places a new value in the program counter. It is
as if our agent who is executing our program written in the Step 1,
Step 2, ..., Step N form has a box in which the number of the next
step is kept. When the agent encounters the "Perform Step 1 next"
instruction, it places a 1 in this box. Upon completing a given

step, the agent looks in the box to determine which step to do next.

The jump instruction appeared in FORTRAN as a Goto instruction. Statements could be labeled with a string of digits (we have used the term unsigned integer for such a string), and

        Goto < unsigned integer >

was the instruction to execute next the statement with the given label. At the machine level, this was accomplished by placing the location of the labeled instruction in the program counter.

The Goto statement was easy to use and easy to translate into a machine instruction. But, as Edgser W. Dijkstra pointed out in a short, but significant, article in the Communications of the ACM, number 11 (1968), entitled, "Goto Statement Considered Harmful", the presence of the Goto statement made programs difficult to read and understand. More importantly, such programs were more likely to contain errors. Use of Goto statements was often characterized as having a "spaghetti effect" because of the appearance of the resulting flowcharts.

The Goto statement may be appropriate in a program when the program has found a serious error condition and recovery requires the invocation of an error handling procedure that has been incorporated in the program. The Goto statement may also be appropriate in a procedure which is searching for some item, and which, in the midst of nested control statements, discovers that the item is found. Then, the natural action is to go to the end of the procedure.

16.1   GOTO Statement

In order to label a statement as a target for a GOTO statement, labels must be declared. The label section precedes all other declaratory sections and begins with the reserved word LABEL. It contains a list of labels separated by commas and terminated by a semicolon. Each label is an unsigned integer, usually restricted to at most four digits. Any statement in the executable part may be labeled by prefixing the statement with a label followed by a colon. An example of the declaration and use of a label is:

```
        LABEL 99;
        ...
        BEGIN
        ...
            99 : Writeln ('Error Encountered');
            Recover;
        ...
```

The GOTO statement is a statement of the form:

        GOTO < statement label >

where statement label is a label declared in the scope of the
current block. The effect is to execute next the statement that has
been so labeled.

The result of jumping into a structured statement such as a
WHILE-DO statement by having a labeled statement within the WHILE-DO
is unpredictable, and this practice should be considered an error
(even if this is not prohibited by the compiler).

It amounts to a step backward in time to show how the IF-THEN
statement and the GOTO statement together can be used to create
iteration and simulate statements such as the REPEAT-UNTIL
statement. Consider the program in listing 16.1:

```
        PROGRAM RepeatUntil (Input, Output);

        LABEL 1;

        VAR Response : Char;

        BEGIN
        1 : Writeln ('If finished respond Y');
        Readln (Response);
        IF NOT ((Response = 'Y') OR (Response = 'y'))
            THEN
                GOTO 1;
        Writeln ('Finished')
        END.
```

                        Listing 16.1

The user of this program could never discover, without looking at
the source program, whether a GOTO and label was used or whether the
executable part of the program was written as:

```
REPEAT
    Writeln ('If finished respond Y');
    Readln (Response)
    UNTIL NOT ((Response = 'Y') OR (Response = 'y'));
Writeln ('Finished')
```

In Chapter 19, in the section on sorting, an example will be given in which a GOTO is used to jump out of a loop after the purpose of the loop has been achieved.

One of the newer programming languages, Ada, sponsored by the United States Department of Defense, is based on Pascal. It has a structured control statement which allows the creation of loops which have the flowchart depicted in figure 16.1. It is a repetition of performing actions S, testing for termination, and performing actions T.

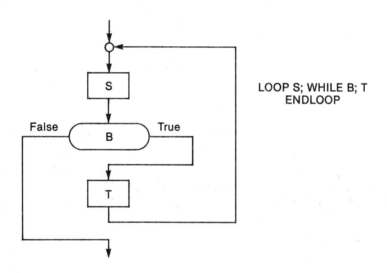

LOOP S; WHILE B; T
ENDLOOP

Figure 16.1   Exiting from the Interior of a Loop

The statement is structured because there is only one entry and one exit path, but the test for termination appears in the interior of the loop. This statement may be coded in Pascal as:

```
        REPEAT
            S;
            IF NOT B
                THEN
                    GOTO 99;
            T
            UNTIL False
    99 :
```

The UNTIL False may seem somewhat surprising. False is an expression which can never be True, so the normal exit from the REPEAT-UNTIL loop has been effectively closed. An alternate rendition of this flowchart is:

```
        WHILE True DO
            BEGIN
            S;
            IF NOT B
                THEN
                    GOTO 99:
            T
            END
    99 :
```

Since there seems little point in encouraging the use of GOTO's, we have omitted exercises in this chapter.

16.2 Summary

The GOTO statement transfers control to a labeled statement. Labels must be declared in the first declaratory section and introduced by the reserved word LABEL. A label is an unsigned integer, usually consisting of at most four digits. To label a statement, precede the statement by the label and a colon.

The GOTO statement should be used sparingly. Two possible uses are to respond to an exceptional condition or to create a loop in which the natural exit is neither at the beginning nor at the end of the loop but in the interior.

CHAPTER 17

Pointers

Sections

17.0   Introduction

     Allocation of memory for data objects is divided into static
allocation and dynamic allocation. Static memory allocation demands
that the amount of memory be fixed and known at the time the program
is compiled. Dynamic memory allocation does not demand that the
amount of memory be known at the time of compilation but rather
permits the size of memory to vary during the execution of the
program. As an example, static allocation requires that array sizes
be fixed. Greater flexibility is achieved if a program may request
additional memory as it is needed.

     Memory required by procedures is drawn from a region called a
stack. When a procedure is invoked, it obtains memory from the
"top" of the stack, and, when the execution of the procedure is
completed, the memory is returned to the "top" of the stack. Since
the amount of memory needed by a procedure can be computed at the
time of compilation, the need can be computed statically, but the
memory is actually made available dynamically.

     Using dynamic memory allocation, memory can also be demanded
for storage of individual data objects. This type of memory is
drawn from a complementary region of memory called a heap. To
access this memory requires a new data type called a pointer. From
the perspective of the computer system, a pointer is an address of
some location in the heap; from the perspective of the programmer,
a pointer is a data type which may, in turn, reference a memory
location containing a specified data type. In a program, there can
be as many types of pointers as there are data types available to
the program.

     Pointers are commonly used to create various lists, in
particular, those whose size cannot be predicted at the time of
compilation. As an introduction to both lists and pointers, the
first section presents an array of records which is designed so that
it can be used as a list. It includes pointer-like indices to the
preceding and succeeding list elements in the array.

     Pointers are introduced in the second section. There are two
operations that can be performed on a pointer. It may be assigned a
value, either the value of another pointer or the special value NIL,
indicating that the pointer does not currently point to any
location. Alternatively, the pointer may be dereferenced, an
operation which yields the value of the data object to which it
points.

Two standard procedures act on pointers. The procedure New
(< pointer >) supplies from the available memory of the heap a
memory cell of appropriate size to which the pointer then points.
Dynamic memory no longer required by a program may be returned to
the available memory in the heap by a procedure Dispose
(< pointer >).

The next section uses pointers to create the structure for a
family tree. The manipulation of this tree-like structure requires
the creation of another structure, also called a stack, in order to
"remember" positions in the tree.

The final section illustrates the use of variant records as
objects dynamically created by the procedure New. This method of
storage of variant records may be used to create variables whose
data type is a union of the data types of the variants. As an
example, a union of types is created which permits the access of the
individual bits in the internal representation of data.

17.1 Linked Lists

Often, one would like to use a portion of the memory of the
computer as one uses a looseleaf book or a box for index cards.
Initially, the structure is empty. One may insert an object of a
fixed size, for us a page, until the space available is exhausted.
The insertion can be performed at the front, between two adjacent
objects, or at the end. Any object can be deleted. If an interior
object is deleted, the two surrounding objects become adjacent.

With respect to these operations of insertion and deletion, an
array of records can be manipulated so that insertion and deletion
of a record appear to the user to behave in this fashion. The key
to this technique is to include a component in the record which
indicates the next record. This corresponds to the continuation
message in a newspaper or magazine that directs the reader to a
later page where an article is continued. Some kinds of processing
a record are made easier if a record contains an indicator of the
position of the preceding record. This corresponds to the use of
the phrase, continued from page such and such, at the head of a
continuation page.

     We shall construct an example of this management of memory in
which the informational or data field of each record is a line of
thirty characters. This field can be replaced by a more useful
field, say a page or a mailing address, in a more realistic
application. For ease in developing the program, we shall also
restrict the book to a small number of pages, in this case a mere
five.

     Each record will consist of three fields: the index of the
preceding record, the data, and the index of the following record.
The definitions are:

     InfoType = ARRAY [1..30] OF Char;
     ItemType = RECORD
                  PriorIndex, NextIndex : IndexType;
                  Info : InfoType
                  END

     We can picture a typical object of ItemType in figure 17.1:

     PriorIndex   Info   NextIndex

     | | | |

                          Figure 17.1

     Let us postpone the description of IndexType for the moment.
The array of records that we wish to manage as if it were a
looseleaf book will be declared by:

     LooseLeaf : ARRAY [1..MaxIndex] OF ItemType

where, for us MaxIndex is 5. If all five records are in our
looseleaf book in their natural order, the array will appear as
indicated in figure 17.2:

LooseLeaf

	PriorIndex	Info	NextIndex
[1]	?		2
[2]	1		3
[3]	2		4
[4]	3		5
[5]	4		?

Figure 17.2

Since it is the first page, LooseLeaf [1] has no predecessor.
Similarly, since it is the last page, LooseLeaf [5] has no
successor. In these cases, 0 will indicate the page has no
predecessor or no successor. We can now specify IndexType as
0..MaxIndex.

Operations on a List

What functions do we wish to perform? The program should
certainly be able to open the looseleaf book and view the first page
as the current page. We should be able to read the current page.
We should be able to move the position of the current page toward
the final page or toward the initial page, unless we are at the rear
or front, respectively. If there is another unused page available,
we should be able to insert a new page. We should be able to delete
the current page, in which case it should be returned to the
collection of unused pages, and have the adjacent pages close up.
If we intend the program to be a prototype, we should be able to
store and retrieve the "book" from an external file. And we should
be able to terminate the program.

The program can be developed top-down by using a menu format
for the operations. Operations still to be developed may be entered
as stubs. If some care is spent choosing the order in which the
operations will be developed, those already fully developed and
tested may aid in uncovering errors in those developed at a later
time. This suggests that priority be given to insert and read. One
can also construct what amounts to a scaffolding, by temporarily
including an operation which prints the entire array LooseLeaf.

This operation can then be removed when the program is completed.

The initial step of the program will require the user to indicate if a file is to be read into LooseLeaf since the first time the program is used there will not exist a permanent file. The looseleaf book will be held in the form of a full book of unused pages with the first available page set to 1. To indicate that there is no current page, we can set a variable CurrentPage to 0.

Insertion

As pages are inserted into LooseLeaf, a page will be removed from the front of the unused pages. The CurrentPage will then be given the value of the index of the newly inserted page. By an appropriate sequence of insertions and movements of the current page, the array LooseLeaf will appear as in figure 17.3. (The information on the three pages is arranged in the order: Don't... , Leave... , Now...).

LooseLeaf

	PriorIndex	Info	NextIndex
[1]	0	Don't...	3
[2]	3	Now...	0
[3]	1	Leave...	2
[4]	0		5
[5]	4		0

CurrentPage = 2,   FirstAvailablePage = 4

Figure 17.3

Deletion

The info on the current page is Now.... This page is deleted by closing up the NextIndex of preceding page and the PriorIndex of the succeeding page, and by returning the current page to the unused pages. The value of CurrentPage would be changed appropriately.

The modified data space would appear as in figure 17.4:

LooseLeaf

	PriorIndex	Info	NextIndex
[1]	0	Don't...	3
[2]	0	Now...	4
[3]	1	Leave...	0
[4]	2		5
[5]	4		0

CurrentPage = 3,   FirstAvailablePage = 2

Figure 17.4

If we were dealing with a large array, the processing time required to close up the chain of currently active pages is small and fixed, whereas, if we repositioned array entries, the processing time would be large and would grow with the size of the array.

The fields PriorIndex and NextIndex have been used to "point" to an object of ItemType. In the next section, we shall introduce a data type called pointer. Pointers may be used to give us access to, or to direct us to, any data object. Also, since they may be directed at newly created instances of the data objects, we are saved the trouble of keeping track of the first available object and of creating the objects themselves dynamically. The size of the structure we build, e.g., our looseleaf book, is constrained by the memory capacity of the computer rather than by some predeclared limit such as the size of an array.

Conceptually, the use of the links PriorIndex and NextIndex has allowed us to view the records in the array as separate objects, each with a set of labeled tabs in these two link fields. The list currently in use in the example is obtained by pasting together the records at corresponding tabs. For example, since:

LooseLeaf [1] . NextIndex = 3

LooseLeaf [3] . PriorIndex = 1

these two pages can be considered as linked so that LooseLeaf [1] is followed by LooseLeaf [3]. This type of structure, where there are

two links directed from an object to two neighbors and both
neighbors have reciprocal return links, is called a doubly linked
list.

17.2   Pointers

     A pointer may be thought of as a data object which "points" to
a memory cell in much the same way that indices were used in the
previous section to point to array elements. Pointers are a novel
type of data object in that we do not manipulate the value of a
pointer in the same way that we manipulate the values of other data
objects. It may help to think of a pointer as an address, an
address which the computer operating system hides from us. There is
one constant value, called NIL, which may to be assigned to a
pointer, but a pointer whose value is NIL does not point to any data
object. (This is similar to the use of 0 in the previous section as
a possible value of PriorIndex and NextIndex to indicate that these
indices were not "pointing" to any array element.)

Declaration of Pointer

     When a pointer is declared, the data type of the objects to
which it will point must be specified. Suppose that ItemType is a
type identifier, either previously defined in the TYPE section, or
integer, real, Boolean, or Char. A declaration such as:

     VAR
          Ptr, PtrItemType, P, Q : ^ItemType;

creates four pointers, each of which may point to an object of
ItemType. (These pointers, however, do not point to any object
until action by the executable part of the program creates a data
object that they point to.) These pointers are said to be bound to
the type ItemType, which is also called the base type of the
pointer.

     The general form of the definition is:

          < list of pointer variables > : ^ < data type > ;

or, if a type is being declared, the form is:

    < pointer variable > = ^ < data type > ;

    The declaration of a pointer may use structuring constructs, or
pointers may themselves appear in the definition of other types and
structures. The following would be acceptable declarations:

    VAR
        PointerList : ARRAY [1..100] OF ^ItemType;
        IDPtr : ^RECORD
                    Name : PACKED ARRAY [1..30] OF Char;
                    Age : 0..999;
                    END

    If the circumflex is not available in a given character set,
some other character may be used. The up-arrow and the character @
are two common substitutes.

    Pointer types may be created in the TYPE section. Here is an
example:

    TYPE
        String = PACKED ARRAY [1..10] OF Char;
        Tabs = ARRAY ['A'..'Z'] OF ^String;
        PtrChainType = ^ChainType;
        ChainType =
            RECORD
            Info : ARRAY [1..30] OF Char;
            LeftLink, RightLink : PtrChainType
            END;

    Pointer types may be defined prior to the definition of the
type to which they are bound. This is reasonable since a pointer is
an address and the compiler can allot a memory cell to store an
address before the structure being addressed has been fully
described. In the above example, this permits the pointer to
ChainType to be defined before ChainType itself is defined. Unless
this were the case, ChainType could not be defined since the
definition of PtrChainType uses ChainType and the definition of
ChainType uses PtrChainType.

Procedure New

    Before describing some of the more important uses of pointers,
it is probably wise to give some simple examples. Suppose that the
following have been declared:

```
    VAR   X, Y, Z : ^Integer;
```

    The above declaration creates three pointers. To create memory
cells to which they may point, use must be made of a memory
management procedure, New, which allots an appropriate memory cell
from a pool of available memory (the heap). To deposit in, or to
assign a value to, any one of these cells, the name of the pointer
followed by a circumflex acts as a window to the cell. In effect,
this name followed by the circumflex functions as if it were a
variable of type integer.

Example, Pointer to an Integer

    Here is an annotated description of the effect of certain
instructions on the relevant data space of a program:

    Initially:

    X, Y, Z undefined.

    After: New (X); New (Y)

    Z undefined
                 -------   -------
    X ----> | ? | Y ----> | ? |
                 -------   -------

    After the assignments: X^ := 8; Y¨ := -5; Z := NIL

                 -------   -------
    X ----> | 8 | Y ----> | -5 | Z ---->
                 -------   -------

    After the assignments: Z := Y; New (Y) { the order of these
statements is important }

                 -------   -------   -------
    X ----> | 8 | Z ----> | -5 | Y ----> | ? |
                 -------   -------   -------
```

    A pointer, such as Z, may have assigned to it the value of
another pointer of the same base type, such as Y.  The instruction Z
:= Y creates a situation in which both Z and Y point to the same
memory cell.  Consequently, not only is it true that Z^ = Y^ (the
memory cells that the two pointers point to now contain the same
```

value because they are the same cell), but also a subsequent
assignment of a new value to Y¨ will automatically assign the same
value to Z^. Thus, the sequence of statements:

    New (Y);   Y¨ := 17;   Z := Y;   { now Z^ = 17 }
    Y^ := 3;   { now Z^ = 3 }

terminate with the effect:

```
                       -------
          Y, Z ---->  |   3   |
                       -------
```

Compare this with the effect of the statements:

    New (Y);   New (Z);   Y^ := 17;   Z^ := Y¨;   Y := 3

The effect of this sequence is:

```
              -------                      -------
   Y ---->  |   3   |          Z ---->  |  17   |
              -------                      -------
```

Multiple calls to the procedure New may leave memory cells
unreachable. The sequence of statements:

    New (X);   New (Y);   X^ := 5;   Y¨ := 6;   New (X);   X¨ := Y¨

has as its effect:

```
    -------             -------             -------
   |   5   |   Y ---->  |   6   |   X ---->  |   6   |
    -------             -------             -------
```

The first memory cell can no longer be referenced by a pointer and
the memory space is effectively lost space for the duration of the
program.

Procedure Dispose

    There is a standard procedure, Dispose, which returns a memory
cell to the unused pool of memory in the heap. It is recommended
practice to set each pointer to NIL immediately after the cell that
it points to has been returned to the memory pool by Dispose. This
prevents a program from unwittingly using the pointer to reference a
cell before the pointer is made to point to another cell. More

importantly, if a cell is a record which contains pointer fields,
the pointers in the pointer fields should be set to NIL prior to the
disposal of the cell.

The previous sequence of statements, which created a situation
in which there was no way to reference the cell containing 5, should
be replaced by a sequence of statements, such as the following,
which includes Dispose (X):

```
New (X);  New (Y);  X¨ := 5;  Y := 6; ...
{ processing here may use X^ }  Dispose (X);  X := NIL;
{ any reference here to X¨ will generate a run-time error }
...; New (X);  X¨ := Y^
```

The expression < pointer variable > ^ is said to dereference
the pointer. Dereferencing a pointer which is NIL generates a
run-time error message. It would be preferable to generate such a
message rather than to allow a program to produce spurious results
because there was an inadvertent dereferencing of a pointer such as
X after Dispose (X) and before the next New (X).

Linked Lists Using Pointers

Pointers may be used to create linked lists. Nodes are created
as records with one or more fields consisting of links or pointers
which point to other nodes of the same type. A simple linked list
could be created using nodes declared by:

```
PtrNode = ^Node;
Node =
    RECORD
    Data : DataType;
    NextNode : PtrNode
    END
```

If Head is a PtrNode, then, provided Head¨ is not NIL,
Head . Data would be the data in the first node and Head¨ . NextNode
would point to the second node in the list, if one exists. If so,
Head¨ . NextNode^ . Data is the data in the second node.

A procedure, using a linked list, to print the data in
successive nodes in the list is given below. This provides a model
for other types of processing, in which successive nodes in a linked
list are to be examined. Note how the condition Ptr = NIL is used
to terminate the processing. Encountering a NIL pointer generates
an end-of-list signal.

```
          PROCEDURE PrintLinkedList (Head : PtrNode);
          VAR    Ptr : PtrNode;
          BEGIN
          Ptr := Head;
          WHILE Ptr <> NIL DO
              BEGIN
              Print Ptr^ . Data;
              { Move to next node }
              Ptr := Ptr~ . NextNode
              END
          END; { PrintLinkedList }
```

17.3   Family Trees

     Pointers may be used to keep track of the ancestral
relationships in a genealogical or family tree. The structure of
such a tree consists of a base node containing the name of the
person whose lineage is being represented, and, for each node
containing a name, links or edges pointing toward each of the two
parents of the person represented by that node. Eventually, there
are ancestors who have either one or zero parents. We shall use
pointers for these links, and we shall indicate the absence of a
parent by a NIL pointer.

Node in a Family Tree

     A typical node in a diagram of such a tree contains three
fields. The first contains the name of the individual, and the
other two are pointers to another node of this type, one for each
parent. The initial example will use as its base node the node
depicted in figure 17.5:

```
        PtrMom            Name            PtrDad
       --------------------------------------------
       |  NIL | Popeye               |  NIL |
       --------------------------------------------
```

                        Figure 17.5

This describes the situation in the movie "Popeye" where Popeye is searching for his father (presumably in a sequel, he will search for his mother). Since Popeye does not know the identity of either of his parents, initially both of the pointer fields are NIL. It is convenient to define both a type which is a pointer to a record of this form and the type of the record itself. The program in listing 17.1 creates the structure in figure 17.5:

```
PROGRAM Orphan (Input, Output);

{ Create  Popeye's family tree }

CONST
    NameSize = 14;

TYPE
    NameString = PACKED ARRAY [1..NameSize] OF Char;
    PtrPersonType = ^PersonType;
    PersonType =
        RECORD
        Name : NameString;
        PtrMom, PtrDad : PtrPersonType
        END; { PersonType }

VAR
    MeSelf : PersonType;

BEGIN
WITH MeSelf DO
    BEGIN
    Name := 'Popeye
    PtrMom := NIL;
    PtrDad := NIL
    END;
Writeln ('Family Tree of ', MeSelf . Name)
END.
```

Listing 17.1

The types PtrPersonType and PersonType each depend on the other. We could define PersonType directly by the definition:

```
PersonType =
    RECORD
    Name : NameString;
    PtrMom, PtrDad : ^PersonType
    END; { PersonType }
```

This form highlights the recursive nature of the definition. We
will need to use the pointer type as a parameter so in the sample
program we have defined the pointer type separately. A pointer is a
simple or scalar type and it may therefore be used as a value
returned by a function.

     The possibility exists of confusing a pointer and the data
object to which it points. This is less likely if, in declaring the
identifiers for pointers, nomenclature is adopted that uses Ptr as a
prefix.

     Suppose Popeye finds his father. We would now (dynamically)
create a record in which his father's name is stored and alter
MeSelf . PtrDad so that it points to this new node. This could be
coded as:

```
          New (MeSelf . PtrDad);
          WITH MeSelf . PtrDad^ DO
            BEGIN
            Name := 'Me Poppa
            PtrMom := NIL;
            PtrDad := NIL
            END
```

Create

     It is convenient to code this using a function which we will
call Create. This function will have a local variable available to
point to the new node, it will insert the name that it is given as
an argument in the name field, and it will set the parent pointers
to NIL. Coding for Create is given in listing 17.2:

```
FUNCTION Create (Info : NameString) : PtrPersonType;

{ Function Create returns a pointer to a memory cell
     of type PersonType which contains Info in the
     name field, and with PtrMom and PtrDad set to NIL }

VAR  Ptr : PtrPersonType;
BEGIN
New (Ptr);
WITH Ptr^ DO
   BEGIN
   Name := Info;
   PtrMom := NIL;
   PtrDad := NIL
```

```
      END;
   Create := Ptr
   END;  { Create }
```

                              Listing 17.2

Enlarging the Tree

     Now, if Popeye also finds his mother, the main part of the
program can include the instructions:

```
        MeSelf . PtrMom := Create ('Me Momma      ');
        MeSelf . PtrDad := Create ('Me Poppa      ');
```

We shall devise a more convenient way to enlarge the tree, but,
using the current method, the tree could now be enlarged by
statements such as:

```
        MeSelf . PtrMom^ . PtrMom := Create ('Momma''s Momma ');
        MeSelf . PtrDad^ . PtrMom := Create ('Poppa''s Momma ');
```

     In the ancestral chains being constructed in this growing tree,
ancestors must be entered in the proper order. Suppose the tree
currently has the form of figure 17.6:

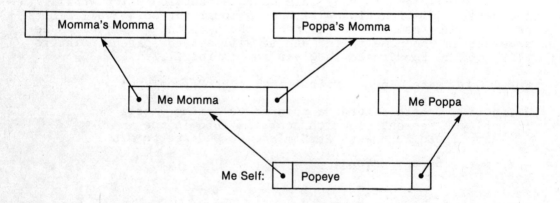

                  Figure 17.6 Popeye's Family Tree

An attempt to enter a fourth generation, such as paternal great-grandparent, with the code:

```
MeSelf . PtrDad^ . PtrDad^ . PtrDad :=
                              Create ('Eric?         ')
```

will result in a run-time error because

```
        MeSelf . PtrDad^ . PtrDad = NIL
```

Consequently, it cannot be dereferenced to obtain the following record:

```
        MeSelf . PtrDad^ . PtrDad^
```

Printing the Tree

Printing the contents of the tree is surprisingly simple when viewed as a recursive procedure. We begin with the base node. First, we print the name in the node. Second, if the node has a female parent, we print her tree. Third, if the node has a male parent, we print his tree. If we think of this as a procedure PrintTree which takes as its argument the node whose tree we are printing, the general form of PrintTree is:

```
        PrintTree (Node)
           BEGIN
           Write (Name in Node);
           PrintTree (Mother of Node);
           PrintTree (Father of Node)
           END
```

As this stands, we will obtain a list of the names in the tree without any indication of their relationship to the person at the base. To include this information, we can use a scheme of indentation in which the name of a parent is indented three spaces with respect to its child. This can be done by creating a global variable Indentation, which is increased by say 3 each time we (recursively) print a parent and which is reduced by 3 each time we complete printing the tree of the parent. Initially, indentation is set to 0.

The code for PrintFamilyTree is given in listing 17.3:

```
PROCEDURE PrintFamilyTree (Node : PersonType);

{ Print the names in the tree with base Node, indenting the
    trees of the parents with three blanks }

CONST  Blank = ' ';
VAR  Index : 0..Maxint;

BEGIN
WITH Node DO
   BEGIN
   FOR Index := 1 TO Indentation DO
      Write (Blank);
   Writeln (Name);
   IF PtrMom <> NIL
      THEN
         BEGIN
         Indentation := Indentation + 3;
         PrintFamilyTree (PtrMom¨);
         Indentation := Indentation - 3
         END;
   IF PtrDad <> NIL
      THEN
         BEGIN
         Indentation := Indentation + 3;
         PrintFamilyTree (PtrDad¨);
         Indentation := Indentation - 3
         END
   END
END; { PrintFamilyTree }
```

Listing 17.3

If the tree is as indicated in figure 17.6, PrintTree (MeSelf)
will produce the following:

```
Popeye
   Me Momma
      Momma's Momma
   Me Poppa
      Poppa's Momma
```

Building a Tree

As a further exercise in using pointers, we shall develop an
interactive program which presents the user with a menu of
operations that can be performed to build and examine a family tree.
As we have seen before, a menu creates a desirable format for the
user, and also aids the development process by describing the
procedures needed and allowing procedures already written to aid in
debugging other procedures. Perhaps another advantage of the menu
type of program is that the designer is forced to use it during its
development and by becoming a user is more likely to appreciate the
needs of the user.

The user will be asked initially to enter the name of the
person at the base of the tree. The user will be able to control a
current position in the tree as it grows. Here are the definitions
we shall use of OperationType:

```
TYPE
    OperationType = (CurrentName, EnterFather, EnterMother,
        Help, MovetoChild, MovetoFather, MovetoMother,
        MovetoBase, PrintTree, ReplaceName, Terminate);

VAR
    Operation : OperationType;
```

To "move" about in the tree, we will change the value of a
pointer which points to the current position in the tree. This is
one of the reasons why it will be more convenient to declare two
pointers of PersonType by the following:

```
VAR
    PtrBase, PtrCurrent : PtrPersonType;
```

and use PtrBase^ as a substitute for the node MeSelf in the earlier
example. The initialization procedure is given in listing 17.4:

```
PROCEDURE Initialize;
VAR  Name : NameString;
BEGIN
PrintDescription;
Writeln ('Enter name of person at base of tree');
Writeln ('Enter at most ', NameSize : 3, ' characters');
GetString (Name);
PtrBase := Create (Name);
PtrCurrent := PtrBase;
PrintMenu;
PtrStack := NIL
```

```
END; { Initialize }
```

Listing 17.4

The procedure Create is described in listing 17.2. A prototype for
the creation of a GetString procedure is given in an earlier
chapter, in listing 9.2. PrintDescription describes how to use the
program and PrintMenu describes how to choose menu items. PtrStack
will be explained later. (Setting PtrStack to NIL corresponds to
the fact that initially there are no previous positions in the tree
that must be remembered.)

The main part of the program is given in listing 17.5:

```
BEGIN { Main }
Initialize
REPEAT
   Obtain (Operation);
   CASE Operation OF
      CurrentName  : Writeln (PtrCurrent¨ . Name);
      EnterFather  : InsertFather;
      EnterMother  : InsertMother;
      Help         : PrintMenu;
      MovetoChild  : Recall (PtrCurrent);
      MovetoFather : MoveFatherSide (PtrCurrent);
      MovetoMother : MoveMotherSide (PtrCurrent);
      MovetoRoot   : WHILE PtrStack <> NIL DO
                        Recall (PtrCurrent);
      PrintTree    : BEGIN
                     Indentation := 0;
                     PrintFamilyTree (PtrRoot^)
                     END;
      ReplaceName  : SetNewName (PtrCurrent);
      Terminate    :
      END { Case of Operation }
   UNTIL Operation = Terminate
END.
```

Listing 17.5

We will not include the code for the procedure Obtain. In four
of the procedures, little remains to be described: Terminate
requires no action; CurrentName requires one Write statement; Help
permits the user to display again the menu options and the means of
choosing them; and PrintTree requires the procedure PrintFamilyTree
of listing 17.3.

SetNewName overwrites the name field in the current node. The code for this procedure is in the next listing, 17.6:

```
PROCEDURE SetNewName (Ptr : PtrPersonType);
VAR NewName : NameString;
BEGIN
Writeln ('Enter new name');
GetString (NewName);
Ptr^ . Name := NewName
END; { SetNewName }
```

Listing 17.6

Insertion in a Tree

The procedure InsertMother guards against the insertion of a new node as the target of PtrCurrent^ . PtrMom, if a mother has already been created for the person named in the current node. The code for this procedure is in the next listing, 17.7:

```
PROCEDURE InsertMother;
VAR  NewName : NameString;
BEGIN
IF PtrCurrent^ . PtrMom = NIL
   THEN
      BEGIN
      GetString (NewName);
      PtrCurrent^ . PtrMom := Create (NewName)
      END
   ELSE
      Writeln (PtrCurrent^ . Name, ' already has a mother')
END; { InsertMother }
```

Listing 17.7

The procedure InsertFather is obtained by replacing Mom by Dad in PtrMom and by replacing Mother by Father.

Remembering, Using a Stack

The four remaining procedures cause the pointer to be moved to the current node. Two of them, moving to the child and moving to the base, require the recall of previous pointers. In order for this "remembering" to function properly, moving to a parent must

place the position to be remembered in some sort of structure that
is capable of recalling this position when needed. The structure
used for this purpose retrieves the most recently stored item first.

     This type of structure, called a stack, is an essential
structure in many applications. It is an example of a last in-first
out (LIFO) method of storage, often compared to a stack of trays in
a cafeteria. The author's experience is that it describes the pile
of unfinished tasks which accumulates on a desk. (And which is then
moved in toto to another archival form of storage such as a box, and
then eventually discarded when archival storage overflows, on the
theory that if it has not been attended to by now, it is no longer
of any importance.) In a computer, the portion of memory used for
remembering where procedures have been suspended and what are their
local variables is called a stack because it is managed in this last
in-first out fashion.

     A stack may be implemented as an array, where an index
indicates the most recently stored item. In our case, this would
require putting an upper limit on the number of generations allowed.
A technique which avoids this constraint is to implement the stack
as a linked list, which looks like the structure in figure 17.7:

Figure 17.7   A Stack, Implemented as a Linked List

     The stack, which is pointed to by PtrStack, is declared by:

```
TYPE
    StackNode =
        RECORD
        Item : ItemType;
        Link : ^StackNode
        END;

VAR
    PtrStack : ^StackNode;
```

Initially, PtrStack = NIL, which will indicate that there is nothing
to remember and that the current node is the base of the family
tree.

The latest item placed on a stack is often said to be on top of the stack, and the action of putting an item on top of a stack is referred to as pushing the item onto the stack. The procedure MoveMotherSide is given in listing 17.8:

```
PROCEDURE MoveMotherSide (VAR Ptr : PtrPersonType);

BEGIN
IF Ptr^ . PtrMom = NIL
   THEN
      Writeln (Ptr^ . Name, ' has no mother')
   ELSE
      BEGIN
      Push (Ptr);              { Remember this position }
      Ptr := Ptr^ . PtrMom        { change position }
      END
END; { MoveMotherSide }
```

                        Listing 17.8

The code for MoveFatherSide is similar to this.

Push

    What remains is to develop Push. Push consists of the following steps:

    1. Obtain a new stack node.
    2. Place the value of the pointer Ptr in the Item field.
    3. Insert this new stack node at the front or top of the
        stack pointed to by PtrStack. This is done by:
            first, giving the Link field of the new stack node
               the value of PtrStack, and
            second, giving PtrStack a value which points to the
               new stack node.

Listing 17.9 accomplishes this. (ItemType would be declared as equal to PtrPersonType in this application.)

```
PROCEDURE Push (NewItem : ItemType)

{ Place NewItem in the Item field at the top of a stack
    pointed to by PtrStack }

VAR  PtrNewNode : ^StackNode;
```

```
BEGIN
New (PtrNewNode);
PtrNewNode^ . Item := NewItem;
PtrNewNode^ . Link := PtrStack;
PtrStack := PtrNewNode
END; { Push }
```

Listing 17.9

The situation after the second instruction has been executed is depicted in figure 17.8.

Figure 17.8

The instruction PtrNewNode^ . Link := PtrStack yields figure 17.9.

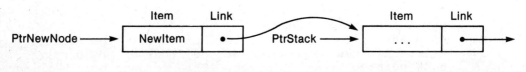

Figure 17.9

Finally, PtrStack := PtrNewNode yields figure 17.10.

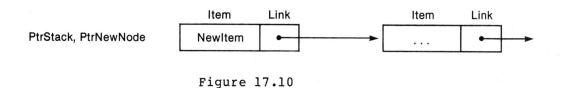

Figure 17.10

    Note that Push works properly if the stack is empty, that is, if PtrStack = NIL. The result in this case is shown in figure 17.11.

Figure 17.11

Recall

    All that remains to complete the program is to develop the procedure Recall. This procedure consists of removing the top item from the stack, replacing the actual parameter CurrentPtr by the value of this top item, and disposing of the node just removed from the stack. An attempt to do this when the current node is the base of the tree should result in a message indicating that a move to a child is not possible. This will be the case if, and only if, the stack is empty. Recall is given in listing 17.10.

```
    PROCEDURE Recall (VAR Ptr : PtrPersonType);

    VAR  PtrTemp : PtrPersonType;

    BEGIN
    IF PtrStack = NIL
        THEN
```

```
        Writeln (Ptr^ . Name, ' is at base of tree')
     ELSE
        BEGIN
        PtrTemp := PtrStack;
        PtrStack := PtrStack^ . Link;
        Ptr := PtrTemp^ . Item;
        { the following three steps are good housekeeping }
        PtrTemp^ . Link := NIL;
        PtrTemp^ . Item := NIL;
        Dispose (PtrTemp)
        END
   END; { Recall }
```

Listing 17.10

Figure 17.12 shows before and after snapshots of the effect of the first two statements in the ELSE clause. The third statement, the assignment Ptr := PtrTemp^ . Item, gives Ptr the value that was stored in what is the top node of the stack before it is returned to available memory by the last three statements. Setting the pointer PtrTemp^ . Link to NIL breaks the connection of this node to the stack before the node is returned to heap.

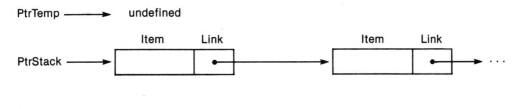

PtrTemp := PtrStack ;

PtrStack := PtrStack^ .Link ;

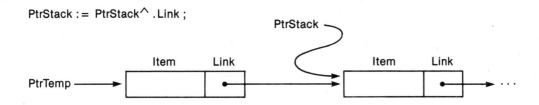

Figure 17.12   Removing the Top of a Stack

The action performed by Recall on the Stack is most commonly called Pop, because we are popping the top entry off the Stack. We have used Recall so as not to confound the familial relationships.

17.4 Variant Structures

Pointers to Variant Records

    Pointers may point to records which have a variant structure.
Consider the variant type below:

```
    TYPE
        VariantType = (Numeric, Textual);
        VType =
            RECORD
            Link : ^VType;
            CASE Variant : VariantType OF
                Numeric : (Number : Integer);
                Textual : (Line : ARRAY [1..80] OF Char)
            END;
    VAR
        PtrV : ^VType;
```

Either variant of VType has three components. The two possible
templates are:

```
        Link        Variant    Number
        ------------------------------
        |         | Numeric |         |
        ------------------------------

        Link        Variant          Line
                             [1] [2]   ..      [80]
        ----------------------------------------  --------
        |         | Textual |   |   |   |       |   |   |
        ----------------------------------------  --------
```

    Without any indication of the value of the variant field, New
(PtrV) forces the system to allocate the maximum amount of space,
which in this case would be for the second variant. In contrast,
the value of the variant field may be supplied to the procedure New,
in which case the exact amount of space for the specified variant is
allocated. New (PtrV, Numeric) would store the variable PtrV^
efficiently. If there are nested variants, they can be supplied to
New in the order of their nesting. If memory that has been
allocated with variants specified is freed using the procedure
Dispose, the same variants must be supplied to Dispose in the same
order as were supplied to the procedure New.

Unions of Types Using Variant Records

If we know how a computer allocates static memory for the
various data types, it is possible to use the variant record to
create a union of data types which enables us to treat a memory cell
as one of the several data types in that union. In particular, one
of the data types may permit us to examine the individual bits in
the cell.

We shall assume that we have a computer which stores each of
the data types Integer, Real, Boolean, and Char in a 32-bit memory
cell. Define a variant type by:

```
VariantType = (Int, Float, Bool, Ch, Bits);
CellType =
    RECORD
    CASE VariantType OF
        Int   : (Decimal : Integer);
        Float : (Floating : Real);
        Bool  : (TruthValue : Boolean);
        Ch    : (Character : Char);
        Bits  : (Bit : PACKED ARRAY [0..31] OF 0..1)
    END;
```

If a variable Cell of CellType is declared, it may be treated
as any one of the five types, Integer, Real, Boolean, Char, and
PACKED ARRAY [0..31] OF Char. In each case, we refer to the same
memory cell. Cell . Float refers to the contents as a real number,
whereas Cell . Ch refers to the same contents as a character. For
example, the statements:

```
Cell . Int := MaxInt;
FOR BitPosition := 31 DOWNTO 0 DO
    Write (Cell . Bit [BitPosition] : 2);
Writeln
```

treat the contents of the variable Cell as first an integer using
the selector Int, and next as a PACKED ARRAY using the selector Bit.
This fragment will reveal, in a 32-bit computer, what bit pattern is
used to store the value of MaxInt.

17.5   Summary

Arrays of records may be organized into more flexible list-like structures by including components which contain the indices of preceding and succeeding entries. These indices function in much the same way as do pointers. A pointer variable consists of a value pointing to an object of a given data type. The form of the declaration is either of the forms below:

```
< pointer variable >  =  ^ < data type > ;
< list of pointer variables >  : ^ < data type >;
```

for TYPE and VAR declarations, respectively. Given the declaration:

```
Ptr : ^ItemType;
```

Ptr points to an object of ItemType, and Ptr˜ denotes that variable. The procedure call New (Ptr) allocates storage for the variable Ptr^ during program execution, that is, dynamically. The storage may be freed for subsequent reassignment by Dispose (Ptr).

A pointer may be assigned the value NIL, which indicates it does not point to a data object, or it may be assigned the value of another pointer. These are the only assignments that may be made to pointers. Provided that memory has been allocated by New (Ptr), Ptr^ functions just like a variable of type ItemType. The operation of obtaining the contents of the cell that Ptr points to by applying the suffix ^ to Ptr is called dereferencing the pointer Ptr.

Pointers provide a flexible method for creating linked data structures. A simple linked list of Nodes may be created by using a structure such as:

```
NodeType =
    RECORD
    Info : DataType;
    Link : ^NodeType
    END;
```

Declarations of pointers may be recursive, as above, or a pointer type may be declared before the data type to which it points is declared, as in the following:

```
        LinkType = ^NodeType;
        NodeType =
            RECORD
            Info : DataType;
            Link : LinkType
            END
```

More complicated structures, in which each node has several link fields, can be created in a similar fashion.

Pointers may point to records with variant structure. If efficient usage of space is required, New and Dispose may be called with the values of the tag field (whether the tag field is actually present as a component or not). A variant record may be used to create a user-defined data type consisting of a union of data types.

Exercises for Chapter 17

1. The data in each of the nodes of a linked list (using pointers) is an integer. Write a procedure which finds the sum of the integers in the list.

2. The data in each of the nodes of a linked list (using pointers) is a word contained in a string of length 8. Write a procedure which finds the word in the list which precedes all the other words in dictionary order.

3. A doubly linked list is created using pointers which can be thought of as pointing to the right and to the left. Write procedures to: (1) delete a node from a nonempty, doubly linked list; (2) insert a node to the right of a given node; and (3) insert a node in an empty, doubly linked list. Write a procedure to print, left to right, all the data in a doubly linked list.

4. A queue is a structure to which a component can be added at what is called the rear, and from which, if it is not empty, a component can be removed from what is called the front. This is sometimes called a first in-first out (FIFO) structure. Implement a queue as a linked list using pointers to the front and rear. Write the addition and removal of a component as separate procedures, and write a Boolean function which determines if the queue is empty or

not empty.

5. If a family tree is created using pointers, it cannot be stored
permanently in a file. The purpose of this exercise is to recreate
the same tree-like structure in an array of records in which the
pointers are replaced by indices to other array components. In this
way, a family tree originally created using pointers may be stored
in a permanent file.

Define a type by:

```
PNodeType =
    RECORD
    Name : NameString;
    PMom, PDad : 0..MaxIndex
    END
```

Let FamilyTree be ARRAY [1..MaxIndex] OF PNodeType. Rewrite the
family tree program so that, instead of storing the name of a family
member in a node of PersonType, the name is stored as FamilyTree
[NextAvailableNode], where NextAvailableNode is originally 1 and is
incremented after a new component is adjoined. Use the fields PMom
and PDad to store indices to the mother and father, respectively.
Can you now augment the program so that it can store and retrieve a
family tree stored in a file?

6. Use variant records to create a data type consisting of a union
of data types and thereby discover what code is used by your
computer system to store the characters in the character set.

CHAPTER 18

Simulation

Sections

18.0   Introduction

A computer simulation consists of the execution of a program which models or imitates a sequence of events. Usually we are interested in the values of certain variables either in the course of or at the end of the simulation. These values represent the

state of the system being modeled. The manner in which the program
alters these values imitates the manner in which the actual system
changes states.

Some simulations are intended to be deterministic, i.e., the
values of the variables representing a state of the system and the
relations or equations governing the system completely determine the
next set of these values. Other simulations are intended to be
probabilistic, i.e., the next state of the system depends, in part,
on some seemingly unpredictable occurrence. In this chapter, we
will examine both types of simulation.

18.1 Deterministic Simulations

Constant Growth

A physical object is moving and its velocity is increasing by a
fixed amount each unit of time. The sequence of successive values
is an example of an arithmetic series, a series in which each value
differs from its predecessor by this fixed amount. To simulate such
a system, we may use:

```
    Velocity := InitialVelocity;
    FOR Time := 1 TO Eternity DO
        BEGIN
        Velocity := Velocity + Difference;
        Writeln (Time, Velocity)
        END
```

If the initial state of this system is InitialVelocity = 5,
Eternity = 3, and Difference = 2, the output from this fragment will
be:

```
    1        7
    2        9
    3       11
```

The change in this series from one term to the next is
constant. This growth (or decline, if Difference were negative) is
called linear since the points on a graph of Velocity versus Time
lie on a straight line. The final amount can be expressed in terms
of the initial amount and the number of time periods. The formula
is:

Velocity = InitialVelocity + (Eternity * Difference)

Multiplicative or Exponential Growth

Most growth processes are not linear. Under ideal conditions, and for a limited period of time, a colony of bacteria of a given initial size will grow multiplicatively. For each successive unit of time the population will be roughly equal to the population present the preceding period multiplied by some constant. This constant determines the rate of growth.

In the next fragment, we will use real numbers since the rate of growth is in general a real number:

```
Bacteria [0] := InitialCount;
FOR Time := 1 TO Eternity DO
   BEGIN
   Bacteria [Time] := Ratio * Bacteria [Time - 1];
   Writeln (Time, Bacteria [Time] : 10 : 0)
   END
```

We have called the constant Ratio since it is the ratio of the new value to the old value. If we did not wish to retain the successive values of the population in the array Bacteria, we could write:

```
OldAmount := InitialAmount;
FOR Time := 1 TO Eternity DO
   BEGIN
   NewAmount := Ratio * OldAmount;
   Writeln (Time, NewAmount : 10 : 0);
   OldAmount := NewAmount
   END
```

Given these initial values--InitialAmount = InitialCount = 100.0, Eternity = 4, Ratio = 1.5--the output produced is:

```
1        150.
2        225.
3        338.
4        506.
```

A sequence of numbers in which each successive number is a fixed multiple of the preceding number is called a geometric series. If the ratio is greater than 1.0, the successive values increase without bound. If the ratio is less than 1.0, the successive values

decrease and approach closer and closer to zero. (Here we are
assuming a positive initial value.)

        This behavior is more obvious if the ratio is written in the
form:

        Ratio = 1.0 + Rate

where Rate is the rate of change from one time period to the next.
This is the form that the compound interest formula takes, where the
computation is:

        NewAmount := (1.0 + InterestRate) * OldAmount

The final amount can be represented as a function of the
InitialAmount and the number of time periods by the formula:

        FinalAmount = ((1.0 + InterestRate) ** Eternity) *
                                        InitialAmount

where ** is the symbol for exponentiation. This is called
exponential growth because the number of time periods appears in the
exponent.

A More Realistic Model, Stable Value

        It is unreasonable to expect unlimited growth. In many
populations, it is more reasonable to assume that there exists an
upper limit to the population and, as the current population
approaches this upper limit, the rate of increase falls. This
suggests that the computation:

        NewAmount := (1.0 + Rate) * OldAmount

should be modified so that Rate is multiplied by a factor which
approaches 0.0 as the population approaches a bounding value.
Denote this upper limit, called the carrying capacity, by S and the
current population by P. The factor:

        (S - P) / S

has the property that we desire.

        Consider the fragment:

```
        OldPop := InitialAmount;
        FOR Time := 1 TO Eternity DO
            BEGIN
            NewPop := (1.0 + Rate * (S - OldPop) / S)) * OldPop;
            Writeln (Time, NewPop : 10 : 0);
            OldPop := NewPop
            END
```

Given InitialAmount = 100.0, Rate = 0.5, S = 150.0, and Eternity = 8, the output produced from this fragment is:

```
1        117.
2        130.
3        138.
4        144.
5        147.
6        148.
7        149.
8        150.
```

Notice that the values are approaching the carrying capacity, S. After eight periods, the rounded off value is 150.

Effect of Varying the Growth Rates

It is interesting to contrast these results with results obtained by using other values of Rate. If Rate is 2.0, the first value of NewPop is greater than 150. This causes the expression S − OldPop to be negative for the next period and the population falls below 150. The long-term effect creates an oscillation of the population above and below the stable value, as the population approaches the carrying capacity.

If the Rate is equal to S / InitialAmount, the first value of NewPop will be S. If, for some period, the population has the value S, subsequent values of the population will continue to equal S.

If Rate is 0.0, the assignment reduces to NewPop := OldPop. If Rate is less than 0.0, and InitialAmount < S, NewPop will be smaller than OldPop, and the successive values of NewPop will decrease, moving away from S. If S is very large relative to InitialAmount, the expression (S − OldPop) / S will be close to 1, and, provided Rate is also relatively small, the successive values of the population will approximate a geometric series.

Another general observation that can be substantiated
analytically without running the program is that, if Rate is
positive and less than (2 * S) / OldPop, the successive values will
approach S.

Supply and Price, Two-Variable Simulations

Consider the interrelationship between the supply and the price
of a commodity during consecutive time periods. The classical
economic model assumes that there are stable or equilibrium values,
say S for supply and P for price, and that, if these values are
attained at the beginning of the same time period, they will persist
until some outside event intervenes. If the current values of price
and supply are not both at their respective equilibrium values, then
there will be a change in price based on the difference of the
current supply from S, and similarly a change in supply based on the
difference between the current price and P.

Using the prefixes Old and New, the relationships are
characterized by the assignment statements:

```
NewPrice  := OldPrice - C1 * (OldSupply - S);
NewSupply := OldSupply + C2 * (OldPrice - P)
```

The constants C1 and C2 are assumed to be positive, and the signs in
front of them are chosen so that an oversupply, that is, a supply
greater than S, will depress the new price, whereas a price greater
than P will increase the supply.

A fragment to simulate the mutually dependent relation of price
and supply would assume that values for S, P, C1, C2, and
InitialPrice and InitialSupply had been established. The code could
then be:

```
OldPrice := InitialPrice;
OldSupply := InitialSupply;
FOR Time := 1 TO Eternity DO
   BEGIN
   NewPrice := OldPrice - C1 * (OldSupply - S);
   NewSupply := OldSupply + C2 * (OldPrice - P);
   Writeln (Time, NewPrice, NewSupply);
   OldPrice := NewPrice;
   OldSupply := NewSupply
   END
```

Given appropriately chosen initial values, the price and supply will increase and decrease in a cyclic fashion.

Predator and Prey

     Another example of a system whose successive states are
determined by updating two variables arises in the field of ecology.
This simulation models the relation between predator and prey. A
simple version assumes that one of the species, the prey, would have
unbounded growth in the absence of the other. For the other, the
predator, it is assumed that in the absence of the prey, the
predator would become extinct. It is also assumed that the number
of prey in the next period is adversely affected by the number of
predators, whereas the larger the number of prey the larger the
subsequent number of predators.

     The two update assignments are:

        NewPrey := (1.0 + A1 - A2 * OldPred) * OldPrey;
        NewPred := (1.0 - B1 + B2 * OldPrey) * OldPred

Signs have been chosen so that the four constants A1, A2, B1, B2 are
nonnegative.

     The constant A1 measures the intrinsic rate of growth of the
prey, as can be seen by setting A2 to 0.0 so that the predator has
no effect on the prey. A relatively large value of A2 indicates
that the predator significantly reduces the population of the prey.
The combined effect of A1 and A2 is not too drastic if

        A1 - A2 * OldPred

is close to 0.0, or equivalently, A2 is close to A1 / OldPred.

     Similarly, B1 is the rate of decline of the predator population
in the absence of the prey. The change in the number of predators
is not too great if B2 is close to B1 / OldPrey.

     If, for some period, we have the following equalities:

        A2 = A1 / OldPred
        B2 = B1 / OldPrey

then, from this period on, the successive values of the pair of
numbers NewPrey and NewPred will remain unchanged. A set of these
four constants satisfying these relations with respect to the
initial values of prey and predator establish a stable situation.

The code for this simulation, assuming values of Eternity, the four constants Al, A2, Bl, B2, and the two initial values which we will call PredStart and PreyStart, is:

```
NewPrey := PreyStart;
NewPred := PredStart;
FOR Time := 1 TO Eternity DO
   BEGIN
   NewPrey := (1.0 + Al - A2 * OldPred) * OldPrey;
   NewPred := (1.0 - Bl + B2 * OldPrey) * OldPred
   Writeln (Time, NewPrey : 10 : 0, NewPred : 10 : 0);
   OldPrey := NewPrey;
   OldPred := NewPred
   END
```

For certain values of the rates Al, A2, Bl, and B2, the stable population levels vary in a cyclic fashion. To detect these phenomena, one must take small values of Al and Bl, which amounts to taking a short unit of time for each update. This tends to simulate a more continuous process, as opposed to the more discrete simulation obtained by taking longer time units.

Longer Time-Dependence

In the type of situation above, the values of a set of variables for one period determine the set of corresponding values for the next period. In another type of situation, the past history for several earlier periods determines the state of the system in the next period.

An example of this type, which was formulated by Leonardo de Pisa (also known as Fibonacci) about 1210 A.D., is a system in which the new state is determined by the previous two periods. He considered a population whose size during the next period is the sum of the sizes during the two preceding periods.

To begin a simulation of such a population, we must have initial population values for two periods. A simulation in which the initial population values are 1 for both previous periods, and in which the successive values are stored in an array F, is coded by:

```
F [1] := 1;
F [2] := 1;
FOR Time := 3 TO Eternity DO
    BEGIN
    F [Time] := F [Time - 1] + F [Time - 2];
    Writeln (Time, F [Time])
    END
```

The resultant sequence of numbers, 1, 1, 2, 3, 5, 8, 13, ... , with
F [1] and F [2] included, is called the Fibonacci sequence.

If the numbers in this sequence need not be retained, we may
store sufficient information to generate the series using the three
variables NewF, RecentF, and OldF. The code in this case could
read:

```
OldF := 1;
NewF := 1;
FOR Time := 1 TO Eternity DO
    BEGIN
    NewF := RecentF + OldF;
    Writeln (Time, NewF);
    OldF := RecentF;
    RecentF := NewF
    END
```

Note that the last two assignments must be in the order given.

18.2   Random Number Generation

To perform simulations involving chance or random events, we
must create a source of seemingly unpredictable numbers. If one has
access to the hardware of a computer, this can be accomplished by
sampling transient phenomena or "noise". Another source related to
the computer hardware involves accessing an internal clock, if it is
available, and sampling some of the digits of the current time, in
particular those giving the current millisecond. The major
drawbacks of both of these techniques is that they use nonstandard
features, and they may not be as unpredictable as one might expect.

Linear Congruential Method

The technique that we shall use is based on performing
arithmetic operations to obtain a "next" integer. One begins with
an initial number called the seed. Let this be denoted by X [0].
Each successive number is generated by the assignment:

        X [N + 1] := (A * X [N] + C) MOD M

We shall refer to the constants A, C, and M as Multiplier, Shift,
and Modulus, respectively. If these three numbers are well chosen,
the sequence of numbers generated by this process, called the linear
congruential method, has many of the properties that one would
normally associate with a random sequence of integers.

Criteria for a Good Generator

An excellent discussion of techniques of generation and of
possible acceptance tests for random-like sequences is contained in
Volume 2 of Donald Knuth's "The Art of Computer Programming". He
lists six criteria that should be applied to obtain a good linear
congruential generator:

  i)   X [0] should be chosen arbitrarily;

  ii)   The Modulus should be large;

  iii) If the Modulus is a power of 2, choose the Multiplier
        so that
                  Multiplier MOD 8 = 5;

  iv)   The Multiplier should be large, preferably satisfying
        the relation

    (Modulus / 100) < Multiplier < (Modulus - Sqrt (Modulus));

  v)   The Shift should be odd;

  vi)   Use the more significant digits of X [N].

The number of bits used to store an integer varies from
computer to computer. (See Appendix D for a discussion of some of
the details.) A good choice is to take one half of the number of
bits, raise 2 to this power, and set the modulus to the resultant
value. The following expression should yield this value:

        2 * Round (Sqrt (1 + Maxint DIV 2))

     This will ensure that the arithmetic operations do not generate
overflow by exceeding Maxint. It also fulfills the purpose of
requirement ii), which is to establish a substantial range for the
possible values of X, in this case 0..(Modulus - 1).

     The purpose of conditions iii) and v) is to ensure that each of
the values in this range appears before the sequence repeats itself.
To satisfy iv) we may calculate the multiplier as follows: divide
the modulus by 2--this will be a multiple of 8--and add 5, giving a
value which leaves a remainder of 5 when divided by 8. Given a
modulus equal to 65536, this yields a value of 32773 for the
multiplier. If we take the addend as 1, the formula for the next
number becomes:

        X [N + 1] := (32773 * X [N] + 1) MOD 65536

     When the input of X [N] to the expression on the right is odd,
the resultant output X [N + 1] is even. Conversely, when the input
is even, the output is odd. Thus, the least significant or
rightmost digit shows extreme regularity. (If the numbers are
represented in base two notation, the least significant digits are
alternately 0 and 1.) Behavior of this sort leads to requirement
vi). Below, we shall illustrate how the more significant digits are
sampled.

     To achieve the requirement i) of obtaining an arbitrary seed,
one frequently allows the user to select the seed. By choosing the
same seed, one expects to obtain exactly the same results. If the
process is to be repeated, but with a different seed, the last
number generated by the previous process can be used as a seed for
the repetition.

     To sample the more significant digits and satisfy requirement
vi), we assume that the next number will appear at each position in
the interval 0..(Modulus - 1) with equal likelihood. We then divide
this interval into adjacent segments whose sizes are proportional to
the probabilities of occurrence of the various events.

     We will give two short examples, tossing a coin and spinning a
dial, where this random number generator is used. These examples
will be followed by an extensive discussion of a simulation of a
random walk.

Tossing a Coin

    For the simulation of tossing a coin, the two possible events
are the appearance of a head or the appearance of a tail. A fair
coin means that these events are equally likely. We divide the
interval 0..(Modulus - 1) into two equal segments. A number in the
first segment is taken to represent the toss of a head (or tail),
and a number in the second segment is taken to represent the toss of
a tail (or head).

    Given Modulus = 65536, 32768 = Modulus DIV 2. For any X [N],

        X [N] DIV (Modulus DIV 2)

will be either 0 or 1. (This remainder of X [N] upon division by
Modulus DIV 2 is the highest or most significant bit in the
representation of X [N] as a binary number.) Assume that the values
of the array X have already been generated. Code for generating a
sequence of tosses of a fair coin would be:

```
        FOR Time := 1 TO Eternity DO
            BEGIN
            Toss := X [Time] DIV (Modulus DIV 2);
            CASE Toss OF
                0 : Writeln ('Tails');
                1 : Writeln ('Heads')
                END { Case of Toss }
            END
```


Spinning a Dial

    Similarly, the interval of possible values 0..(Modulus - 1)
could be divided into four equal parts to correspond to the four
compass points. Successive spins of a dial could then be generated
by the code:

```
        FOR Time := 1 TO Eternity
            BEGIN
            Spin := X [Time] DIV (Modulus DIV 4);
            CASE Spin OF
                0 : Writeln ('North');
                1 : Writeln (' East');
                2 : Writeln ('South');
                3 : Writeln (' West')
                END { Case of Spin }
            END
```

In general, a number in the range 0..M is generated by the expression:

        X [Time] DIV (Modulus DIV M)

If the random number generation technique is reasonably good, the number of times the dial points to each of the four compass points should, in the long run, be approximately equal to one-fourth of the total number of spins. If, however, each of the four numbers were exactly one-fourth the total, the random number generator would be very poor because it would be too regular.

18.3 Probabilistic Simulations

Random Walk

A random walk simulates or models random motion of a particle. For each period of the simulation, the particle moves in one of several directions, the particular direction of motion chosen in a random-like fashion.

Let a particle initially be placed at the midpoint of a segment. Movement will be confined to one of two directions, Left or Right. For each period, the current position is displayed, the direction of next motion is obtained, and, if moving the particle in that direction will keep it within the boundaries of the segment, the particle is moved. This iteration is continued until the particle "walks off" the segment.

This description leads to a first version of the program:

```
    Initialize;
    REPEAT
       Display;
       GetNextMove;
       TestIfDone
       IF NOT Done
          THEN
              MakeNextMove
       UNTIL Done;
    Report
```

Since a priori there is always the possibility that the
particle never leaves the confines of the segment, we shall also
count the number of moves and terminate the repetition if a maximum
number of moves is exceeded. A variable Count will be introduced,
and it will be incremented each time a move is made. The test for
termination will be modified to read:

        UNTIL Done OR (Count >= Maximum)

There is a temptation to use Count = Maximum here. Resist this
temptation, for, if inadvertently Count should initially exceed
Maximum, equality will never occur. In a test for the end of a
loop, do not depend on strict assumptions about the behavior
expected if the test can be formulated so as to avoid making those
assumptions.

Development of the Program

Recall that a stub is a temporary version of a procedure which
may be no more than the BEGIN END delimiters or an output message
asserting that the procedure has been invoked. To expand the above
program, we will perform the following five steps: (1) expand
Initialize; (2) expand Display; (3) insert a stub for GetNextMove;
(4) temporarily have TestIfDone set the Boolean variable Done to
True; (5) insert stubs for MakeNextMove and for Report.

This will produce an executable program which can be used to
test the procedure Display by displaying the initial position of the
particle. As further benefit, we will have a program, sometimes
called a driver program, which can be used to test or drive the
remaining procedures.

To define the segment, we declare two global integer constants,
LeftEnd and RightEnd. At this stage of development, the procedure
Initialize will establish the values of four global variables. The
variables and their initial assignments are:

        CurrentPosition := (LeftEnd + RightEnd) DIV 2;
        Count := 0;
        Done := False
        Maximum := 100 * (RightEnd - LeftEnd)

To display the particle, at each unoccupied position we will
print the character +, and at the occupied position we will print
the character X. Assuming the segment is relatively short, we can
surround each of these characters with a blank. Listing 18.1 is the

code for Display:

```
PROCEDURE Display;
{ Display segment containing a particle marked by X
  with unoccupied positions marked by + }
VAR Place : LeftEnd..RightEnd;
BEGIN
FOR Place := LeftEnd TO RightEnd DO
   IF Place = CurrentPosition
      THEN Write (' X ')
      ELSE Write (' + ');
Writeln
END; { Display }
```

                    Listing 18.1

We have modified the indentation style of the IF-THEN-ELSE slightly
to conserve space in the source code.

     With LeftEnd = -5, RightEnd = 5 and the assignment Done := True
in the procedure TestIfDone, we have a program which can be executed
and which produces the output:

        + + + + + X + + + + +

     Work remains to be done on GetNextMove, TestIfDone,
MakeNextMove, and Report. The first three of these must share a
variable Move. Although Move, in this context, could be either -1
for a move left and +1 for a move right, we will define a data type
MoveType = (Left, Right) and declare Move : MoveType as a global
variable. This structures the data in a form which can more easily
be generalized to movement in more than one direction.

     For a moment, let us ignore the probabilistic nature of the
simulation and code GetNextMove as:

```
PROCEDURE GetNextMove (VAR Move : MoveType);
BEGIN
Move := Right  { Temporary assignment }
END; { GetNextMove }
```

     The procedure TestIfDone requires the values of CurrentPosition
and Move. It determines if the value of Done should be set to True
by testing if the move would carry the particle beyond the endpoints
of the segment. The code for this procedure is:

```
PROCEDURE TestIfDone (CurrentPosition : Integer;
                      Move : MoveType;
                      VAR Done : Boolean);
{ If Move would carry the CurrentPosition off the segment,
    Done is set to True, otherwise it is set to False }
BEGIN
CASE Move OF
   Left  : IF CurrentPosition = LeftEnd
              THEN Done := True
              ELSE Done := False
   Right : IF CurrentPosition = RightEnd
              THEN Done := True
              ELSE Done := False
   END { Case of Move }
END; { TestIfDone }
```

                          Listing 18.2

The two ELSE clauses may be deleted provided that Done has the value
False upon invocation of the procedure. The body of this procedure
has been written in what is hoped to be a readily understandable
form. It is possible to write the body as a "one-liner":

```
Done := ((CurrentPosition = LeftEnd) AND (Move = Left)) OR
        ((CurrentPosition = RightEnd) AND (Move = Right))
```

Either of these two pieces of code has the same effect. We prefer
the first version since it more clearly expresses the intent of the
procedure.

      The change in CurrentPosition induced by MakeNextMove can be
coded in the form of a CASE statement. This can be placed "in line"
rather than in a separate procedure created for this purpose. The
code in the main portion of the program is then:

```
IF NOT Done
   THEN
      BEGIN { Make next move }
      CASE Move OF
         Left  : CurrentPosition := CurrentPosition - 1;
         Right : CurrentPosition := CurrentPosition + 1
         END; { Case of Move }
      Count := Count + 1
      END
```

The Report section will print the number of moves made by the particle if it wandered off the segment or will give a message stating that the number of moves was excessive. As currently designed, this version of the program can be executed. It should terminate in five moves.

The remaining feature that must be incorporated is the random-like generation of the next move. In the procedure Initialize, the user will be asked to supply a seed for the random number generator. This value will be assigned to a global variable Random. The procedure GetNextMove must then replace the current value of Random with a next value and, in the manner in which we tossed a coin in the previous section, give Move either the value Left or Right. The code for this is:

```
PROCEDURE GetNextMove (VAR Move : MoveType);
{ This procedure modifies the global variable
  Random as a side effect }
BEGIN
Random := (32773 * Random + 1) MOD Modulus;
CASE Random DIV (Modulus DIV 2) OF
    0 : Move := Left;
    1 : Move := Right
    END { Case of Random }
END { GetNextMove }
```

Listing 18.3

Summary of the Program

```
PROGRAM Stagger (Input, Output);

CONST
    LeftEnd = -5;
    RightEnd = 5;
    Modulus = 65536;

TYPE
    MoveType = (Left, Right);

VAR
    CurrentPosition : LeftEnd..RightEnd;
    Done : Boolean;
    Maximum, Count : 0..Maxint;
    Move : MoveType;
    Random : 0..Modulus;
```

```
PROCEDURE Initialize;
BEGIN
CurrentPosition := (LeftEnd + RightEnd) DIV 2;
Done := False;
Count := 0;
Maximum := 100 * (RightEnd - LeftEnd);
Writeln ('Enter an integer in the range 0..',
                             Modulus - 1 : 5);
Readln (Random)
END; { Initialize }

PROCEDURE Display;
{ See listing 18.1 }

PROCEDURE GetNextMove (VAR Move : MoveType);
{ See listing 18.3 }

PROCEDURE TestIfDone (CurrentPosition : Integer;
                      Move : MoveType;
                      VAR Done : Boolean);
{ See listing 18.2 }

BEGIN { Main }
Initialize;
REPEAT
   Display;
   GetNextMove (Move);
   TestIfDone (CurrentPosition, Move, Done);
   IF NOT Done
      THEN
          BEGIN { Make next move }
          CASE Move OF
             Left  : CurrentPosition := CurrentPosition - 1;
             Right : CurrentPosition := CurrentPosition + 1
             END; { Case of Move }
          Count := Count + 1
          END
   UNTIL Done OR (Count >= Maximum);
{ Report }
IF Done
   THEN
       Writeln ('Number of moves needed to fall off is ',
                 Count : 5)
   ELSE
       Writeln (Maximum : 5, ' moves reached')
END.
```

We have been careful to declare variables, such as
CurrentPosition, by using subranges. This type of declaration
requires that we test to discover if the next move might take the
object beyond the limits of the line segment before we perform the
actual updating of the CurrentPosition in MakeNextMove. If we
attempted to assign a value to CurrentPosition outside this range,
we would create a run-time error and the program would be
terminated. An alternate scheme may be used here. Enlarge the
range so that it includes a border of positions around the previous
boundary. One then updates CurrentPosition without testing, and
follows that with a test to see if CurrentPosition is now one of the
new border positions. If so, Done is set to True.

In this particular program, it might not seem necessary to
separate the program steps into so many different procedures. We
have done so because, in other programs involving the simulation of
random movement, these particular steps may be more complicated and
should be developed separately.

We will not reproduce the output of this program here since it
frequently takes a large number of moves before the object staggers
off the line segment. An interesting question is: how many moves
are to be expected before the object leaves the segment?

18.4   Summary

In many simulations, a set of variables determines the state of
the system being simulated. A new state of the system is determined
by updating the values of these variables. If the new values are
determined solely by the past history of the system, the simulation
is deterministic. A simple form of a deterministic simulation is:

    NewValue := F (Old Values)

More complex forms may involve several variables and nonlinear rates
of change.

The update function F may depend on a random event, yielding a
probabilistic simulation. This requires the generation of a
random-like sequence of numbers. One technique, called the linear
congruential method, computes a next integer by the formula:

```
       NextNumber := (Multiplier * LastNumber + Shift)
                              MOD Modulus
```

NextNumber is then in the range 0..(Modulus - 1). Six criteria are
given for the choice of Multiplier, Modulus, Shift, and the starting
number or seed.

    To use NextNumber as a sample of K equally likely events,

```
       NextNumber DIV (Modulus DIV K)
```

yields an integer in the range 0..(K - 1). If K = 2, the resulting
value, 0 or 1, can be taken as heads or tails. If K = 4, the
resulting value--0, 1, 2, or 3--can be taken as a compass point.
Simulations based on coin tossing and spinning a dial can be created
using this technique of generating random numbers.

Exercises for Chapter 18

1. Initially a body of pure water contains 100 million gallons of
water and has a daily flow of 0.95 million gallons. After a certain
date, the body of water also receives 0.05 million gallons per day
of pollutants, and the flow of the resulting mixture of water and
pollutants becomes 1.0 million gallons per day. Write a program
which computes the percent of pollutants in the body of water over a
period of time. Does the percent approach a stable value?

2. Each month, 0.3 percent of the population of Georgia migrates to
Florida and 0.1 percent migrates to Alabama. Each month, 0.2
percent of the population of Florida migrates to Georgia and 0.1
percent to Alabama. Each month, 0.4 percent of the population of
Alabama migrates to Florida and 0.2 percent to Georgia. Assume
initial populations in Florida of 20 million, in Georgia of 15
million, and in Alabama of 10 million. Assume there is no other
influence on the population of these three states. Write a program
which computes the population of the three states over a period of
several years.

3. A certain animal species has a maximum life span of 5 years.
For each year a table is given for the percent of the female
population who survive to the following year and the average
contribution of a female of that age group to the reproduction of

female animals. The table is:

Age Group	Percent Survive	Average Births
0	40	0.0
1	75	1.0
2	70	1.8
3	55	0.6
4	0	0.2

Assume an initial population of 1000 female animals in each age group. Simulate the population for 20 years.

4. Write a procedure which simulates the throwing of a pair of dice and returns the sum of the two faces. Write a procedure which throws a pair of dice a certain number of times, and returns the frequency with which the sum of the faces is 2, 3, ..., 12.

5. Write a program in which a particle simulates a random walk on a two dimensional grid. You may want to produce a display of the current position periodically rather than after every move. Have the display distinguish between current position, positions previously visited, and positions that have not been visited.

6. A single server queue consists of a single service station, such as a check out counter, and a waiting line served on a first in-first out basis. Create a probabilistic simulation of a single server queue in which, for each unit of time, there is a 0.25 probability that a single customer joins the queue. Also suppose that each customer is equally likely to require 1, 2, 3, 4, or 5 units of time for service. If the unit of time is a minute, simulate the queue for an hour. Have the program report the maximum length of the queue and the average time a customer waits on the queue.

7. Write a procedure which simulates the dealing of four bridge hands from a standard playing deck of 52 cards.

CHAPTER 19

Searching and Sorting

19.0   Introduction

Storing vast amounts of information in a computer system would be useless if that information could not be easily retrieved. Small quantities of information may be stored nonsystematically, e.g., as it arrives or wherever there is room; large amounts of information must be stored systematically, and in a form which permits efficient retrieval.

As a familiar example, a large store of information is contained in a dictionary, where words are stored according to an order inherited from the position of characters in the alphabet. We say that information is sorted if it is arranged on the basis of a

comparison between two items that indicates which comes first. As
we know from looking up a word in a dictionary or a telephone number
in a phone book, it is much easier to find an item when we are
examining a sorted store of information than when we are examining
an unsorted store of information.

Efficient storage and retrieval of information is a vast and
growing field. Management of large data bases depends on efficient
techniques to find and manipulate information. Volume 3 of The Art
of Computer Programming by Donald Knuth, subtitled "Searching and
Sorting," is a compendium of such techniques. In an introductory
text such as this one, it is possible to consider only a few of the
simpler algorithms. The study of these techniques is continued in
subsequent courses, such as Data Structures, Design and Analysis of
Algorithms, or Theory of Data Base Management.

19.1 Sorting

Sorting by Insertion

The class list program of an earlier chapter allows the user to
create an alphabetized list by making insertions according to the
scheme:

1) the first entry is placed in the first position;

2) each subsequent entry is inserted so that the alphabetic
   ordering of the list is preserved.

This scheme may be used to sort any data for which it makes sense to
assert that one item precedes another.

If we store the information for each individual on a separate
piece of paper and are making insertions by simply shuffling the
papers, then insertion of a new sheet automatically moves the
following items back. This is what we might use if each individual
record is stored on a separate index card or looseleaf sheet. But,
if we have stored the information in an array, the actual insertion
must be preceded by the movement of the trailing data.

To illustrate this process, assume that an array of integers,
List, has been created containing entries in the elements List [1]
to List [Size]. Here is a more precise description of a procedure
which will sort this list by creating a new list, SortedList:

```
If Size > 0
   Then SortedList [1] := List [1]
For Position := 2 To Size Do
   { Insert List [Position] in the array SortedList [1],
       ..., SortedList [Position - 1], so that the
       enlarged list remains sorted }
```

We shall embed this description in a program in which the details of the actual insertion procedure are unspecified. Here is such a program:

```
PROGRAM InsertionSort (Input, Output);

{ Sort a list of integers by repeated insertions in a
sorted list, each insertion maintaining the sorted list }

CONST
    MaxLength = 100;
TYPE
    MaxRange = 1..MaxLength;
    ListType = ARRAY [MaxRange] OF Integer;
VAR
    List, SortedList : ListType;
    Position : MaxRange;
    SizeofList : Integer;

PROCEDURE GetList (VAR RawList : ListType;
                   VAR Size : Integer);
BEGIN
END; { GetList }

PROCEDURE Insert (NewItem : Integer;
                  VAR GrowingList : ListType;
                  OldLength : Integer);
BEGIN
END; { Insert }

PROCEDURE ProduceOutput (NewList : ListType);
BEGIN
END; { ProduceOutput }

BEGIN
GetList (List, SizeofList);
IF SizeofList > 0
    THEN
        SortedList [1] := List [1];
FOR Position := 2 TO SizeofList DO
    Insert (List [Position], SortedList, Position - 1);
```

```
    ProduceOutput (SortedList);
    END.
```

The procedure Insert can be developed in more than one way. We
shall assume that the sorting is to be done so that the larger
entries appear first in the sorted list. Our method will be to
start from the rear of the current sorted list, compare the NewItem
to successive elements in the list, and move each list element one
position toward the rear, until we find the position in which we
should insert the NewItem. One may think of this technique as
initially placing a hole at the rear of the list and moving the hole
forward (by moving list elements backward) as long as the list
element is less than the NewItem. Listing 19.1 is the code for
Insert.

```
    PROCEDURE Insert (NewItem : Integer;
                      VAR GrowingList : ListType;
                      OldLength : Integer);
    { Assume GrowingList of length OldLength is sorted with
        larger entries first
      Produce GrowingList of length OldLength + 1 containing
        NewItem and sorted with larger entries first }

VAR
    PlaceFound : Boolean;
    PossiblePlace : MaxRange;

BEGIN
PossiblePlace := OldLength + 1; { Start at rear }
PlaceFound := False;
{ Move list elements back one position until place is
    found in which to insert NewItem }
WHILE NOT PlaceFound DO
    BEGIN { Compare }
    IF GrowingList [PossiblePlace - 1] < NewItem
        THEN
            BEGIN { Move list element back and go forward }
            GrowingList [PossiblePlace] :=
                GrowingList [PossiblePlace - 1];
            PossiblePlace := PossiblePlace - 1
            END
        ELSE
            PlaceFound := True;
    IF PossiblePlace = 1 { NewItem goes at front }
        THEN
            PlaceFound := True
    END;
{ PossiblePlace is now available as place of insertion }
```

```
    GrowingList [PossiblePlace] := NewItem
    END; { Insert }
```

Listing 19.1

The variable PossiblePlace points to the current position of
the hole in the list.

Exchange Sort

Another algorithm for sorting involves comparing adjacent
entries and interchanging the entries if they are out of order.
This action of comparison and, if necessary, interchange is
continued in a systematic manner until the entire array has been
sorted.

It is helpful in discussion of many algorithms, particularly
sorting algorithms, to first examine how these algorithms work in
small instances. We shall look at an algorithm called the exchange
sort, or sometimes called the bubble sort, by first examining how it
works on short lists. In the example, we shall assume that the list
is to be ordered by placing smaller entries before larger entries.

An array consisting of a single value is a sorted list; this
is a trivial statement. If we are presented with an array List of
Integers of length 1, to sort the list we do nothing. If we have a
list of length 2, then we can sort the list by comparing List [1]
and List [2]. If they are already in the proper order, which, in
our example, would be if List [1] < List [2] is True, then we do
nothing. If they are not in proper order, i.e., List [1] < List [2]
is False, then we exchange the two entries.

The process of comparison and interchange may be described by:

```
IF List [1] < List [2]
    THEN { do nothing }
    ELSE { interchange }
        BEGIN
        Temporary := List [1];
        List [1] := List [2];
        List [2] := Temporary
        END
```

Note that, since we are dealing with a sequence of statements which
are executed sequentially, to interchange the value of List [1] and
the value of List [2], we must first place one of the values in a

temporary location. If, instead of what is written for the
interchange portion of the code, we had written:

        List [1] := List [2];
        List [2] := List [1]

then, after execution of the above statements, List [1] would
contain the identical value as List [2].

    We could have organized the code so that an IF-THEN statement
was used instead of an IF-THEN-ELSE by testing to see if the two
entries were out of order, that is, List [2] < List [1], and
interchanging the values if they were out of order. We have chosen
to organize the code in the form of an IF-THEN-ELSE statement and
test for the order desired (rather than its negation).

    Consider a list with three elements. To illustrate the
process, we will use as an initial value of the list:

```
List
     [1]    |    [2]    |    [3]
  ----------|-----------|----------
     15     |     7     |    11
```

The algorithm that we have in mind will first sort the sublist
consisting of the first two elements in exactly the same fashion as
the previous example. In this case, since List [1] < List [2] is
false, the two values are interchanged to obtain:

```
List
     [1]    |    [2]    |    [3]
  ----------|-----------|----------
     7      |    15     |    11
```

    We next perform a procedure on this list very much like
inserting the value 11 in an appropriate place. Starting at the
tail end of the list, we shall first compare the current values of
List [2] and List [3]. If they are in the proper order, then the
list of three elements is already sorted. In our example, this is
not the case. Therefore, we interchange the values of List [2] and
List [3] to obtain:

```
List
     [1]    |    [2]    |    [3]
  ----------|-----------|----------
     7      |    11     |    15
```

It may be the case that the entry 11 has found its final place, but we cannot be certain of that until we have compared the values of List [1] and List [2]. Perhaps at this point, we can begin to see this sorting technique as an iterative process.

If we had a list of four elements, then we can say that, since we know how to sort the sublist consisting of the first three elements, we may assume that the first three have been sorted. Then, to finish the sorting of the list, we compare the pair of elements List [3] and List [4], interchange them if necessary, then compare the pair List [2] and List [3], interchange if necessary, and finally compare the pair List [1] and List [2] and interchange if necessary.

Now let us generalize this process. Suppose that we have a list of a specified length given by the value of a variable Length. We build larger and larger sorted sublists by first sorting the first two elements, then the first three, and so on. The next to last step will be to sort the list of (Length - 1) elements, and the final step will consist of sorting the list of Length elements. Listing 19.2 is one way of coding this:

```
FOR Sublength := 2 TO Length DO
   { Sort the sublist of length Sublength }
   FOR Position := Sublength DOWNTO 2 DO
      IF List [Position - 1] < List [Position]
         THEN { do nothing }
         ELSE { interchange }
            BEGIN
            Temporary := List [Position - 1];
            List [Position - 1] := List [Position];
            List [Position] := Temporary
            END

            Listing 19.2
```

Efficiency

If the list is of length n, the procedure makes one comparison to sort the sublist of length two, two comparisons to sort the sublist of length three, and so on to n-1 comparisons to sort the sublist of length n. This is a total of 1 + 2 + ... + (n-1) = n*(n/2) comparisons. The expected number of comparisons can be halved by noting that in sorting a sublist, the sublist is sorted once there has been no interchange as a result of a comparison. On average, this should happen about halfway through the sublist.

Counting the number of comparisons for the insertion sort in a similar fashion, assuming that on the average an insertion is made halfway down the array, yields an average of n*(n/4) comparisons for sorting an array of length n. In what follows, we shall be able to modify the exchange sort so that, the average, n*(n/4) comparisons need be made. Speeding up the process by a factor of two is good, but for sorting large lists whose length can be of the order of a five- or six-digit number, the number of comparisons is still a number with more than 10 digits. Faster sorting algorithms are available, many of them with an expected average number of comparisons which, for a list of length 5 digits, may require only a 6-digit number of comparisons. Nevertheless, the simpler algorithms such as insertion sort and exchange sort are useful for short lists and for lists that are nearly sorted.

Returning to the exchange sort, we can consider this set of statements in listing 19.2 as a procedure which requires as input an array of a specified length and which returns the array rearranged so that the array elements are arranged in order of precedence, smaller elements first. The heading, as a procedure, and appropriate declarations of local variables, would be:

```
PROCEDURE ExchangeSort (VAR List : ListType;
                        Length   : Integer);
{ The procedure sorts, in place, an array List, by the
  exchange method.  Smaller elements are placed first }

VAR
    Sublength, Position : Integer;
    Temporary : ItemType;
```

To speed up the algorithm, we can modify the control of the iteration which sorts the sublist. We will compare adjacent entries (from the rear forward) until no interchange is made. If we assume that the previous sublist, that is, the sublist with one fewer entry, is sorted, then, as in the insertion sort, the current sublist is sorted when what had been its last entry has found its appropriate position by the sequence of exchanges. The current sublist is sorted and there is no need to continue the comparisons to the front of the list. Listing 19.3 contains this version:

```
PROCEDURE Exchange1Sort1 (Var List : ListType;
                          Length   : Integer);
{ The procedure sorts, in place, an array List, by the
  exchange method.  Smaller elements are placed first.
  Adjacent elements are compared from the rear of the
  sublist toward the front.  A sublist is declared
  sorted when no interchange need be made }
```

```
VAR
    Sublength, Position : Integer;
    Sorted : Boolean;
    Temporary : ItemType;

BEGIN
FOR Sublength := 2 TO Length DO
    { Sort the sublist of length Sublength }
    BEGIN
    Sorted := False;
    Position := Sublength;
    REPEAT
        IF List [Position - 1] < List [Position]
            THEN { sublist is sorted }
                Sorted := True
            ELSE { interchange and decrease Position }
                BEGIN
                Temporary := List [Position - 1];
                List [Position - 1] := List [Position];
                List [Position] := Temporary;
                Position := Position - 1
                END
        UNTIL (Sorted) OR (Position = 1)
    END
END; { Exchange1Sort1 }
```

Listing 19.3

If the comparison is the most time-consuming operation, then
this modified version is more efficient. It does, however, require
after each comparison, the testing of the condition (Sorted) OR
(Position = 1).

The only circumstance in which Position = 1 will become True is
when the item whose place is currently being sought is smaller than
all of those that were in front of this item, and the place in which
it will come to rest is the first position.

Listing 19.4 is a version of the exchange sort in which the
original code is modified so that, instead of doing nothing if there
is no interchange, we use a GOTO statement to transfer control
outside the inner loop.

```
PROCEDURE Exchange2Sort (VAR List : ListType;
                             Length   : Integer);
{ The procedure sorts, in place, an array List, by the
    exchange method.  Smaller elements are placed first.
```

Control is transferred outside the loop which sorts
each sublist by a GOTO statement, when no interchange
has occurred. }

```
LABEL 30;
VAR
    Sublength, Position : Integer;
    Temporary : ItemType;
BEGIN
FOR Sublength := 2 TO Length DO
    BEGIN { Sort the sublist of length Sublength }
    FOR Position := Sublength DOWNTO 2 DO
        IF List [Position - 1] < List [Position]
            THEN
                GOTO 30 { sublist is sorted }
            Else { interchange }
                BEGIN
                Temporary := List [Position - 1];
                List [Position - 1] := List [Position];
                List [Position] := Temporary
                END;
    30 :
    END
END; { Exchange2Sort }
```

Listing 19.4

In this example, the GOTO statement has been used to respond to
an exceptional condition, namely, that the sublist is sorted, and it
transfers control from inside a loop to another portion of a
program, in this case, an enveloping loop. The GOTO statement
should be used with great discretion. It should never be used to
transfer control from outside a loop to the inside of a loop. The
presence of a GOTO statement violates one of the tenets of
structured programming, that each loop and branch should have a
single entrance and single exit. A procedure with more than one use
of the GOTO statement should most likely be rewritten, since the
presence of GOTO's make the flow of control difficult if not
impossible to understand.

Sorting a File, Merge Sort

The sorting techniques examined so far are applicable to
information stored in the data space of the program, where
individual items are available in an indexed fashion. These
techniques cannot be used to sort files. As a technique for sorting

files, we shall consider a process which merges together two smaller
files. The two smaller files are assumed to be sorted already, and,
in merging these files, the combined file produced is also sorted.

Let Upper and Lower be two files for which it makes sense to
compare Upper^ and Lower^. (If this is not the case, then one can
substitute a function of the two file components which returns True
if the first component precedes the second component and False
otherwise.) A file Combined will be produced by repetitively
adjoining a component taken from either Upper or Lower on the basis
of this comparison. This action will terminate when one of the two
files has been exhausted. The file which has not been exhausted
will then be appended to Combined.

The first stage is similar to the operation of a switch which
transfers a file component, as indicated in figure 19.1:

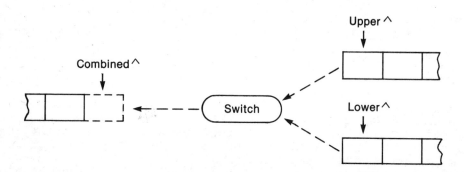

Figure 19.1 Merge Sort

The two stages of the merging process are described by:

```
WHILE (Upper not exhausted) AND
                     (Lower not exhausted) DO
     IF Upper^ precedes Lower^
        THEN
             Transfer from Upper to Combined
        ELSE
             Transfer from Lower to Combined;
  IF Upper not exhausted
     THEN
          Transfer remainder of Upper to Combined
```

```
        ELSE { Lower not exhausted }
            Transfer remainder of Lower to Combined
```

The transfer of a component is accomplished by the procedure of listing 19.5. Recall that files must be passed as reference parameters.

```
        PROCEDURE Transfer (VAR Source, Target : FileType);
        BEGIN
        Target" := Source";
        Put (Target);
        Get (Source)
        END; { Transfer }
```

Listing 19.5

Since moving the remainder of a file is an iteration of the Transfer procedure, the merging process can be coded as:

```
        WHILE (NOT Eof (Upper)) AND (NOT Eof (Lower)) DO
            IF Upper^ < Lower'
                THEN
                    Transfer (Upper, Combined)
                ELSE
                    Transfer (Lower, Combined);
        IF NOT Eof(Upper)
            THEN { Move remainder of Upper to Combined }
                WHILE NOT Eof (Upper) DO
                    Transfer (Upper, Combined)
            ELSE { Move remainder of Lower to Combined }
                WHILE NOT Eof (Lower) DO
                    Transfer (Lower, Combined)
```

To produce the sorted files Upper and Lower, small segments of the file to be sorted can be read into appropriate arrays, and the arrays can be sorted and then read into Upper and Lower. This strategy of solving a large problem by dividing it into several smaller problems is called "divide and conquer". We will see another application of this principle in the next section when we consider a search technique called binary search.

19.2   Searching

Frequently, a search must be performed to discover whether a given piece of information is stored in a given structure. In the simplest form, given the piece of information and the structure to be searched, one wishes to know if the piece of information is present. This suggests that a function Present be defined so that Present (X, S) = True if the item X is found in the structure S and False otherwise.

Searching a Sequential File

If the structure S is a sequential file, the function Present takes the form:

```
    FUNCTION Present (SearchItem : ItemType;
                      VAR S : FileType) : Boolean;
    VAR Found : Boolean;
    BEGIN
    Reset (S);
    Found := False;
    WHILE (NOT Eof (S)) AND (NOT Found) DO
        IF SearchItem = S^
            THEN
                Found := True
            ELSE
                Get (S);
    Present := Found
    END; { Present }
```

In the above algorithm, SearchItem and S¨ are of the same type. If S is a file of Records and the question is whether there is a record with a specified component, the condition tested in the IF statement becomes SearchItem = S^ . C, where C stands for the appropriate field identifier.

Linear Search of an Array

Suppose we are searching an array, called Data, rather than a file. Instead of using the Get procedure to examine successive elements, we increment an index, and, instead of using Eof (DataFile) as an indicator of whether or not there are more elements

to be examined, we use a comparison of the current value of this
index with the last array index. The function Present would now be:

```
FUNCTION Present (SearchItem : ItemType;
                  VAR Data : ArrayType;
                  FirstIndex, LastIndex : IndexType)
                  : Boolean;

VAR
    Found : Boolean;
    Index : IndexType;
BEGIN
Found := False;
Index := FirstIndex;
WHILE (NOT Found) AND (Index <= LastIndex) DO
    IF SearchItem = Data [Index]
        THEN
            Found := True
        ELSE
            Index := Index + 1;
Present := Found
END; { Present }
```

If the array to be searched is not very large, we may use the
following search method: starting at the beginning of the list,
successive entries are tested until either a match is found or there
remain no more list elements to examine. This method is called
linear search for two reasons: because we have conceptually
organized the information as if it were laid out along a line and
searched the information in the same order; and because the number
of comparisons tends to grow at the same rate as the length of the
list being searched.

For some purposes, it may suffice simply to know whether or not
the item has been found. One might, however, wish to know more,
such as the position in the array. This information is readily
available since, at the time that Found is set to True, the current
value of Index is the position in the array where the match for
SearchItem is stored. We say that Index points to this place. To
retain this information for later use, one could enlarge the THEN
clause of the IF-THEN statement to the compound statement:

```
BEGIN
Found := True;
Position := Index
END
```

We could rewrite this process as a procedure with Position and Found declared as reference parameters. We must use a procedure rather than a function here because we are returning two pieces of information, the values of Found and Position (with the understanding that Position is considered to be undefined if Found is False).

The order in which the array elements are examined can be reversed. We may begin with the last index and decrement index. The code then reads:

```
Found := False;
Index := LastIndex;
WHILE (NOT Found) AND (FirstIndex <= Index) DO
    IF SearchItem = Data [Index]
        THEN
            Found := True
        ELSE
            Index := Index - 1
```

If SearchItem is not found, the final value of Index will be FirstIndex - 1. Since array indices such as FirstIndex are normally 1, this value of Index will be 0 if SearchItem is not found.

Using a Sentinel

A variation of the linear search makes use of this previous observation. The array is declared so that there is a position with index 0 available. Such a declaration might be

```
Data : ARRAY [0..MaxSize] OF ItemType
```

Then, prior to the search, the SearchItem is placed in position 0, i.e., Data [0] is assigned the value SearchItem. Now, the match must occur, but, if the value of SearchItem was not in the original list, it will occur when Index has the value 0. This special item is called a sentinel.

As an example, here is a fragment that uses a sentinel to ensure that eventually Found must get the value True:

```
    Data [FirstIndex - 1] := SearchItem;
    Index := LastIndex;
    Found := False;
    WHILE NOT Found DO
        IF SearchItem = Data [Index]
            THEN
                Found := True
            ELSE
                Index := Index - 1
```

The sentinel technique also lends itself to description using the REPEAT-UNTIL statement. It could be coded by the scheme:

```
    Data [FirstIndex - 1] := SearchItem;
    Index := LastIndex + 1;
    REPEAT
        Index := Index - 1;
        UNTIL SearchItem = Data [Index]
```

The linear search technique is expensive in terms of computing time. If there is a small probability that the search item will be found, then most of the time that the list is searched the number of comparisons made will equal the length of the list. In this case, the processing time required grows at the same rate as the length of the list. Even if it were certain that the list contained a given item each time a search were made, it would be just as likely (unless the list has been organized in some particular fashion) that the item is toward the end of the list as that the item is toward the front of the list. In that case, regardless of the end at which the search is initiated, on average we should expect to make as many comparisons as half the length of the list. Again, if the length of the list were doubled, we could expect to double the time, or the number of comparisons, needed to search the list.

We have given a brief introduction to the subject of the organization of lists of information which make search techniques faster and more efficient. Conceptually, since a number of the more inefficient techniques are simpler, they are introduced first. This is not to say that these techniques should not be used. If the lists are short, or sometimes if they are nearly sorted, some of the simpler techniques are as good as, or better than, the more complex ones. Frequently, there is a trade-off between the greater speed inherent in a more complex algorithm and the overhead in terms of extra bookkeeping that these algorithms demand.

Binary Search

     If a sorted list is to be searched and it is stored in an array
so that individual elements are randomly accessible, then other
methods may reduce dramatically the number of comparisons or probes
that must be made to find an item of information. One technique
that can be used is called binary search. Binary search consists of
repetitively dividing a portion of the list in half and confining
the subsequent search to one of the two halves. Since the list is
sorted, the decision of which half to continue to search can be made
by comparing the item sought with the list item in the middle of the
portion of the list currently being examined.

     For simplicity, let the array be an array of nonnegative
integers, arranged in ascending order, and assume that the item
sought is somewhere in the list. We can conceive of starting with
an array List of integers in which the indices run from an initial
index First to a final index Last. Two quantities derivable from
First and Last are the length of the array, Last - First + 1, and
the middle index, (First + Last) DIV 2. The assumption that the
list is sorted is that

     List [First] <= ... <= List [Middle] <= ... <= List [Last]

Let Item be the identifier associated with the integer in the list
for which we are searching. We shall compare Item with List
[Middle]. If Item = List [Middle], then we have found the item. If
Item < List [Middle], then we should continue our search among the
items whose indices are in the range First to Middle - 1.
Similarly, if Item > List [Middle], we should continue our search
among the items whose indices are in the range Middle + 1 to Last.
Here is an outline of this procedure:

```
Middle := (First + Last) DIV 2;
IF Item = List [Middle]
    THEN
        Item found, Item = List [Middle]
    ELSE
        IF Item < List [Middle]
            THEN
                Continue search in range First to Middle - 1
            ELSE
                Continue search in range Middle + 1 to Last
```

     Continuing the search in the range First to Middle -1 consists
of repeating the process above but giving Last the value of Middle -
1. Similarly, continuing the search in the range Middle + 1 to Last
is a repetition of the process in which First has the value of

Middle + 1. Since the number of repetitions of the procedure is not
known in advance, the repetition may be controlled by WHILE NOT
Found DO. This leads us to encode the search as follows:

```
{ Binary search;  Search for the Position of Item
     in the array List in the range First to Last.
   It is assumed that the array List of integers is
     sorted in ascending order }
Found := False;
WHILE NOT Found DO
   BEGIN
   Middle := (First + Last) DIV 2;
   IF Item = List [Middle]
      THEN
         BEGIN
         Found := True;
         Position := Middle
         END
      ELSE { decide which half in which to
                         continue search }
         IF Item < List [Middle]
            THEN { continue search in half
                      First to Middle - 1 }
               Last := Middle - 1
            ELSE { continue search in half
                      Middle + 1 to Last }
               First := Middle + 1
   END;
```

It is instructive to trace through an execution of this
algorithm. Suppose that we consider a list with seven entries:

List

[1]	[2]	[3]	[4]	[5]	[6]	[7]
3	8	12	15	16	20	27

and that we are searching for the position occupied by Item = 20.
In this case, the initial values of First and Last will be 1 and 7,
respectively. The variables that are assigned values during the
execution of the binary search are: Middle, Found, Position, Last,
and First. Also two expressions are evaluated; Item = List
[Middle] and Item < List [Middle]. Here is a table of the
successive values as the procedure unfolds:

Middle	Found	Position	Last	First	Item = List[M]	Item < List[M]
undef 4	undef	undef	7	1		
					False	
				5		False
6						
					True	
	True	6				

In this case, the WHILE-DO loop is iterated twice. One can
check that the maximum number of iterations is 3 in the cases where
the position of the item sought is either 1, 3, 5, or 7, that it is
2 iterations for positions 2 and 6, and only 1 iteration for
position 4. In the first group of cases, in which the maximum
number of iterations occurs, First and Last have the same value.

Here is a table of the positions, the binary representation of
the position, and the number of iterations required if the item
sought occupies the given position in a 15-element array. (In the
case where the item sought must be in the list, the last iteration
is superfluous.)

Position	Binary Representation of Position	Number of Iterations
1	0 0 0 1	4
2	0 0 1 0	3
3	0 0 1 1	4
4	0 1 0 0	2
5	0 1 0 1	4
6	0 1 1 0	3
7	0 1 1 1	4
8	1 0 0 0	1
9	1 0 0 1	4
10	1 0 1 0	3
11	1 0 1 1	4
12	1 1 0 0	2
13	1 1 0 1	4
14	1 1 1 0	3
15	1 1 1 1	4

Note that the maximum number of iterations, 4, when used as an
exponent in 2**4 (2 raised to the 4th power), yields binary 10000 or
16 in decimal, and that this is one more than the length of the

array.   The average number of iterations is:

$$(8*4 + 4*3 + 2*2 + 1*1) / 15 = 3.266$$

For a linear search of a list of the same length, the maximum number of iterations of the loop in the linear search algorithm is 15, while the average is 8.

The improvement for longer lists is much more dramatic, as shown by the following table:

List Length	Binary Search Maximum No. of Iterations	Linear Search Average No. of Iterations
7	3	4
15	4	8
31	5	16
63	6	32
1,023	10	512
65,535	16	32,768
1,048,575	20	524,288

Note that, in the case of linear search, the number of iterations grows at the same rate as the length of the list. If the length of the list doubles, the average computation of the linear search also doubles. But in the case of the binary search, if the length of the list doubles, the maximum number of iterations increases by only one.

Suppose that the item being sought was not in the list. In this case, we could not be sure that Found would be set to True. Therefore, we must expect that the condition for terminating the iteration will be more complicated. It will depend on either finding the item or reaching a point beyond which the search cannot be continued.

A search procedure will usually be in one of three states: the search is actively going on, the item being sought has been found, or the search has revealed that the item is not present. A technique for organizing the search is to use a variable with a value corresponding to one of these three conditions as a control variable. Let us declare

StateofSearch : (StillLooking, Found, NotThere);

It may be that we do find Item in the List, and, if and when we do, we can set StateofSearch equal to Found. If, however, Item is not

in the List, then what should be the final iteration of the search
will occur with First = Last = Middle. In this case, preparation
for the next iteration will result in giving either First or Last a
value such that Last will be less than First. We can use this
condition to test for the absence of Item from the List.

Here are the appropriate modifications of binary search:

```
PROCEDURE BinarySearch (Item : ItemType;
                        VAR List : ArrayType;
                        InitialIndex, FinalIndex : IndexType;
                        VAR Present : Boolean);
{ List assumed to be sorted in increasing order }
VAR
    First, Middle, Last : IndexType;
    StateofSearch = (StillLooking, Found, NotThere);
BEGIN
StateofSearch := StillLooking;
First := InitialIndex;
Last := FinalIndex;
WHILE StateofSearch = StillLooking DO
    BEGIN
    Middle := (First + Last) DIV 2;
    IF Item = List [Middle]
        THEN
            BEGIN
            StateofSearch := Found;
            Position := Middle
            END
        ELSE { decide in which half in which
                                    to continue search }
            IF Item < List [Middle]
                THEN { continue search in half
                                    First to Middle - 1 }
                    Last := Middle - 1
                ELSE { continue search in half
                                    Middle + 1 to Last }
                    First := Middle + 1;
    IF Last < First
        THEN
            StateofSearch := NotThere
    END;
CASE StateofSearch OF
    Found     : Present := True;
    NotThere  : Present := False
    END;
END; { Binary Search }
```

19.3   Summary

The items in one array can be moved to another array by
systematically inserting each element of the first array in the
second, so that, after each insertion, the current version of the
second array is sorted. This method is called insertion sort.
Another method for sorting an array rearranges the entries of the
array so that larger and larger sublists of the array are sorted.
Starting with a sublist of the first two elements, they are compared
and exchanged, if necessary, so as to sort this small sublist. At
each stage, there is initially a sorted sublist. The element
following the sublist is compared with consecutive elements of the
sublist, and exchanged if necessary, until this next element finds
its appropriate position. This process is called an exchange sort.
Both of these methods can be extremely slow for large arrays.

Sorting a sequential file can be accomplished by segmenting the
file into smaller pieces, sorting the smaller pieces, and then
merging these pieces to produce a sorted version of the orginal
file.

A structure such as a file or an array can be searched for the
presence of an item by examining successive items of the structure
until either a match is found or the structure is exhausted. A
variation of this straightforward search technique can be applied to
arrays. Create a special position at the front of the array
(usually with index = 0), and store the item sought in this first
position. This sentinel guarantees that, if the search is begun at
the rear of the array, a match will be found. If the position of
the match is not this special, first position, then the item was in
the original unaugmented array.

When an item is sought in a sorted array, there is a dramatic
decrease in the number of comparisons that must be made if a binary
search technique is used. This technique consists of repetitively
using a comparison of the item sought with the item at the middle of
a subrange of the array. After this comparison, a decision is made
as to whether the item has been found, or if not, in which of the
two halves of the subrange to continue the search.

Exercises for Chapter 19

1. Apply merge sort to sort an array. Can you think of a divide and conquer method which would allow the merge sort technique to be applied recursively?

2. Let X be an array of integers. Write a procedure which will search X for the presence of a component whose value is in the range (Y - Error) to (Y + Error), where Y and Error are integers and Error is positive.

3. Write a procedure to search a simple linked list for a given item.

4. Write a procedure to search a family tree for an ancestor with a given name.

5. In a golf tournament, the lower the score the higher the contestant finishes. Each finishing position carries with it a cash award, and the higher the finish the larger the award. Write a program which allows you to enter the cash award for a certain number of positions and a list of contestants (possibly larger than the number of cash awards) and their scores. Have the program order the contestants by score and compute the award for each contestant. Two or more contestants who have the same score tie for the highest finishing position available to them, but their payoff is an equal share in the total awards for the several positions that they share. For example, if two contestants tie for second, and second pays $10000 and third pays $6000, they each receive $8000.

6. If, starting from the front of an array and continuing to the rear, adjacent entries are compared and interchanged if the second precedes the first, the process will terminate with the smallest entry in the last position and with larger entries working or bubbling their way forward. Develop an algorithm which applies this process to smaller and smaller subarrays of integers in order to sort the array.

7. A textfile can be used as a file of words, by following each word with <EOL>. Write a program to sort such a file.

Appendices

ASCII Code

Seven bits are used to represent a character. The bits may be used to represent a decimal or base ten integer in the range 0 (for binary 000 0000) to 127 (for binary 111 1111). A compact tabular presentation uses the sixteen low-order bits, 0000 to 1111, as row indices and the eight high-order bits, 000 to 111, as column indices. The nonprintable characters are denoted by abbreviations or mnemonic names. Examples are BEL for bell, CR for carriage return. SP is used for the printable character blank or space. The printable characters are in the range ASCII 32 (010 0000) to ASCII (111 1110). On most terminals ASCII characters 1 through 26 are generated by simultaneously pressing the control key and an alphabetic key, the combination is denoted by CTRL/A through CTRL/Z.

High-Order Bits

Low-Order Bits	0 0 0	0 0 1	0 1 0	0 1 1	1 0 0	1 0 1	1 1 0	1 1 1
0 0 0 0	NUL	DLE	SP	0	@	P		p
0 0 0 1	SOH	DC1	!	1	A	Q	a	q
0 0 1 0	STX	DC2	"	2	B	R	b	r
0 0 1 1	ETX	DC3	#	3	C	S	c	s
0 1 0 0	EOT	DC4	$	4	D	T	d	t
0 1 0 1	ENQ	NAK	%	5	E	U	e	u
0 1 1 0	ACK	SYN	&	6	F	V	f	v
0 1 1 1	BEL	ETB	'	7	G	W	g	w
1 0 0 0	BS	CAN	(	8	H	X	h	s
1 0 0 1	HT	EM	)	9	I	Y	i	y
1 0 1 0	LF	SUB	*	:	J	Z	j	z
1 0 1 1	VT	ESC	+	;	K	[	k	{
1 1 0 0	FF	FS	,	<	L	\	l		
1 1 0 1	CR	GS	-	=	M	]	m	}
1 1 1 0	SO	RS	.	>	N	^	n	~
1 1 1 1	S1	US	/	?	O	_	o	DEL

Table of Standard Functions and Procedures

Standard Functions

Functions are listed by tabulating name, description, argument type, and value type. They are listed in the order arithmetic functions, transfer functions, predicate or Boolean function, and other. In the case of arithmetic functions that may take arguments of two different types, each type is listed on a separate line with the corresponding value on the same line.

Function	Description	Argument	Value
Arithmetic			
Abs	absolute value	integer	integer
		real	real
ArcTan	arc tangent	integer	real (radian)
		real	real (radian)
Cos	cosine	integer (radian)	real
		real (radian)	real
Exp	exponential (base e = 2.71828..)	integer	real
		real	real
Ln	natural logarithm (base e = 2.71828..)	integer	real
		real	real
Sin	sine	integer (radian)	real
		real (radian)	real
Sqr	square	integer	integer
		real	real
Sqrt	square root	integer	real
		real	real

Function	Description	Argument	Value
Transfer			
Chr	character of ordinal	integer	character
Ord	ordinal of character	character	integer
Round	rounded to nearest integer	real	integer
Trunc	truncate	real	integer
Predicate			
Odd	odd	integer	Boolean
Eoln	end-of-line	textfile	Boolean
Eof	end-of-file	textfile	Boolean
Other			
Pred	predecessor	integer character user-defined Boolean	integer character user-defined Boolean
Succ	successor	integer character user-defined Boolean	integer character user-defined Boolean

File Handling Procedures

Put   Appends the current value of the buffer variable
to the file. File must be opened for writing with
the Rewrite procedure. Eof (< file variable >) must
be true before execution and will continue to be
true after execution. After execution the buffer
variable is considered to be undefined.

Get   Advances the current file position to the next
             component of the buffer variable. If no next
             component exists, the Eof (< file variable >)
             becomes true and the value of the buffer variable
             is undefined. Not applicable if Eof (< file
             variable >) is true before execution.

Reset   Resets the current file position to the beginning
             for the purpose of reading. Consequently the buffer
             variable is assigned the value of the first element
             of the file and Eof (< file variable >) becomes false
             if the file is not empty. If the file is empty,
             Eof (< file variable >) will be true and the value of
             the buffer variable is undefined.

Rewrite   Replaces the current value of the file with the empty
             file. Eof (< file variable >) becomes true and a new
             file may be written.

Page   Instructs the output device to move to a new page
             before printing the next line of the textfile.

Read   Obtains from the specified file the data required by
             the input list. Items in the input list are separated
             by commas. When reading an Integer or Real from a
             textfile, blanks and <EOL> marks are skipped until
             an initial digit is encountered and the input file
             pointer is left pointing to the character immediately
             after the last digit of the last number read. If no
             file is specified, the standard file Input is assumed
             as a default.

Readln   Only appropriate for textfiles. Same as Read, except
             that after the input list has been read, the file
             pointer is moved past the next <EOL>. Subsequent
             reading from the input textfile will therefore
             commence at the beginning of the next line.

Write   Appends to the output file the values of the expressions
             listed in the output list. Items in the output list
             are separated by commas. Integers, Reals, Booleans,
             and Strings may be written to a textfile and will be
             converted to characters. If no output file is
             specified the standard file Output is assumed as a
             default.

Writeln   Only appropriate for textfiles. Same as Write, except
             that after the output list is transmitted an <EOL> is

placed in the output file. Subsequent writing will
start on a new line.

Dynamic Allocation Procedures

New — Allocates an appropriate unit of memory and assigns
to the pointer supplied as a parameter to New a value
which makes the pointer reference this unit of
memory.

New with variants — Allocates an appropriate unit of memory
according to the supplied variants. The tag field
values must be listed after the pointer as paramenters
in the order of their declaration. The tag field
values must not be changed during execution.

Dispose — Returns the unit of memory referenced by a pointer to
unallocated memory. If variants were supplied when
the memory was allocated by New, they must be
identical in the parameter list for Dispose.

Data Transfer Procedures

Pack (Source, Start, Target)

        Source : ARRAY [M..N] OF T;
        Start : Integer;
        Target : PACKED ARRAY [U..V] OF T;

    Packs Source [I], ..., Source [I + V - U] into consecutive
components of the array Target by making the assignments

        Target [U] := Source [I];
        ...
        Target [V] := Source [I + V - U]

    Therefore, it is required that M <= I and I + V - U <= N.

Unpack (Source, Target, Start)

        Source : PACKED ARRAY [U..V] OF T;
        Target : ARRAY [M..N] OF T;
        Start : Integer;

    Unpacks Source [U], ..., Source [V] into the consecutive
components Target [I], ..., Target [I + V - U] by making the

assignments

```
    Target [I] := Source [U];
    ...
    Target [I + V - U] := Source [V]
```

Memory, Bits and Bytes

Digital Computers store information by means of "bistable" devices, that is, devices that are capable of assuming one of two states. The status of some particular bistable devices might be represented by

```
ON          or   OFF
OPEN        or   CLOSED
HIGH        or   LOW
ODD         or   EVEN
CLOCKWISE   or   COUNTERCLOCKWISE
```

Using zero and one, the information represented by status = 0 or status = 1 is called a "bit"

Some of the means of storing information or bits are:

```
Punched cards and punched paper tape
Relays
Magnetizable ferrite cores
Magnetizable tape, disks, and drums
Flip-flops (semi-conductor devices)
Bubble memory (magnetic domains)
```

The status of a small collection of memory elements can be written as a string of zeros and ones. A string of 8 bits is called a "byte" and is normally the amount of memory required to store a single character.

ASCII (American Standard Code for Information Interchange) uses 7 bits to represent or encode a character. 7 bits are capable of assuming 128 different bit patterns, which is more than sufficient to allow a unique pattern to be assigned to the various printable characters that might appear on the keyboard of a terminal or on a printer and also to various control characters such as carriage return (CR), backspace (BS), line feed (LF), bell (BEL), escape (ESC), etc. A high order or leftmost bit may be added as a means of error checking. This bit is called a "parity" bit. The parity bit

together with the 7 ASCII bits thereby use a byte to transmit a
character. ASCII code is tabulated in Appendix A.

Transmitting with even parity, each character code would be
prefixed with a bit whose value will make the number of ones in the
byte even. Thus in sending characters we would have

character	Even Parity ASCII code
A	0 100 0001
B	0 100 0010
C	1 100 0011

Bits may be transmitted sequentially (one after another) along
a single wire, in which case a graph of voltage (high = 1, low = 0)
versus time might appear as follows

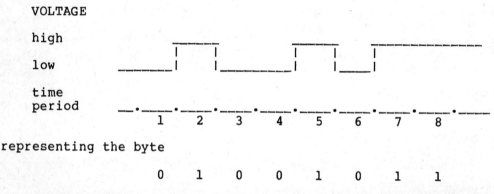

representing the byte

                    0   1   0   0   1   0   1   1

A group of bits may be transmitted along a corresponding group
of parallel wires. The corresponding diagram for four wires would
then look like

```
WIRE NO.

          high                    _____
     1                             |
          low          _____|


          high
     2
          low          _____

          high          _____
     3                             |
          low                      |_____

          high          _____
     4
          low

TIME PERIOD       ___._____._____.___
                      1      2
```

representing

```
          0    1
          0    0
          1    0
          1    1
```

The number of bits of data that can be sent along the parallel wires in a computer's communications channel or bus is usually referred to as a "word" for that computer. For the current generation of microcomputers the word size is a byte, although 16-bit microcomputers are now available. 16 and 32 bits are the word size of some popular minicomputers. Larger word sizes appear on the larger computers, called mainframes.

Computation speed depends on the length of time period needed to send a word and the word size. The length of the time period needed to send a word is related to the amount of time needed to insure that the voltages have stabilized at their appropriate values.

Memory is generally measured by bytes. Larger memory units are K = 1,024. Thus

1 K bytes = 1,024 bytes = 2 raised to the tenth power bytes

8 K bytes = 8,192 bytes = 2 raised to the thirteenth power

bytes.

As memory gets cheaper and also comes in larger units one also refers to mega or million bytes by using M. Small floppy or flexible disks on microcomputers will store about 1/2 megabytes, whereas so-called hard disks on larger machines can now store in the hundred megabyte range.

A bit can have one of two values, two bits can have four or two squared values. A byte or 8 bits can have 2 raised to the 8th power or 256 different values. An IBM punched card has 12 rows and 80 columns, so it has 12 * 80 = 960 bits. The number of different ways in which one such card could be punched is 2 raised to the 960th power (about one followed by 300 zeros).

As another example, in transmitting a black and white news picture, it might be subdivided into small squares so that it consisted of a grid of 100 by 100 small squares. Each square could be one of 8 or 2 cubed different shades, ranging from white to black (thus 3 bits are needed to represent a specific shade). The picture could then be transmitted using 100 * 100 * 3 = 30,000 bits or about 1,000 32 bit words. A typical display for a computer terminal consists of twenty-two eighty character lines, with each character position consisting of a matrix of dots, sometimes called "pixels", measuring 5 columns by seven rows. The information as to which dots in the entire screen are on and which are off therefore requires 22 * 80 * 5 * 7 = 61,600 bits.

Each data item, be it an integer, a real, a Boolean, or a character is stored by means of a specific pattern of bits in a particular memory location. Because we are using a high level language such as Pascal we do not need to concern ourselves with specific details of storage. Nevertheless it is useful to realize that different data types require different amounts of storage and that one of the purposes of the declarations in the early part of a Pascal program is to allow the compiler to make proper storage allocation for the various data types in the program. (Another purpose is to aid the programmer by having the compiler check for proper use of types in the instructions, such as the compatibility of types on the two sides of the assignment operator.)

Generally, as we have seen, 8 bits, or a byte, is used for the storage of a character. On some computers 32 bits are used to store an integer. The number of bits used will directly determine the value of Maxint, the largest positive integer. If 32 bits are used for an integer, the value of Maxint is stored as a zero bit followed by thirty-one one bits, i.e.,

```
0 1 1 1     1 1 1 1     1 1 1 1     1 1 1 1
1 1 1 1     1 1 1 1     1 1 1 1     1 1 1 1
```

This pattern of bits is used to represent 2 raised to the 31st power minus 1.

A more compact notation for describing long sequences of bits is hexadecimal (for base sixteen) notation. Sixteen different hexadecimal digits are used to represent the sixteen different bit patterns available with four bits. The table of correspondences is

Hexadecimal Digit	Bit Pattern
0	0 0 0 0
1	0 0 0 1
2	0 0 1 0
3	0 0 1 1
4	0 1 0 0
5	0 1 0 1
6	0 1 1 0
7	0 1 1 1
8	1 0 0 0
9	1 0 0 1
A	1 0 1 0
B	1 0 1 1
C	1 1 0 0
D	1 1 0 1
E	1 1 1 0
F	1 1 1 1

Using hexadecimal notation the bit pattern for the value of Maxint on a 32 bit machine can be written as 7FFF FFFF.

Representing Integers

We use positional notation to write numbers, with the base of the system (also called the radix) the number ten. A string of digits, such as 358, represents the same integer as the expression

    3 * 100 + 5 * 10 + 8 * 1

where the 3, 5, and 8 are multiplied by the base ten raised to the second, first, and zeroth power, respectively. Each digit contributes an amount which is related to its position in the sequence, with the rightmost digit the units digit, the preceding digit the tens digit, and so on.

Leading zeros, such as the first zero in 05076 may be deleted without changing the value of the number being represented. But a zero after the first significant or non-zero digit cannot be deleted without altering the value of the number being represented.

Positional notation can be used to represent numbers using bases other than ten. In particular, the base two representation, or binary representation, is a convenient technique for representing numbers in digital computers. Only two digits, 0 and 1, are needed, and the two digits correspond to the two possible values of a bit. Other convenient bases are eight, which gives rise to an octal representation, and sixteen, which gives rise to a hexadecimal representation. Eight digits, 0..7, are used in octal. A hexadecimal system requires sixteen digits. The usual scheme is to use 0..9, A, B, C, D, E, F.

Here is a table of various representations of the numbers zero through sixteen:

Name	Binary	Octal	Decimal	Hexadecimal
zero	0	0	0	0
one	1	1	1	1
two	10	2	2	2
three	11	3	3	3
four	100	4	4	4
five	101	5	5	5
six	110	6	6	6
seven	111	7	7	7
eight	1000	10	8	8
nine	1001	11	9	9
ten	1010	12	10	A
eleven	1011	13	11	B
twelve	1100	14	12	C
thirteen	1101	15	13	D
fourteen	1110	16	14	E
fifteen	1111	17	15	F
sixteen	10000	100	16	10

The powers of two have an especially simple representation in the binary system. The following table gives some of these representations.

Exponent	Binary	Decimal
0	1	1
1	10	2
2	100	4
3	1000	8
4	1 0000	16
5	10 0000	32
10	100 0000 0000	1024
15	1000 0000 0000 0000	32768

In each case we have a 1 followed by the same number of trailing 0's as the exponent.

The range of integer values available with a given computer will depend on the number of bits used to store an integer. If sixteen bits are used, 65,536 different integers can be stored. Usually about half of these will be negative integers.

A common technique for storing both negative and positive integers is to use the binary representation for positive integers, and a representation called the two's complement form for negative integers. The representation of a negative integer in this form can be obtained from its corresponding positive value (the absolute value) by "complementing" each bit of the absolute value and adding 1. The complement of a bit whose value is 1 is 0 and the complement of a bit whose value is 0 is 1.

The representation of -1 in a sixteen bit integer representation would be obtained by complementing

0000 0000 0000 0001

to obtain

1111 1111 1111 1110

and adding 1 to obtain the two's complement representation

1111 1111 1111 1111

Syntax Diagrams and BNF

Many of the syntactic rules for the proper formation of
programs may be described by substitution rules. The rules
prescribe the replacement of one syntactic term by a combination of
terms consisting of entities such as reserved words, identifiers,
grammatical marks, or other syntactic terms. A well-formed program
is obtained by starting with a single syntactic term, such as
program, and performing continued replacements until only elements
that may appear in the source program remain. The technique is
similar to the generation of an English sentence, beginning with the
syntactic term sentence, and using a sequence of substitutions such
as the following:

< sentence >   ====>   < noun phrase > < transitive verb > < object >

< noun phrase >   ====>   < adjective > < noun >

< transitive verb >   ====>   hit

< object >   ====>   < noun phrase >

< adjective >   ====>   the

< noun >   ====>   clock

< noun >   ====>   hour

The syntactic terms are enclosed in angle brackets, whereas the
English words and grammatical marks are not. The words and
grammatical marks are called terminal symbols. They appear in the
sentence or sentences that may be generated by these rules. The
syntactic term sentence is referred to as the starting term and a
sequence of substitutions such as:

< sentence > ====> < noun phrase > < transitive verb > < object > .

   ====> < adjective > < noun > hit < noun phrase > . ====>

The clock hit < adjective > < noun > . ====>

The clock hit the hour .

is called a derivation or a parse of the sentence "The clock hit the hour."

A common notation for indicating permissible substitutions, called the Backus-Naur form (abbreviated BNF) uses the symbol ::= in place of the arrow to denote the relation "may be replaced by". When there is a choice among substitution rules, the several allowable replacements for a given term are listed to the right of the replacement operator, ::=, separated by |. Thus, in the English language sample, we would write

< noun > ::= clock | hour

indicating that the syntactic term noun may be replaced by either the word clock or the word hour. A comparable situation in Pascal is the substitution rule

< relational operator > ::= = | <> | < | <= | >= | > | IN

This replacement rule indicates that there are seven relational operators.

Another method of presenting this information is by a diagram, called a syntax diagram. A syntax diagram is a collection of nodes and directed arcs. There is one entry arc and one exit arc. A single arc may split into several arcs and several arcs may combine into a single arc. Arcs pass through nodes. The nodes contain syntactic terms or terminal elements of the source program. Each syntax diagram corresponds to a substitution rule for that syntactic term. Following a path from the entry node to the exit node indicates that the syntactic term may be replaced by the terms encountered in the nodes along the path in the order in which they have been visited.

Using relational operator as an example, the corresponding syntax diagram is:

< relational operator >

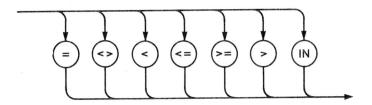

This particular substitution replaces the term relational operator
by one of the seven terminal character strings that may appear in a
source program. Syntactic terms may appear on the right of the
substitution operator and therefore within the nodes in syntax
diagrams. The substitution rule for expression:

   < expression > ::= < simple expression > | < simple expression >

                   < relational operator > < simple expression >

yields the syntax diagram

   < expression >

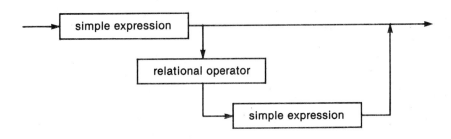

Substituting for < relational operator > we obtain a syntax diagram
which indicates how an expression may be defined using simple
expression. The resulting diagram is:

< expression >

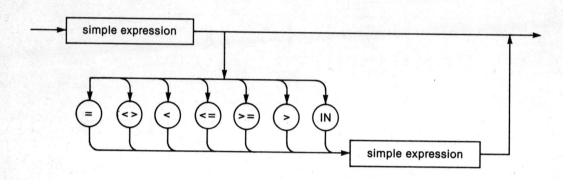

If this diagram is used to define the grammar of Pascal, it indicates that we are owed a definition of simple expression.

Syntax diagrams can indicate an indefinite number of replacements. For example, an identifier is defined as a letter followed by any number (including zero) letters or digits. In an extended version of BNF, the braces, { and }, are used to indicate "zero or more occurrences." The BNF definition of identifier is then:

< identifier > ::= < letter > { < letter > | < digit > }

The corresponding syntax diagram is:

< identifier >

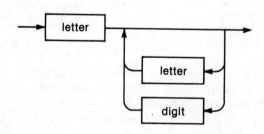

In particular, < letter > < digit > < letter > < letter > is an instance of an identifier obtained by looping through the lower nodes in the diagram three times.

Syntax diagrams may be organized in a bottom-up fashion starting with the definition of the terms closest to the terminal elements of the language (in Pascal this would be terms such as letter, digit, identifier) and building toward the starting term program. We have organized the set of syntax diagrams at the end of this Appendix in a top-down fashion, starting with the definition of program.

Consider the syntax diagram for program given below:

< program >

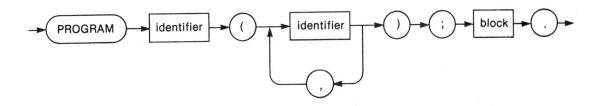

A certain amount of contextual information is not contained in this diagram. One such item is that the first identifier encountered in traversing the diagram is the program name. Also, the remaining identifiers listed between the parentheses are file names. Where appropriate we will note after a diagram some of this contextual information.

The diagrams are based on those in Jensen and Wirth. We have adopted some of their conventions: syntactic terms appear in rectangular nodes without angle brackets; terminal symbols are printed in uppercase within oval nodes; the term character is not specified in a syntax diagram, but is assumed to include uppercase alphabetic characters, digits, the space or blank, and characters necessary for grammatical marks.

< program>

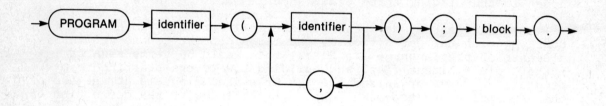

< identifier >

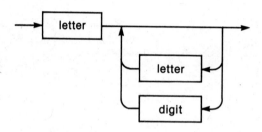

< letter >

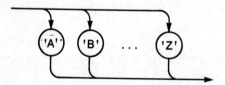

< digit >

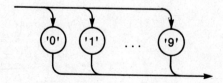

< block >

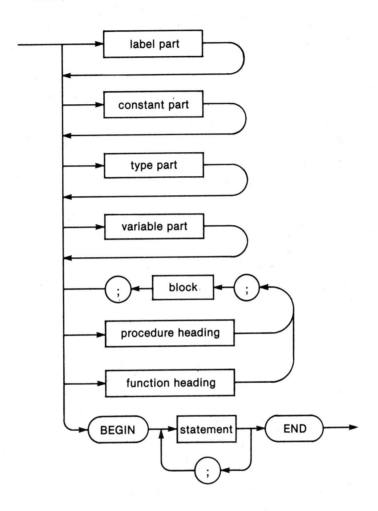

< label part >

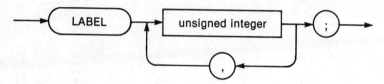

< constant part >

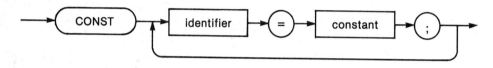

Note: identifier is a constant identifier

< unsigned integer >

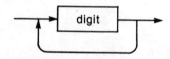

< constant >

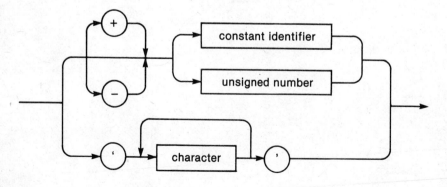

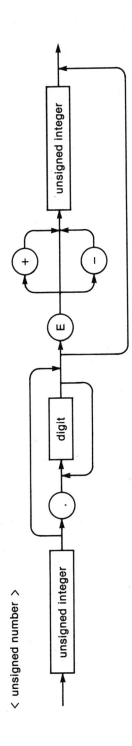

< type >

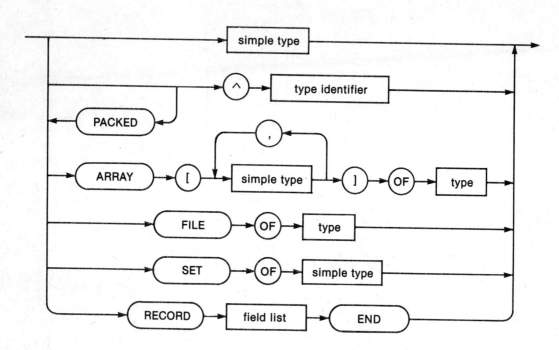

< type part >

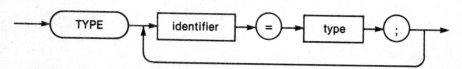

Note: identifier is a type identifier

< simple type >

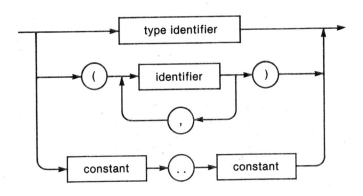

< field list >

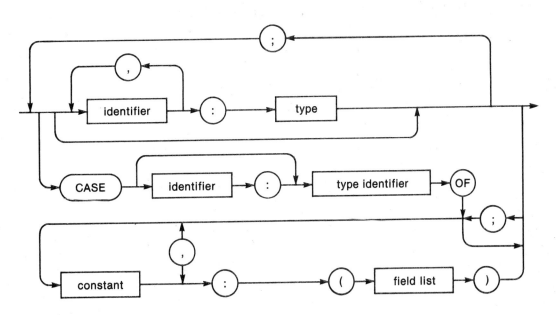

< variable part >

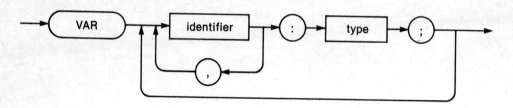

Note: identifier is a variable identifier

< procedure heading >

Note: identifier is a procedure identifier

< function heading >

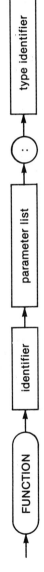

Note: identifier is a function identifier

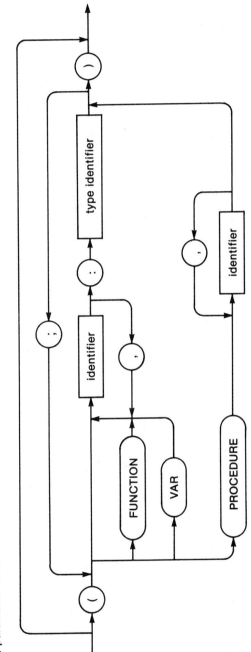

< statement >

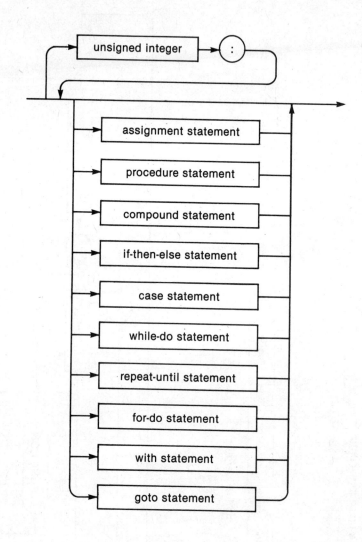

< assignment statement >

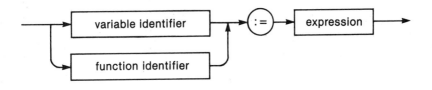

< procedure statement >

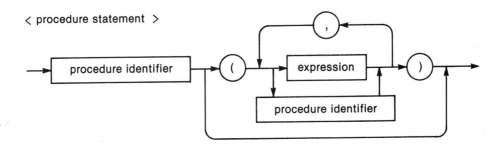

< compound statement >

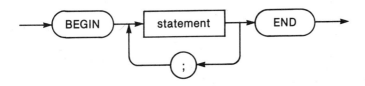

< if-then-else statement >

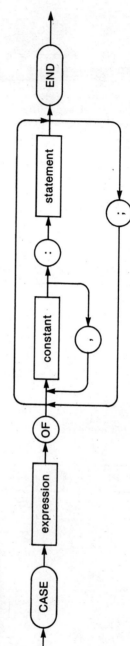

< case statement >

< while-do statement >

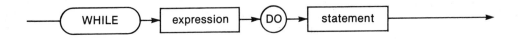

< repeat-until statement >

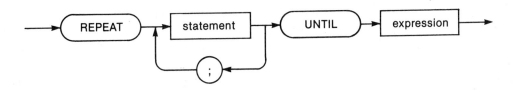

< for-do statement >

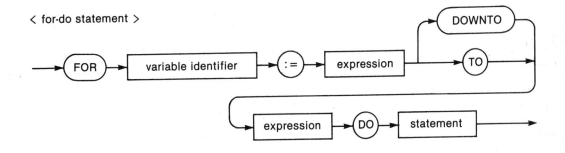

< with statement >

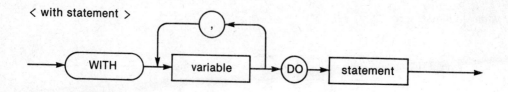

< goto statement >

< expression >

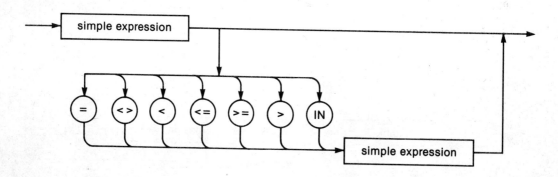

< simple expression >

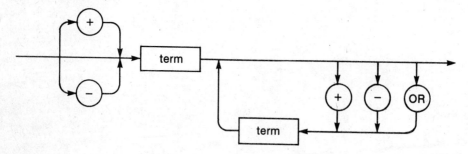

< term >

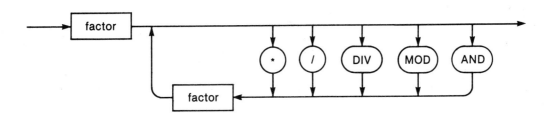

< factor >

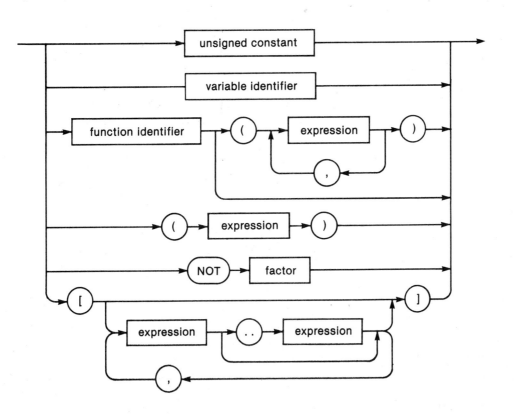

Bibliography

Aho, Alfred V., John E. Hopcroft and Jeffrey D. Ullman.
   "The Design and Analysis of Computer Algorithms." Addison
   Wesley, 1974.

Alagic, Suad and Michael A. Arbib. "The Design of Well-
   Structured and Correct Programs." Springer-Verlag, 1978.

Arbib, Michael A., A. J. Kfoury and Robert N. Moll. "A Basis
   for Theoretical Computer Science." Springer-Verlag, 1981.

Baase, Sara. "Computer Algorithms: Introduction to Design and
   Analysis." Addison-Wesley, 1978.

Backhouse, Roland C. "Syntax of Programming Languages: Theory
   and Practice." Prentice-Hall, 1979.

Bennet, William R., Jr. "Scientitic and Engineering Problem-
   Solving with the Computer." Prentice-Hall, 1976.

Coleman, Derek. "A Structured Programming Approach to Data."
   Springer-Verlag, 1979

Denning, Peter J., Jack B. Dennis and Joseph E. Qualitz.
   "Machines, Languages, and Computation." Prentice-Hall, 1978.

Dijkstra, Edsger W. "A Discipline of Programming."
   Prentice-Hall, 1976.

Gill, Arthur. "Applied Algebra for the Computer Sciences."
   Prentice-Hall, 1976.

Hamming, Richard W. "Coding and Information Theory." Prentice-
   Hall, 1980.

Hopcroft, John E. and Jeffrey D. Ullman. "Formal Languages and
   their Relation to Automata." Addison-Wesley, 1969.

Horowitz, Ellis and Sartaj Sahni. "Fundamentals of Data
   Structures." Computer Science Press, 1976.

Horowitz, Ellis and Sartaj Sahni. "Fundamentals of Computer Algorithms." Computer Science Press, 1978.

Jensen, Kathleen and Niklaus Wirth. "Pascal User Manual and Report." Springer-Verlag, 1974.

Kernighan, Brian W. and P. J. Plauger. "Software Tools." Addison-Wesley, 1976.

Knuth, Donald E. "The Art of Computer Programming Volume 1/ Fundamental Algorithms." Addison-Wesley, 1968.

Knuth, Donald E. "The Art of Computer Programming. Volume 2/ Seminumerical Algorithms." Addison-Wesley, 1969.

Knuth, Donald E. "The Art of Computer Programming. Volume 3/ Sorting and Searching." Addison-Wesley, 1973.

Ledgard, Henry F., John F. Hueras and Paul A. Nagin. "Pascal with Style: Programming Proverbs." Hayden Book, 1978.

Ledgard, Henry F. and Michael Marcotty. "The Programming Language Landscape." Science Research Associates, 1981.

Lewis, Harry R. and Christos H. Papadimitriou. "Elements of the Theory of Computation." Prentice-Hall, 1981.

Linger, R.C., H. D. Mills and B.I. Witt. "Structured Programming: Theory and Practice." Addison-Wesley, 1979.

Minsky, Marvin L. "Computation: Finite and Infinite Machines." Prentice-Hall, 1967.

Nievergelt, J., J.C. Farrar, E.M. Reingold. "Computer Approaches to Mathematical Problems." Prentice-Hall, 1974.

Organick, Elliot I., Alexandra J. Forsythe and Robert Plummer. "Programming Language Structures.", Academic Press, 1978.

Pohl, Ira and Alan Shaw. "The Nature of Computation: An Introduction to Computer Science." Computer Science Press, 1981.

Prather, Ronald E. "Discrete Mathematical Structures for Computer Science." Houghton Mifflin Company, 1976

Standish, Thomas A. " Data Structure Techniques."
   Addison-Wesley, 1980.

Stone, Harold S. "Discrete Mathematical Structures and their
   Applications." Science Research Associates, 1973.

Tennent, R. D. "Principles of Programming Languages."
   Prentice-Hall, 1981.

Wetherell, Charles. "Etudes for Programmers." Prentice-
   Hall, 1978.

Wirth, Niklaus. "Systematic Programming: an Introduction."
   Prentice-Hall, 1973.

Wirth, Niklaus. "Algorithm + Data Structures = Programs."
   Prentice-Hall, 1976.

Wulf, William A., Mary Shaw and Paul N. Hilfinger.
   "Fundamental Structures of Computer Science." Addison-
   Wesley, 1981.

Index